The History of
Street Literature

The History of
Street Literature

The Story of Broadside Ballads, Chapbooks, Proclamations,
News-Sheets, Election Bills, Tracts, Pamphlets, Cocks,
Catchpennies, and other Ephemera

Leslie Shepard

Singing Tree Press

Book Tower   Detroit   Michigan 48226

OTHER BOOKS BY LESLIE SHEPARD

The Broadside Ballad:
A Study in Origins and Meaning (1962)

John Pitts, Ballad Printer of Seven Dials,
London 1765-1844, with a short account
of his predecessors in the
Ballad and Chapbook Trade (1969)

Library of Congress
Cataloging in Publication Data

Shepard, Leslie
    History of street literature

    Bibliography: p.
    1. Street literature. I. Title.
Z1029.3.S5   082   72-12953
            ISBN 0-7153-5881-2

Contents

List of Illustrations

Preface

This book is not intended to be a conventional history, with copious footnotes, every detail discussed to death, and all the reader's work done by the author. Street literature is an elusive subject, in which emotions, moods, and tendencies are often more significant than facts, for street writers were never over-critical on the score of accuracy. The factual discussion here is primarily a framework, for many volumes could be written on printing history alone, although they might not help anyone to write a ballad.

Folklore, from which street literature developed, is essentially a shared experience, falsified by over-detachment or too much scholarly apparatus, and much of this story can be told only by implication. I have tried to communicate some of the feeling of street literature and its background, hence the many examples in facsimile. Whilst we also need detailed studies of individual aspects, the present work attempts a general overall view of the scope and development of street literature, as much for the man in the street as for the scholar. In blurring tidy divisions between literature and life I hope that readers may be stimulated to discover another way of looking at the whole question of literature and its functions.

Facts are also important in their proper context, and the books listed in the Bibliography will add valuable documentation. I have included some titles dealing with European and American traditions of street literature similar to those in Britain. Inevitably I have been obliged to include some factual material from my earlier books and lectures on ballads and chapbooks, but the present work has a wider scope.

The trade catalogue of James Catnach, London, has been reproduced in full in the Appendix, as an example of the stock of the most celebrated ballad and chapbook printer of the nineteenth century. Many songs in this list have passed into the repertoire of traditional folk singers.

I should like to thank many friends who have supplied me with useful information, or assisted in other ways, in particular Mr W. N. H. Harding, of Chicago, Mr R. S. Thomson, Hartford, Huntingdon (who located the Catnach catalogue), Mr John Foreman ('The Broadsheet King'), London, Mr Peter Stockham, of Dillon's University Bookshop, London, Mr Frederick G. Ruffner and Mr James M. Ethridge, both of Detroit. I am particularly indebted to Mr Sol Biderman, who introduced me to the *literatura de cordel* of Brazil, on which he is the expert; the verses quoted are from his own translations. Some material in the chapter SURVIVALS was first published in my article 'The Ballads Today', *New Society*, 20 December 1962.

I gratefully acknowledge the following permissions: the British Museum, for reproduction of two Black-Letter ballads, *The Lover's Tragedy* and *Oppertunity Lost* (Nos 13 and 68 in Collection Shelf Mark C.22.f.6); The Syndics of the University Library, Cambridge, for reproduction of the Catnach *Catalogue of Songs and Song Books* from the Madden Collection. Other items are from my own collection.

LESLIE SHEPARD

The primitive ballad, then, is popular, not in the sense of something arising from and suited to the lower orders of a people. As yet, no sharp distinction of high and low exists, in respect to knowledge, desires, and tastes. An increased civilization, and especially the introduction of book-culture, gradually gives rise to such a division; the poetry of art appears; the popular poetry is no longer relished by a portion of the people, and is abandoned to an uncultivated or not over-cultivated class—a constantly diminishing number. But whatever may be the estimation in which it may be held by particular classes or at particular epochs, it cannot lose its value. Being founded on what is permanent and universal in the heart of man, and now by printing put beyond the danger of perishing, it will survive the fluctuations of taste and may from time to time serve, as it notoriously did in England and Germany a hundred years ago, to recall a literature from false and artificial courses to nature and truth.

PROFESSOR FRANCIS JAMES CHILD
[from article 'Ballad Poetry' in *Johnson's Universal Cyclopaedia*, New York, 1894]

1: The Varieties of Street Literature

The Varieties of Street Literature

IT MAY SURPRISE MANY READERS TO BE TOLD THAT THERE IS A WHOLE field of literature that has been persistently ignored by literary historians.

Street literature is concerned with the cheap ballad-sheeets, pamphlets and other ephemera of the masses, which circulated from the dawn of printing right up to the end of the nineteenth century, a literature often more influential than books.

Histories of books and authors give a very one-sided view of the growth and development of literature as a cultural and political force. Books were produced by professional writers for the privileged few who could afford them, and the themes and language of books, like their fine bindings, generally reflected the outlook of sophisticated society. In the first four centuries of printing, books were mainly for church dignitaries, noblemen, scholars, merchants, and gentlemen with private libraries, not for the masses.

In modern times there has been much scholarly discussion as to whether there is a continuous line of English literature running from, say, Saxon times through Norman periods to modern English writing, changing its linguistic accent from Old English to modern but still basically reflecting a national scene and its outlook. Certain periods are given arbitrary labels—'Renaissance', 'Augustan', etc. Such views involve a misconception which arises through regarding literature as a succession of 'great works' in recited or printed form which are typical of their times. What they typify is merely the ideas and outlook of an élite.

Of course some literary creations, like the plays of Shakespeare, bridged all divisions of society, whilst works like *The Canterbury Tales* gave a panoramic view of the life of the time. Yet such works, however monumental, are hardly typical of the popular mass views of their period. Ordinary people could not afford to buy or read books until well into the twentieth century, and did not think so clearly about their times. Many of their attitudes and actions were rooted in layers of unconscious traditional response, often confused and contradictory.

Sophisticated literature merely provided, as it were, chapter-headings for the real story of ordinary people, whose own sub-literature of ballad-sheets and pamphlets provided news, diversion, inspiration, fantasy, and political stimulus. It is precisely because of its faults and deficiencies that it is of greater significance historically than the more polished works of sophisticated writers, for that sub-literature was linked to the fierce energies of the crowds that created history, rather than to the culture of its rulers or manipulators. The crude half-truth of a slogan has always been more powerful than a reasonable truth.

Although the invention of printed books extended the scope and subject-matter of written and recited literature, books only emphasised a division between two cultures—the popular culture of the ordinary folk, and the culture of the privileged classes. Until barely a century ago, masses of people were cut off from the world of books which is catalogued in all histories of literature. It was not until the cheap book production of the nineteenth century that many poor and middle-class people could afford to read books—even although many could already read. How, then, did they read?

For some four centuries, the streets had been full of ephemeral literature.

To begin with, there were broadside proclamations, the free history books of the streets. These official notices were fixed to posts which had been painted and ornamented for this purpose, or to the doors of sheriffs and other magistrates. Proclamations were the official notices of new laws, intrigues, battles, and peace treaties [see pages 15 and 16]. People who could not read would hear these proclamations read by others or cried on the streets. It is possible to construct a political history from proclamations alone, and indeed they have been invaluable source material for historians.

But above all, the halfpenny and penny broadside ballads were the popular literature of ordinary people from the sixteenth century onwards.

A broadside was a sheet printed on one side, and the text might be verse, prose, picture, or a mixture of all three. The term 'broadsheet' is often used as synonymous with 'broadside', but strictly speaking a broadsheet is either a large uncut sheet printed on both sides, or a pamphlet formed from one. Broadside ballads were sheets of verses, traditional or topical, usually decorated with a crude woodcut. The displayed title with woodcut illustrations set a

AN ACT

Prohibiting Correspondence with *CHARLS STUART* or his Party.

Whereas certain English Fugitives gathering themselves together in the parts of Scotland, did heretofore perfidiously and traiterously Assist the Enemies and Invaders of this Commonwealth, endeavoring with Forreigners and persons of desperate condition, to bring a War upon their Native Countrey ; and in order thereunto, did set up for their Head Charls Stuart, calling him their King, who had formerly been declared a Traitor to the Parliament and People of England ; And whereas afterwards, to divert the said Calamities thereby likely to ensue within the bowels of this Land, It pleased the Lord to direct the Parliament of this Commonwealth to send an Army into Scotland, and to afford them his gracious Assistance and Blessing in so wonderful a maner, that a good part of Scotland is become within the Power of this Commonwealth ; and the said Charls Stuart with his Complices, the Remainder of his Party, finding their own weakness and disability to continue longer in that Countrey, are now fled into England : For prevention therefore of the Mischiefs which may befal divers of the good People of this Nation, in case the said Fugitives be not timely overtaken by the English Army ; And to the end all persons may be further warned, The Parliament of the Commonwealth of England have thought fit to Enact and Declare, and do hereby Enact and Declare, That no person whatsoever do presume to hold any Correspondence with the said Charls Stuart, or with his Party, or with any of them, nor give any Intelligence to them, or to any of them, nor Countenance, Encourage, Abet, Adhere to, or Assist them or any of them, nor do voluntarily afford or deliver, or cause to be afforded or delivered to them or any of them, any Victuals, Provisions, Arms, Ammunition, Horses, Plate, Money, Men, or any other Relief whatsoever, under pain of High Treason. And the Parliament doth hereby Command all persons to use their Endeavors to hinder and stop the March and Passage of the said Charls Stuart and his Party, and of every of them, and to Resist and Oppose them according to such Orders and Directions as they shall receive from the Parliament, or from the Council of State appointed by Authority of Parliament, or from the General of the Forces of this Commonwealth, or from such other persons as shall be thereunto Authorized by them or any of them. And it is further Enacted by the Authority aforesaid, That whosoever shall offend against this Act and Declaration, shall or may be proceeded against by a Councel of War, who are hereby Authorized to hear and determine all and every the said Offences ; and such as shall by the said Councel be condemned to suffer Death, shall also forfeit all his and their Lands, Goods and other Estate, as in case of High Treason. Provided, That no person shall be proceeded against by any Court-Martial or Councel of War for any Offence done against this Act, unless such person be proceeded against, and convicted of such Offence within three Moneths after such Offence committed. Provided, That this Act continue in force till the First day of December, One thousand six hundred fifty one, and no longer. Provided also , and it is hereby Declared, That any person or persons who shall not be tryed by a Court-Martial or Councel of War, for any Offence committed contrary to this Act , shall and may at any time after the said three Moneths, be proceeded against for such Offence, according to the Laws of this Commonwealth, as if this Act had never been made.

Tuesday the 12ᵗʰ of August. 1651.

ORdered by the Parliament, That this Act be forthwith Printed and Published.

Hen: Scobell, Cleric. Parliamenti.

London, Printed by *John Field,* Printer to the Parliament of *England.* 1651.

An important broadside proclamation of 1651

✌ Thurſday, April 26. 1660.

Reſolved by the Lords and Commons in Parliament Aſſembled,

That this Day fortnight be ſet apart for a Day of Thankſgiving to the Lord for Raiſing up His Excellency the Lord General, and other Eminent Perſons who have been Inſtrumental in Delivery of this Nation from Thraldome and Miſery.

Reſolved by the Lords and Commons in Parliament Aſſembled,

That this Day fortnight be the Day ſet apart for a Day of Thankſgiving for both Houſes of Parliament, and within the Cities of London and Weſtminſter, and late Lines of Communication; And this Day Moneth for the Whole Nation.

April 26. 1660.

ORdered by the Lords in Parliament Aſſembled, That theſe Reſolves be forthwith Printed and Publiſhed.

Jo. Browne, *Cler. Parliament.*

LONDON, Printed by *John Macock*, and *Francis Tyton*, Printers to the Houſe of Lords, 1660.

A broadside proclamation of the Restoration, following the decisive victory of General Monk

style for the popular newspapers of the nineteenth century, and the technique of the arresting headline has scarcely changed over the centuries:

THE TRUE DESCRIPTION OF A MONSTEROUS CHYLDE BORNE IN THE ILE OF WIGHT [1564]

MURDER UPON MURDER, COMMITTED BY THOMAS SHERWOOD, ALIAS, COUNTREY TOM: AND ELIZABETH EVANS, ALIAS, CANBRYE BESSE [1635]

A DESCRIPTION OF A STRANGE (AND MIRACULOUS) FISH, CAST UPON THE SANDS IN THE MEADS, IN THE HUNDRED OF WORWELL, IN THE COUNTY PALATINE OF CHESTER [c 1636]

A NEW SPANISH TRAGEDY. OR, MORE STRANGE NEWES
    FROM THE NARROW SEAS [1639]
THE STRANGE AND WONDERFUL STORM OF HAIL,
    WHICH FELL IN LONDON ON THE 18th. OF MAY 1680
THE REPENTING MAIDS SORROWFUL LAMENTATION;
    FOR THE LOSS OF HER TRUE LOVE THAT SHOT
    HIMSELF IN SOHO [1698]
GREAT BRITAIN'S JOY FOR HER MOST GRACIOUS
    MAJESTY QUEEN ANN'S BEING UNANIMOUSLY
    PROCLAIM'D THROUGH ENGLAND, SCOTLAND, AND
    IRELAND [1702]
A NEW SONG ON THE BIRTH OF THE PRINCE OF WALES,
    WHO WAS BORN ON TUESDAY, NOVEMBER 9th, 1841
LAMENTATION & CONFESSION OF J. R. JEFFERY, WHO
    NOW LIES UNDER SENTENCE OF DEATH, FOR THE
    WILFUL MURDER OF HIS LITTLE BOY [1866]

Some news ballads summarised the whole story in a sub-title:

The two inseparate brothers. *OR*

A true and strange description of a Gentleman (an Italian by
birth) about seventeene yeeres of age, who hath an imperfect
(yet living) Brother, growing out of his side, having a head, two
armes, and one leg, all perfectly to be seen. They were both
baptized together; the imperfect is called *Iohn Baptist*, and the
other *Lazarus*. Admire the Creator in his Creatures. To the tune of
The Wandring Iewes

Chronicle [1637]

After such a heading there
seems little more to add, but
there were two parts to the
ballad, of eight and eleven
verses respectively. With a
special woodcut illustration,
this broadside ballad bears
an astonishing resemblance
to any modern sensational
newspaper front-page. Moreover, it appears to be a true
account of an exceptional
abnormality.

Whilst many such news ballads were reasonably accurate reports, others were entirely apocryphal, and a favourite yarn was the story

of the Pig-faced Lady, immensely rich, who needed a husband. This fable lingered in street balladry from 1639 to 1815.

Other broadside ballads covered a wide range of subjects—religious, political, criminal, romantic, amatory, bawdy, humorous, superstitious, moralistic, and tragic. Broadsides were often the spearhead of the protest movements of former times. For more than three centuries the major struggles of politics and religion were mirrored in the street ballad-sheets and news pamphlets, from the harsh dealings between Protestants and Catholics in Tudor and early Stuart times to the clashes of Roundheads and Cavaliers. Criminals and political offenders would have their doleful confessions (many of them ghost-written) sold on the streets where they were executed. But outside these front-page stories there were many ballads on the comedies and tragedies of everyday life. Here are some typical titles:

A LOUE-SICK MAID'S SONG, LATELY BEGUILD,
  BY A RUN-AWAY LOUER THAT LEFT HER WITH
  CHILDE [c 1615]
A MAYDENS LAMENTATION FOR A BEDFELLOW. OR, I
  CAN, NOR WILL NO LONGER LYE ALONE [c 1615]
THE MANS COMFORTABLE ANSWER TO THE MAYDEN
  THAT CAN NOR WILL NO LONGER LY ALONE [c 1615]
THE FAMOUS RATKETCHER, WITH HIS TRAVELS INTO
  FRANCE, AND OF HIS RETURNE TO LONDON [c 1615]
THIS MAID WOULD GIVE TEN SHILLINGS FOR A KISS
  [c 1615]
SIR WALTER RAULEIGH HIS LAMENTATION: WHO WAS
  BEHEADED IN THE OLD PALLACE AT WESTMINSTER
  THE 29. OF OCTOBER. 1618
DAMNABLE PRACTISES OF THREE LINCOLN-SHIRE
  WITCHES [1619]

GOOD SIR, YOU WRONG YOUR BRITCHES [1625]

A WONDER BEYOND MANS EXPECTATION, IN THE PRESERUATION OF EIGHT MEN IN GREENLAND FROM ONE SEASON TO ANOTHER, THE LIKE NEUER KNOWNE OR HEARD OF BEFORE, WHICH EIGHT MEN ARE COME ALL SAFELY FROM THENCE IN THIS LAST FLEET, 1631

KNAVERY IN ALL TRADES, OR, HERE'S AN AGE WOULD MAKE A MAN MAD [1632]

STRANGE NEWES FROM BROTHERTON IN YORKE-SHIRE, BEING A TRUE RELATION OF THE RAINING OF WHEAT ON EASTER DAY LAST, TO THE GREAT AMAIZMENT OF ALL THE INHABITANTS [c 1648]

NO NATURALL MOTHER, BUT A MONSTER. OR, THE EXACT RELATION OF ONE, WHO FOR MAKING AWAY HER OWNE NEW BORNE CHILDE, ABOUT BRAINFORD NEERE LONDON, WAS HANG'D AT TEYBORNE, ON WEDNESDAY THE 11. OF DECEMBER, 1633

THE LAMENTING LADY, WHO FOR THE WRONGS DONE BY HER TO A POORE WOMAN, FOR HAUING TWO CHILDREN AT ONE BURTHEN, WAS BY THE HAND OF GOD MOST STRANGELY PUNISHED, BY SENDING HER AS MANY CHILDREN AT ONE BIRTH, AS THERE ARE DAIES IN THE YEARE [c 1620]

A WARNING FOR ALL GOOD FELLOWES TO TAKE HEEDE OF PUNCKES INTICEMENTS [c 1625]

THE POOR WHORE'S COMPLAINT TO THE APPRENTICES OF LONDON [1668]

MANS AMAZEMENT: IT BEING A TRUE RELATION OF ONE THOMAS COX, A HACKNEY-COACH-MAN, TO WHOM THE DEVIL APPEARED ON FRIDAY NIGHT, IT BEING THE 31st OF OCTOBER, FIRST IN THE LIKE-NESS OF A GENTLEMAN, SEEMING TO HAVE A ROLE OF PAPER OR PARCHMENT IN HIS HAND, AFTER-WARDS IN THE LIKENESS OF A GREAT BEAR WITH GLARING EYES, WHICH SO AFFRIGHTED HIM, THAT IT DEPRIVED HIM OF ALL HIS SENCES [1684]

Such penny and halfpenny sheets constituted a popular literature more versatile than printed books, with best-sellers, and classics of

A New SONG, called
The Lover's Tragedy:
or
PARENTS Cruelty.

To the Tune of, *Charon make haß and Carry me Over.*

A Virgin fair'd by her Vertue and Beauty,
Who by her Parents was greatly lov'd,
To whom she paid all obedience and duty,
rather chusing to be rejected;
A loving youth of Reputation
having her features burn'd,
Who struck with so much love and admiration,
seeing the thoughts of her could cruckue.

To her parent, us'd all indeavours
for to obtain her friend's consent,
But he no means could picture their favour,
which fill'd his heart full of discontent.

He had made many a fair profession,
But what he offer'd they still deny'd;
At last he in a desparting condition,
thus on his sorrows himself cry'd;
Entreating my nearest dearest Behavers,
but a mission Lover complain,
Who upon Earth was her her from hours,
gave in sunder a sympathy disdain.

Banish her Parents (ye Gods) for refusing
a heart so loving, so sad and true,
Which they deserve for so vilely refusing,
to be tormented as bad by you;
But may the Nymph, so fair and cruel,
every Worldly Bliss enjoy,
Since if the languish'd I ye in she know well,
she with a smile would my care destroy.

At last he grew to break a condition,
that there was nothing could yield relief,
Seeing the Virgin who was his Physician,
on whom he sain'd to express his Grief;
Farewell, O cruel Nymph, he cry'd,
I now to Elizium must repair;
There grate a sigh or two, and so he dy'd,
and thus for his curse of all his care.

To the fair Virgin this News was soon carried,
which perhaps struck her with great surprize;
She trowing to see him ere he was buried,
upon She had slain with her killing Eyes.
To the house she sped with expedition,
as if by Cupids Wings remov'd,
Asting at top in a soft low Tone from,
which way the Room where his Corps was lay'd.

When to the Chamber was quickly conducted,
both in a swound on his Bed he lay,
Which sight to on her unkindness reflected
that made her swound in the Room away:
Many hearts came to her assistance,
and so her festival things reply'd,
But Death against them all made such resistance,
that by the Corps so her blour dy'd.

When this sad News came to her Parents,
both in a heavy distraction were,
Running like mad people, crying and staring,
for the sad loss of their Daughter fair;
Tho' they presented their being slighted,
while they were living by their care,
Yet in one Grave they together were buried,
thus was the end of this lovely pair.

FINIS.

This may be Printed, R. P.

Printed for P. Brooksby at the Golden Ball
in Pye-corner.

fiction and non-fiction. Some broadside ballads were even collected into elegant anthologies with names like *A Handefull of pleasant delites*. This particular poetical anthology, printed in 1584, was highly praised by a modern editor as 'one of the most prized of the poetical book gems of the Elizabethan period', but contains only street ballads from broadsides. One of these, 'A new Courtly Sonet, of the Lady Green sleeues', has retained its popularity even today; the full version of eighteen verses published in the *Handefull* has special interest, as it presents the complete wardrobe of an Elizabethan lady of high fashion.

Some broadside ballads suggested themes to authors of books, and a few broadside writers also published more sophisticated literature. Richard Johnson (1573–1659?), poet, prose writer, and author of the deathless work *The Famous Historie of the Seven Champions of Christendome*, wrote a number of popular broadside ballads. Other writers would compose ballads to order, to lampoon some public figure. Some two hundred ballad writers are known by name from the Elizabethan period, including, poets, playwrights, courtiers, and priests, as well as the literary hacks of the taverns. Many ballad-sheets were unsigned (some merely initialled), for the radical political and religious items could result in severe penalties. Other broadsides merely printed the beautiful traditional folk ballads from centuries earlier.

Most of the ballads were sung by the hawkers who sold them for a halfpenny or a penny, and the tunes were either established favourites or new tunes which would become familiar if one bought the sheet of words to jog one's memory. A limited number of broadsides printed a few bars of music notation, but in most instances these were meaningless devices of decorative value only. Some of the broadsides, notably execution papers, were prose reports, but the sixteenth and seventeenth century format was predominantly a musical one.

The hawkers would come bawling through the streets, clutching a sheaf of broadsides or news pamphlets, hot from the press, just like the newspaper sellers of modern times.

The broadside ballad, then, was a kind of musical journalism, the forerunner of the popular prose newspapers, and a continuation of the folk tradition of minstrelsy.

In addition to prose and verse broadsides, there were also sheets

The old blind Man playing on Sticks.

Italian Muficians.

The Country Fidler and his Son

Here's the laft dying Speech and Confefsion

One kind of 'lottery'—a sheet of pictures

of woodcut pictures which could be pasted on walls for decoration, or simply used as materials for imaginative reverie, a kind of poor man's art gallery. Amongst the earliest broadsides are sheets with a wood block illustration of a saint. Several of these are extant from the fifteenth century, and one, a woodcut of St Christopher is dated 1423. Some of these sheets may have been intended for binding into block-books in the period before the development of movable type.

In the nineteenth century, sheets of wood-cut illustrations for children were sold under the name of 'lotteries' [see page 22]. I have found no reliable explanation for the origin of this strange term, although there is a suggestion that these prints were placed between the pages of books and used as a game or 'lottery' by children. On the other hand, the nineteenth century prudery about children's activities would surely have discouraged anything savouring of gambling, and it may be that the term has another origin.

Of course, the illustrated handbills and posters for state lotteries were themselves a colourful part of street literature. The first public English lottery, projected in 1566, was actually drawn in 1569, and Holinshed recorded 'A great lotterie being holden at London, in Poules Church Yard, at the west dore, was begun to be drawne the eleventh of Januarie, and continued daie and night until the sixt of Maie, wherein the said drawing was fullie ended'. In 1826 there was a frenzied outburst of street literature announcing the last state lottery, to be drawn on 18 October of that year, and thousands of posters and handbills were issued; there were elaborate street processions, and sandwich-men paraded with placards.

After a hiatus of 130 years, the state revived lotteries in Britain with the introduction of prizewinning Premium Savings Bonds on 1 November 1956. The public handbills and leaflets advertising this modern lottery are available in post offices throughout the country, but they are of the most staid and dignified character compared to the highly imaginative and exuberant street literature of former times.

In addition to broadsides of various kinds, there has been a torrent of pamphlet literature since printing began—news books, tracts of religious and political controversy, almanacs, and chap-books ('cheap books'). The religious and political pamphlets had a decisive influence on popular opinion and the course of history, and many pamphleteers were hanged and tortured for their seditious

Street advertising for 'The last State Lottery' of 1826

propaganda. In 1715, Myles Davies, an early historian of pamphlet literature, commented on the variety and scope of subject-matter in his *Icon Libellorum, or a Critical History of Pamphlets*, written under the name 'A Gentleman of the Inns of Court':

From Pamphlets may be learn'd the Genius of the Age, the Debates of the Learned, the Follies of the Ignorant, the bevews [bévues] of Government, the Oversights of Statesmen, the Mistakes of Courtiers, the different approaches of Foreigners, and the several encroachments of Rivals; in *Pamphlets*, Merchants may read their profit and loss, Shopkeepers their Bills of Parcels, Countrymen their Seasons of Husbandry, Sailors their Longtitude, Soldiers their Camps and Enemies; thence School-boys may improve their Lessons, Scholars their Studies, Ministers their Sermons, and Zealots their Devisions. *Pamphlets* furnisht Beau's with their Airs, Coquets with their Charms: Pamphlets are as Modish Ornaments to Gentlewomen's Toylets as to Gentlemen's Pockets: Pamphlets carry reputation of Wit and Learning to all that make them their companions: The Poor find their account in Stall-keeping, and in hawking them: The Rich find in them their Shortest Way to the Secrets of Church and State.

Obviously the greater number of pamphlets were beyond the purse of poorer people, for whom even a halfpenny ballad was a luxury, but many found a lucrative profession in selling broadside ballads and pamphlets, particularly the news pamphlets ('news books' and 'corantos') which spread from 1622 onwards.

Almanacs were one of the most profitable types of cheap pamphlet or broadside, and the Company of Stationers of London jealously guarded its monopoly of printed almanacs for two hundred years, until it was successfully challenged by the courageous London bookseller Thomas Carnan in 1773. A few months later, the company's perpetual copyright in almanacs was in danger through a judgement of the Lord Chancellor; in 1775 the Court of Common Pleas decided that the publishing of all almanacs by one organisation could not be upheld. After that the way was clear for rival Old Moores and Poor Robins. Almanacs were very profitable pamphlets. Apart from the conventional enigmatic prognostications, they contained essential information on times and seasons, dates of festivals, holidays, country fairs, and other data needed by farmers and peasants. Some almanacs also listed the roads and routes followed by the pedlars who sold the almanacs throughout the countryside.

In 1774, Samuel Johnson stressed the importance of pamphlet literature to the historian. His perceptive essay 'On the Origin and Importance of Small Tracts and Fugitive Pieces' appeared as an introduction to Osborne's edition of the *Harleian Miscellany* (from the collection of Edward Harley, second Earl of Oxford, 1689–1741), first published in eight volumes 1744–6. In this essay Johnson commented:

> From *Pamphlets*, consequently, are to learned the *Progress* of every debate; the various State, to which the questions have been changed; the artifices and fallacies, which have been used; and the subterfuges, by which reason has been eluded: In such writings may be seen how the mind has been opened by degrees, how one truth has led to another, how the mind has been disentangled, and hints improved to demonstration. Which pleasure, and many others are lost by him, that only reads the *larger Writers*, by whom these scattered sentiments are collected, who will see none of the changes of fortune, which every opinion has passed through. . . .

Pamphlets appealed chiefly to the middle classes. The language and the finer points of religious and political controversy were complex, and besides, the pamphlets were too expensive for most poor readers. Chapbooks were the popular pamphlets of the poor.

A chapbook was a sheet folded in four, eight, twelve, or sixteen, making a small uncut booklet of eight, sixteen, twenty-four, or thirty-two pages, thus described as 4to, 8vo, 12mo, 16mo as in normal book production. But chapbooks were sold uncut and unstitched at a halfpenny or a penny each. The purchaser would slit the pages and lovingly stitch or pin them—a kind of do-it-yourself paperback. The word 'chapbook' seems to have derived from the Anglo-Saxon term *ceap*, in the sense of 'trade', for these pamphlets were sold by pedlars together with pins, ribbons, and other knick-knacks.

The Civil War and Commonwealth period had provoked a flood of political pamphlets, and these must have popularised the chapbook format, as well as stimulated a nostalgia for more romantic themes.

Chapbooks began as a kind of printed folklore. Like broadsides they had quaint woodcut illustrations, but they had a broader scope than the ballads. Chapbooks retold old romances and fairy-tales,

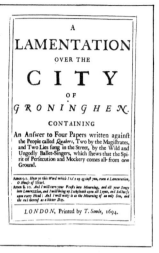

A
LAMENTATION
OVER THE
C I T Y
OF
G R O I N G H E N.

CONTAINING

An Answer to Four Papers written against the People called *Quakers*, Two by the Magistrates, and Two Lies sung in the Street, by the Wild and Ungodly Ballet-Singers, which shews that the Spirit of Persecution and Mockery comes all from one Ground.

Amos 5.1. Hear ye this Word which I take up against you, even a Lamentation, O House of Israel. Amos 8. 10. And I will turn your Feasts into Mourning, and all your Songs into Lamentation, and I will bring up Sackcloth upon all Loyns, and Baldness upon every Head : And I will make it as the Mourning of an only Son, and the end thereof as a bitter Day.

LONDON, Printed by T. *Sowle,* 1694.

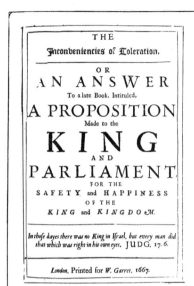

THE
𝕴nconbeniencies of 𝕿oleration,
OR
AN ANSWER
To a late Book, Intituled,
A PROPOSITION
Made to the
K I N G
AND
PARLIAMENT
FOR THE
SAFETY and HAPPINESS
OF THE
KING and *KINGDOM.*

In those dayes there was no King in Israel, but every man did that which was right in his own eyes. JUDG. 17. 6.

London, Printed for *W. Garret.* 1667.

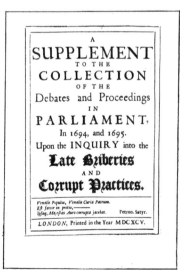

REASONS
OF THE
INCREASE
OF THE
Dutch Trade.

WHEREIN

Is demonstrated from what Causes the *Dutch* Govern and Manage Trade better than the *English* ; whereby they have so far improved their Trade above the *English.*

TREATISE II.

By *ROGER COKE.*

LONDON,
Printed by *J. C.* for *Henry Brome,* at the *Gun* at the *W. g-end* of St. *Pauls.* 1671.

A
SUPPLEMENT
TO THE
COLLECTION
OF THE
Debates and Proceedings
IN
PARLIAMENT,
In 1694, and 1695.
Upon the INQUIRY into the
Late 𝕭riberies
AND
Corrupt 𝕻ractices.

*Venalis Populus, Venalis Curia Patrum.
Est favor in pretio,——
Ipsaq; Majestas Auro corrupta jacebat.* Petron. Satyr.

LONDON, Printed in the Year MDCXCV.

A group of typical pamphlets on diverse subjects

related stories of ancient battles, rehashed superstitions and riddles, interpreted dreams, foretold the future, exhorted sinners to repentance, or simply cracked jokes. These penny histories were the books of poor people, and they coloured their outlook and philosophy.

Many chapbooks were shorter versions of the sixpenny and shilling romances bought by more prosperous readers, and considerable ingenuity was shown by hack writers in digesting substantial works like the ever-popular *Seven Champions of Christendom* to a twenty-four page chapbook. One miracle of condensation was the rendering of *The Canterbury Tales* in twenty-four small pages. Richard Greene's *Pandosto* (also known as *The History of Dorastus and Fawnia*), which provided the plot for Shakespeare's *The Winter's Tale*, cost a shilling in 1588, but the penny chapbook version was a great favourite with poor people. The wide scope of chapbook subject-matter supplied ordinary people with every variety of literature—poetry, songs, fiction, history, folklore, ghosts and marvels. Here are some typical chapbook titles, many of which remained popular from the seventeenth century till the end of the eighteenth century:

The History of Dr. John Faustus, showing how he sold himself to the Devil to have power to do what he pleased for twenty-four years. Also Strange Things Done by Him and His Servant Mephistopheles. With an Account how the Devil came for him, and tore him in Pieces.

The History of the Learned Friar Bacon

The Old Egyptian Fortune-Teller's Last Legacy

The History of Mother Shipton

The History of Valentine and Orson

The Life and Death of St. George the Noble Champion of England

The True Trial of Understanding: or Wit Newly Reviv'd, being a Book of Riddles Adorned with a Variety of Pictures

The Whole Trial and Indictment of Sir John Barleycorn, Knt.

The Foreign Travels of Sir John Mandeville

The Most Lamentable and Deplorable History of the Two Children in the Wood

The Famous and Memorable History of Chevy Chase

The World Turned Upside Down

The Merry Tales of the Wise Men of Gotham

The Famous and Pleasant

HISTORY

OF

PARISMUS,

The Valiant and Renowned

Prince of BOHEMIA.

In Three PARTS.

PART I. Containing his Triumphant Battles fought against the *Persians*, his Love to the Beautiful *Laurana*, the great Dangers he passed in the *Island of Rocks*, and his strange Adventures in the *Desolate Island*

PART II. Containing the Adventurous Travels, and Noble Chivalry of *Parismenos*, The *Knight of Fame*, with his Love to the fair Princess *Angelica*, the *Lady of the Golden Tower*.

PART III. Containing the Admirable Adventures and truly Heroick Atchievements of *Parismenos*, *Knight of the Golden Star*, with his Love to the Fair *Astrea*, Princess of *Austracia*, and other rare Adventures

The Seventh EDITION.

LONDON: Printed for Mess. *Bettesworth* and *Hitch*, at the *Red Lyon*, and *J. Osborne*, at the *Golden Ball*, in *Pater Noster-Row*; *R. Ware*, at the *Sun and Bible* in *Amen-Corner*, and *James Hodges*, at the *Looking-Glass*, on *London-Bridge* 1734.

This Book relates what worthy Deeds were done
By the seven Champions of *Christendom*:
They Giants, Dragons, Monsters, Serpents slew,
And mighty *Pagan* Armies overthrew.
They the damn'd Necromancer's Pow'r did quell,
And them with their Enchantments, sent to Hell:
They acted like the Sons of valiant Sires.
Whose high Atchievements all the World admires.
Read them with *Pleasure* this renowned Story,
Which for your Recreation's set before ye.

The Illustrious and Renown'd

HISTORY

OF THE

Seven famous Champions

OF

CHRISTENDOM.

In Three Parts.

Containing their Honourable Births, Victories, and noble Atchievements by Sea and Land, in divers strange Countries; their Combats with Giants, Monsters, &c. wonderful Adventures, Fortunes and Misfortunes, in Desarts, Wildernesses, inchanted Castles; their Conquests of Empires, Kingdoms; relieving distressed Ladies, with their faithful love to them; *Honour* they won in Jousts and Turnaments; and Success against the Enemies of *Christendom*.

Also, with

The Heroic Adventures of St. *George's* three Sons.

TOGETHER

With the *Manner* of their untimely Deaths; and how they came to be stiled Saints and Champions of *Christendom*.

The Eighth EDITION.

London: Printed for *C. Hitch*, at the *Red Lion*, in *Pater-Noster-Row*, *R. Ware*, at the *Bible and Sun*, in *Ludgate-Hill*, *S. Crowder* at the *Looking-Glass* on *London-Bridge* and *H. Woodgate* at the *Golden Ball*, in *Pater-Noster-Row*. 1759.

Two popular 'small books', often abridged into chapbooks

A Whetstone for Dull Wits, or a Poesy of New and Ingenious Riddles
The Life and Death of Fair Rosamond, concubine to King Henry the
*   Second, showing her being poisoned by Queen Eleanor*
Hocus Pocus, or a New Book of Legerdemain

Like some of the broadsides, there were chapbooks which would outline the whole contents in a heroic title:

Here is a full and true RELATION
Of one MR. RICH LANGLY, A GLAZIER,
Living over against the Sign of the Golden Wheat Sheaf in Ratcliff
Highway, London, that lay in a Trance for two Days and one Night.
He also saw the Joys of Heaven and the Terrors of Hell.
You have also an Account when he came out of His Trance, how he
declared to the Minister, that he had but 5 Days to live in this World,
before he should depart. As soon as the Minister was gone out of the
Room, it is said the Devil appearing to him, and asking of him if he
would Sell his Soul and Body to Him, proffering him in the shape of
a Gentleman, a bag of Gold, but he crying out against it, and saying,
Lord Jesus receive my soul. Having an account how the Devil
Vanished away in a Flame of Fire, you have also in this Book, a
Good and Godly Sermon, that was Preached on him at his Funeral,
by that Reverend and Learned Divine, Dr. Pede, Minister, of the
Parish Church of Clakenwell London.
LICENSED ACCORDING TO ORDER.

Some of the best of the early chapbooks were collected by Samuel Pepys, who also preserved the largest collection of early broadside ballads. Pepys bound his chapbooks into small quarto volumes, titled *Vulgaria*; he also bound up others in four smaller volumes titled *Penny Witticisms; Penny Merriments; Penny Compliments;* and *Penny Godlinesses*. Together with his great collection of some eighteen hundred broadside ballads, the chapbook volumes record a cross-section of the popular reading-matter of the time.

The first great period of broadside ballads and chapbooks extended from the early sixteenth century to the end of the seventeenth century, in spite of periodic harsh legislation against seditious literature. In the eighteenth century, chapbooks were more popular than broadsides, but in the nineteenth century there was a final tremendous outpouring of every kind of street literature, just before the introduction of cheap books and newspapers. Thousands upon thousands of broadsides and chapbooks swept like a tidal wave over the streets and market-places. And as the tide receded, much of this fragile ephemera disappeared, leaving only the souvenirs secured by thoughtful collectors. Few materials are more perishable than paper.

Throughout four centuries of street literature, only a handful of broadminded and far-seeing individuals preserved specimens of the immense variety and vigour of these ephemeral papers.

The broadside ballads collected by Samuel Pepys had earlier passed through other discerning hands. The manuscript title-page gives the following provenance:

My Collection of Ballads; begun by Mr. Selden;
Improv'd by yᵉ addition of many Pieces elder thereto in Time; and the whole continued to the year 1700. When the Form, till then peculiar thereto, vizᵗ of the Black Letter with Picturs, seems (for cheapness sake) wholly laid aside, for that of the White Letter without Pictures.

The reference to 'Black Letter' denotes the 𝕲𝖔𝖙𝖍𝖎𝖈 typeface later superseded by roman letters. But the reference to 'Picturs' is incorrect, for the wood-cut illustrations persisted on the majority of broadside ballads until the mid-nineteenth century.

The Pepys Collection has pride of place as the largest and most complete of its kind. Pepys arranged his five volumes under ten headings:

1. Devotion and Morality
2. History—True and Fabulous
3. Tragedy—vizᵗ Murd.ʳˢ Execut.ⁿˢ Judgm.ᵗˢ of God
4. State and Times
5. Love—Pleasant
6. do.—Unfortunate
7. Marriage, Cuckoldry, &c.
8. Sea—Love, Gallantry, & Actions
9. Drinking & Good Fellowshipp
10. Humour, Frollicks &c. mixt.

These divisions constitute an excellent cross-section of the scope of broadside ballads, and incidentally of Pepys's own personal pre-occupations, for he was truly a man of his time. On the verso of the title-page he quotes Selden's famous statement: 'Though some make slight of Libells; yet you may see by them, how the Wind sits. As take a Straw, and throw it up into the Air; you may see by that, which way the Wind is; which you shall not do, by casting up a Stone.

More solid things do not shew the Complexion of the Times, so well as Ballads and Libells.' This perceptive comment was also quoted by Bishop Percy as a half-title to volume 2 of his famous *Reliques of Ancient English Poetry*, a work drawn more from broadside balladry than from the famous folio manuscript acquired by Percy. The Pepys Collection is housed at The Pepysian Library, Magdalene College, Cambridge.

The next most famous collection is the Roxburghe, at one time the property of John Ker, third duke of Roxburghe. It would be more proper to call this the 'Harleian Ballads' since the collection was basically assembled by Robert Harley, first Earl of Oxford (1661–1724). The collection later passed to James West, President of the Royal Society; then, a year after his death in 1772, it was acquired by Major Thomas Pearson, who added an alphabetical index of first lines. After Pearson's death, the collection was bought for the Duke of Roxburghe in 1788; he had the volumes rebound. At the sale of the Duke's library in 1813, the ballads passed to Benjamin Haywood Bright, who added some additional items, and after his death the collection finally passed to the British Museum in 1845. This great collection contains nearly 1,500 ballads.

Another celebrated collector was Anthony Wood (1632–95), author of *Athenae Oxonienses*, published 1691–2. Only 279 ballads remain in his collection, once at the Ashmolean Museum and now in the Bodleian Library at Oxford. There is evidence that two or three times that number were removed, and found their way into the Roxburghe Collection in Harley's time. The 218 ballads of the Rawlinson Collection at the Bodleian are believed to have come from the ill-fated Wood Collection.

One man who supplied items to Harley was John Bagford (1650–1716), an early pioneer of the study of ephemera [see page 33]. Bagford was a London shoemaker, a self-educated man who became a connoisseur of old books, prints, and coins. He planned a history of printing based on his own collection of title-pages of books. Bagford was employed by various noblemen and gentry to obtain rare items for their libraries. It is generally assumed that he pillaged the Wood Collection, although there is no evidence to show whether the items obtained for other collectors were stolen or simply imprudently supplied to Bagford. Bagford's own collection of three volumes of ballads is now in the British Museum.

JOHN BACKFORD.
Obijt 6. of May Æ. Suæ 60.

Another source listing the variety and scope of broadside ballads is furnished by the registers of the Stationers' Company, London, who required registration of ballads as well as books. The printed *Transcripts* edited by Professor Edward Arber show broadside ballads side by side with the sophisticated publications of their time. Between 1557 and 1709, some three thousand ballad titles were registered. Probably something like three times that number were printed by unlicensed presses. There could have been more than 15,000 different ballads in circulation during that period.

The history of the Black-Letter period of broadside ballads has been exhaustively documented by many specialists, notably the late Professor Hyder E. Rollins of Harvard University. During the nineteenth century, a number of great collections, including the Roxburghe and the Bagford, were reprinted with critical notes by the Ballad Society, London, under the editorship of William Chappell and the Rev Joseph W. Ebsworth. In the twentieth century Rollins was responsible for many brilliant volumes reprinting and annotating selections from the Pepys and related collections.

The largest collection of pamphlets was formed by George Thomason, a seventeenth century bookseller at the Sign of the Rose and Crown in St Paul's Churchyard, London. Between 1641 and 1662 he secured copies of every tract, broadside, news book, or handbill which he thought might be of interest to posterity. The collection of some 22,255 items includes 14,942 pamphlets relating to the Civil War, Commonwealth, and Restoration periods. This heroic collection is now in the British Museum Library, and there is a published catalogue of the items. Pamphlet literature is also well represented by the *Harleian Miscellany*, reissued by Thomas Parks, London, in ten volumes, 1808–13.

There has been no really comprehensive reprinting of chapbook collections, although there are some useful studies and some valuable catalogues. One of the best general surveys is that of Harry B. Weiss, *A Book about Chapbooks, The People's Literature of Bygone Times*, privately printed 1942, reissued by Folklore Associates, Pennsylvania, 1969. A useful survey of literature and printers of chapbooks is *Chapbooks: A Bibliography of References to English and American Chapbook Literature of the Eighteenth and Nineteenth Centuries* by Victor E. Neuburg, London, 1964; new edition, 1972. There is also a delightful review of the subject in *Banbury Chap Books and Nursery Toy Book Literature (Of the XVIII. And Early XIX. Centuries)* by Edwin Pearson, London, 1890, reprinted New York, nd, and London 1970. Of the catalogues of chapbook collections, two deserve special mention: *Catalogue of English and American Chapbooks and Broadsides in Harvard College Library*, Cambridge, Mass., 1905, reprinted Detroit, 1968; and

National Library of Scotland. Catalogue of the Lauriston Castle Chapbooks, Boston, Mass., 1964.

Little was published on the final great period of street literature during the nineteenth century until the pioneer work of Henry Mayhew in his great survey *London Labour and the London Poor*, published from 1851 onwards after Mayhew's preliminary articles in the *Morning Chronicle* in 1849. The definitive edition of his work was published 1861–2, and has been reprinted recently.

Mayhew listed and classified an astounding range of street literature, including love songs, religious tracts, conundrums and riddles, newspapers, lottery tickets, playbills, exhibition papers, magical delusions, almanacs, long-song sheets, song books, children's books, battledores, squibs, political dialogues, 'litanies', 'cocks', 'catchpennies', and other varieties of ephemera. Until Mayhew's time none of this vast world of street literature had been properly studied in relation to the social conditions of the times, and even subsequent investigations have somehow kept street literature apart from the general history of literature as a somewhat disreputable chapter, or a curious and romantic offshoot.

The extraordinary fact is, however, that this kind of literature is the life-blood of popular sentiment and action, for no matter how much policy is planned by politicians and conspirators, or culture directed and exploited by entrepreneurs, it is the inchoate mass of popular feeling, with its strange mixture of truth, untruth, and sheer banality, which is the pulse of history and which has shaped the destiny of nations.

Ballads have always had more influence than polite literature. It is no use arguing that the political ballad 'Lilliburlero' is poor doggerel compared with Dryden's 'Song for Saint Cecilia's Day' published only a few months earlier, for, as Macaulay commented, 'The verses and the tune caught the fancy of the nation. From one end of England to the other all classes were singing this idle rhyme.' Bishop Burnet noted 'perhaps never had so slight a thing so great an effect' in the revolution of 1688. In the same period, another broadside began 'Dryden, thy Wit has catterwauld too long, Now *Lero, Lero*, is the only Song'.

Crowds love lies and half-truths better than truth itself. They are quick, uncomplicated, and capable of instant application. The very banality and sometimes downright dishonesty of much of street literature is a good reason why we should study such things. The epicurean theory of literature that only the best books have historical and aesthetic importance is misleading. Such works have often had the least influence in their times or even later. To understand the phenomenon of man we must study the tremendous popularity of the banal, the grotesque, anti-social and dishonest, side by side with the cheaply printed remnants of noble old romances and the fragments of folk poetry which have a beauty beyond all sophisticated verse.

Ever since the growth of towns and cities, the street and the market-place have been the great theatre of the people, the stage for comedy and tragedy. In medieval times, the folk passion plays were acted out by strolling players, blending verses from oral tradition with the magic of primitive stage technique. At other times the streets and public places have seen the dimly understood remnants of old folk festivals and processions. For centuries the great real-life dramatic spectacle of the streets was the public execution, staged with a sweating cast of thousands and the horrifying vulgarities of crude dishonourable death.

Bawling hawkers have sold ballads, pamphlets and news-sheets, and pedlars have taken cheaply printed ballads and chapbooks to every country village. Throughout history the fairground mountebanks, traders, and other colourful rogues have charmed, lied and cheated their way into the hearts of the crowd, right up to modern times when they have become rich and famous manipulating the masses in newspapers, magazines, and television programmes.

In the past, the streets were the libraries and bookshops of the masses, their primers and reading rooms. Today, with the sensationalist literature of pop revolt and pornography, posters of underground-music groups and political agitation, and the hasty graffiti of bourgeois revolutionaries, they are the scene for provocative demonstrations and the inhuman brutalities of urban warfare.

2: How It Began

How It Began

STREET LITERATURE, IN ITS BROADEST SENSE, IS AS OLD AS MANKIND.
The paintings on the walls of palaeolithic caves in southern
France and northern Spain, circa 30,000–10,000 BC, might be
considered proclamations of a magical society long before letters.
Before the invention of paper, many messages have been carved
laboriously on stones. Long before printing, *gazettas* were written by
hand. The *Acta Diurna* of ancient Rome were announcements of
battles, elections, and calendar events, posted up in public places
and sometimes delivered to individuals, like morning newspapers.
There must have been a high degree of literacy amongst the ancients,
for we know that in the first century AD Apollonius of Tyana quelled
a riot at Pamphylia by a terse message written on a single tablet.
Since those days, printed messages on sheets have more often
provoked and encouraged riots.

To understand the history and function of cheap popular literature,
we must consider the impulses that shaped it.

There are two major forces in human affairs. The first of these is
tradition—a great underground river that nourished the past,
fertilises the present, and gives meaning to the future. Consciously
or unconsciously the whole process of life is shaped by tradition, and
when we abandon it life becomes artificial, grotesque, and meaningless. Tradition is manifest in form and recreated by it, yet mere form
alone, without the spirit which is the essence of tradition, becomes
stereotyped and reactionary.

The second great force is topicality—the newness of things in the
material world. It animates the individual life in the context of
history, compelling re-statement and fresh discovery. Topicality is
for ever running off at a tangent, asking questions, demanding a new
view. At best, topicality refines and revitalises tradition which has
become stagnant and dogmatic; at worst, it leads us away from a
firm design for living, by creating insatiable demands or distracting
with tawdry novelty and slick oversimplifications.

All literature is shaped by these two forces, but books belong to
sophisticated culture. The printed tradition of halfpenny and penny
broadside ballads and chapbook pamphlets stemmed from the

traditional culture of folk music, dance, and story, upon which the technique of printing was superimposed. And printed sheets became as much carriers of tradition as the oral transmission of texts from father to son and grandmother to child. Folk culture is older than printing, but both oral and printed traditions have told the same human story, and some of the noblest insights of mankind, as well as its topical trivia, have been conveyed by the beautiful shapes of letters lovingly written or printed.

There is much mystification about folk music and its origins in the ages before printing. We have been told by one pundit after another that folk song is simply an oral tradition, that it is the spontaneous creation of a nameless group, or that it is the art work of a single talented minstrel. They say it is the musical outburst of a man at work or in love, that it is the music of peasants, or the art of 'a people' (as opposed to the music of birds and insects, perhaps?). It is the music of 'all of us' (and thus the new sound of the Beatles, the Rolling Stones, Bob Dylan, perhaps even Tiny Tim) or it is simply 'the music of the working class'. Obviously it all depends what you mean by 'folk'.

With due respect to many scholars and propagandists who have debated these views, all such explanations are unsatisfactory, because they are a mixture of half-truths, inaccuracies and special pleading. Oral transmission and the conservatism of peasant societies are obvious aspects at a certain time and place, but they are only chapters of a larger story.

Rich men have had their insights as well as the poor, and there is no sin in wealth or beauty—only in the selfish use of it. The great English and Scottish popular ballads sung by the peasantry for centuries descended, in part, from the same stories danced and sung by noble families in Scandinavia centuries earlier, while the troubadours and minstrels who were honoured by kings and princes were ancestors to the rogues and vagabonds of the broadside ballad periods. Superficial distinctions between art and folk culture break down when one considers the great religious song and recitative dramas of the poor people of India (like the *Ram Lila*, performed by dedicated barnstormers over the centuries), for the conventions and techniques are as stylised as classical Western opera.

It can no longer be doubted that the body of European folklore, including tales, music, ballads, rhymes, riddles and ceremonies, is a recasting of the fragments of ancient religion.

The myths and rituals of great religions established a relationship between man and the mystery of his existence through poetry and art that pierced the symbolism of the shapes of the visible world. All art was originally connected with the mysteries of religion and related to the meaning of life, the riddle of the universe. Only in the course of time, the magic spell of religious society was convulsed by natural catastrophes, or the magic circle broken open by warlike invaders. Religions became dogmatic and formal, or too permissive; rival religions fought for political power in place of mystical insight. However and wherever it happened, men became a little more practical and less mystical, to defend themselves from nature, from empire-builders outside or tyrants at home. The centuries of power struggles and holy wars engaged men in topical preoccupations, and tradition became a dream from the past. The old myths were wrenched away from religious meaning and became secularised. Millions of stories of gods and heroes were transmuted into folk tales and ballads, and much later into best-selling novels. The poignancy of folk songs drew their strength from powerful images in which the pangs of separation hinted at the gap between God and man as much as the distance between the parted lovers.

In an earlier book, *The Broadside Ballad* (1962), I have shown how the basic theme of the Scottish love ballad 'The Two Magicians' is expressed in an old Scandinavian folk tale, and long before that in the Hindu scripture *Brihadaranyaka Upanishad* (1st adhyaya, 4th brahmana). Many other ballad themes may be traced to Hindu sources, part of the diffusion of culture from the great Indo-European migrations of ancient times. The old ballad 'Riddles Wisely Expounded' (Child, No 1) is clearly a recasting of the seventy riddles of the rakshasi Karkati in the scripture *Yoga-Vasishtha Maharamayana*, where the life of the individual questioned hangs upon answers which contain metaphysical truths. The complex of 'Cutty Wren' and 'Derby Ram' folk songs concerning the division of gigantic animals has sometimes been ascribed to peasant revolts against rich and despotic landowners, but it has deeper, magical roots, for there are more powerful archetypes in the descriptions of the cosmic spirit Purusha in the Hindu *Rig-Veda*, x, 90. And the story of the third avatar of Vishnu as Vahara the great boar, whose cosmic battle with the demon Hiranyaksha created the mighty

Himalayas, is distantly echoed in the many ballads of 'Old Bangham', 'Blow Your Horn, Hunter', and the comicalities of 'Sir Eglamore'.

A brilliant paper by Charles B. Lewis, *The Part of the Folk in the Making of Folklore* (*Folklore*, March 1935), traces the origins of 'Dabbling in the Dew' and 'Where are you going to, my pretty maid?'. Folksingers will have noticed the recurrent theme of the 'dew' in other songs like 'The Foggy Dew' and 'Blow Away the Morning Dew'. In his book *The Idiom of the People* (1958) James Reeves attempts a lengthy analysis of the theme, and concludes that 'dew' means virginity or chastity. It is not so simple as that.

In his famous *Diary*, Samuel Pepys has an entry for 28 May 1667:
My wife away down with Jane and W. Hewer to Woolwich, in order to a little ayre and to lie there to-night, and so to gather May-dew to-morrow morning, which Mrs. Turner hath taught her is the only thing in the world to wash her face with. . . .
The *Morning Post* newspaper for 2 May 1791 has this note: '. . . on the day preceding, according to annual and superstitious custom, a number of persons went into the fields and bathed their faces with the dew on the grass, under the idea that it would render them beautiful.' Obviously this custom explains why 'Dabbling in the dew makes the milkmaids fair', but there is a strong connection with promiscuity rather than chastity.

The May Games of sixteenth century Britain had much in common with the Maïeroles of medieval France, when only young lovers might enter the sacred wood to gather violets. As Lewis points out, the May Day celebrations were originally a festival of love—but love outside the ties of marriage. These customs go back to the cult of the Phrygian goddess Cybele, officially established in Rome 204 BC and later diffused through Spain and the southern part of Gaul. Cybele was the original May Queen, and her passionate love for Attis, whom she found on a river bank, led to the custom of young men who wished for luck in love to roll naked in the dew on May Day. In due course, Christianity assimilated pagan archetypes and feasts, and the cult of Cybele was superseded by veneration of the Virgin Mary.

There are fascinating side-issues in the probable connection of Robin Hood and Maid Marian with the May Games, arising from the thirteenth century 'Jeu de Robin et Marion' of Adam de la Halle, but the important link is the medieval French *Pastourelle* form, a popular class of verse in the great background of Provençal lyrical song drawn upon by troubadours. Although many *Pastourelles* were by known poet-singers, others were as anonymous as folk songs.

Pastourelles were basically dialogues between a knight and a shepherdess. The knight's impetuous declaration of love is dealt with in various ways. The maid may protest that she is of lowly birth. If the knight offers costly gifts she may say she has a simple shepherd boy as lover and could not be unfaithful. She may even lead the knight on and finally trick him.

Now the dialogue and play between the knight and maid (with sometimes a shadowy third figure of the shepherd lover) are precisely the plot conventions of a whole complex of British folk songs and ballads, notably 'The Knight and the Shepherd's Daughter' (Child, No 110), 'The Baffled Knight' (Child, No 112), 'Lovely Joan' and 'The Green Bushes'. Moreover in the *Pastourelle* dialogue convention, usually crisp and witty, the two main characters address each other as 'Damoisele' and 'Sire', just as in the British nursery song of 'Where are you going to, my pretty maid?'.

Lewis suggests that the dominant elements have Christian analogues, for the Biblical *Song of Solomon* is surely a prototype *Pastourelle*, revolving around three main characters: Solomon himself, the Shulamite maiden, and her shepherd lover. Lewis concluded:

> The source of our folksong and folk customs is religion: on the one hand Christian religion; on the other, pagan. At what date in history these elements of religion turned, the one into folksong, the other into folklore, it is difficult to affirm, and indeed it is a different date in each case; but one may perhaps venture to say that it was when the religious origin of the themes in question was finally forgotten. From that moment on, the theme of our song and the details of our customs changed more rapidly than before, were even simplified or whittled down by this or that trait falling into oblivion, until they now appear as pearls of such pure simplicity and loveliness that only the folk, it is thought, in a far-distant past could have conceived them. Thus folklore and folksong, at least in the cases we have considered, turn out to be the last stage of all in an age-long evolution and not by any means the first beginnings.

Behind the materialistic façade of modern urban society there is still a romantic undercurrent of the oldtime spring games, celebrated March to May, depending on your calendar. Every spring there is an exciting current in the blood of men and maids, and an age-old mystery of life is re-enacted. Two or three characters play out their hierarchical roles on a stage of a strip of green grass, the vegetation of the new year. We do not know how many feet have trodden that stage, but the human story goes on year after year, and a divine tragi-comedy descends as a nursery song.

The oral tradition of songs, ballads and rituals was the forerunner of street literature in peasant society before printing. In the decentralised societies of the past there were always pockets of tradition in which a poor man would remain the carrier of lost mysteries and beautiful insights, in a song which had little to do with his poverty and working conditions, and even less with the politics of the state.

As with the broadsides which overtook them, some of the folk songs were trivial and banal, but the best of them had a timeless meaning that reached to the roots of the human situation. It was an impulse for which mere literary cleverness and topicality could not be a substitute.

Folk song and folklore were not the final stage of religious descent, for urban folklore took over form and themes from the country tradition, and the printed format of broadsides and chapbooks continued and enlarged the fading oral tradition. Even today there are still a few traditional folk singers in Britain, but most of their repertoire was printed on the broadsides which became part of the traditional process.

If ballads, folk songs, and romances were the last flicker of an ancient metaphysical impulse before its transmutation into social and political mythologies, the street literature of broadsides and chapbooks continued to reflect this gleam before they too were supplanted by the sophisticated culture of books. The history of this process is not so much a formal affair of dates and titles, but rather of trends and phases.

So many early broadsides and pamphlets failed to survive that we cannot give any exact reckoning of their scope and subject-matter. We do not know the titles of the one hundred and ninety ballads sold by the Oxford bookseller John Dorne in 1520. His day-book, preserved at Corpus Christi College, shows only that these halfpenny broadsides were sold side by side with Christmas carols, almanacs, ABCs, primers, and school books.

The earliest surviving broadside ballad is an undated untitled political item of a dialogue between 'Luther, the Pope, and a Husbandman' circa 1535. Probably many other broadsides were issued between 1520 and 1535, but we have no record of them.

The early period of broadside balladry was characterised by items of religious and political controversy, which were attacked by repressive legislation. In 1543 there was an Act 'for the Advancement of True Religion and for the Abolishment of the Contrary', specifically directed at 'printed books, printed ballads, plays, rimes, songs, and other fantasies'. Churchmen and politicians were disturbed by the inflammatory power of ballads in the great power struggles between Catholics and Protestants.

Traditional ballads were not at first common on the broadsides. The emphasis was on topicality, and many broadsides were titled 'A New Ballad of——'. Newness was the feature most stressed by the street hawkers and pedlars. But even the most up-to-date broadside compositions were more often than not to be sung to a wistful old ballad or country-dance tune, and so tradition carried topicality on a musical measure. It is possible that old ballads and country songs were eventually printed on broadsides because they did not involve a fee to a ballad writer, but it is more likely that city dwellers sometimes tired of novelty and hungered for tradition.

Many cultured writers took a wistful backward look at traditional themes, and during the eighteenth century sophisticated literature tried to rediscover the romantic tradition of ballads. The antiquarian Bishop Thomas Percy started the first ballad revival with his *Reliques of Ancient English Poetry*, a curious mixture of traditional and broadside verses. Of the 176 pieces in the first edition of the *Reliques* published in 1765, only 45 were from the old folio manuscript acquired by Percy, but by touching up certain ballads, omitting bawdy items and inserting broadside pieces, Percy introduced polite society to traditional balladry, and gave a new impulse to European literature, in the German romantic movement of Herder, and, in Britain, in the work of Scott, Burns, Wordsworth, Coleridge and others. Soon it became possible for cultured gentlemen to collect folk music from uncultured peasants, while the most polished writers tried to copy the accents of ancient balladry. Generally it was the more plodding broadside verse that was mistaken for the older folk style, and real traditional folk-music collecting awaited the broadminded country parsons of the nineteenth century, like the Rev John Broadwood and the Rev Sabine Baring-Gould.

Broadsides preserved something of tradition at a time when folk memory was beginning to fail. Many news items excited a sense of wonder and awe, and much of topicality was not unmixed with superstition. The verse form itself, as well as the music of the ballads, kept city dwellers in touch with an older, more mysterious past. Chapbooks kept alive the ancient legends and folk tales at a time when men were increasingly concerned with practical affairs.

Ballad-sheets were pasted up on the walls of inns and cottages, sold from the stalls in churchyards or market-places, hawked by pedlars up and down the land. Broadsides and chapbooks were the libraries of ordinary people who had nothing else to read and very little leisure for reading. A common man thought very deeply over what he read, and from one or two tattered and well-thumbed chapbooks, with perhaps a family Bible and a few ballad-sheets, a farm labourer in the eighteenth and nineteenth centuries might read by a guttering light in early morning and late night, prizing all literature as a treasure for the mind. From these materials he might evolve a wise philosophy and ethic, integrated with his feeling for tradition and his life in the fields or as a servant in a middle-class house. His hold on tradition was a measure to test the value of new ideas.

So the popular literature of the streets held the last hints of a secret that mankind once knew—the meaning of religion and everyday affairs, the balance between tradition and topicality, the wonder and mystery of the humblest life. There were hints of this still in what was left of religion—the religion of the dedicated life and intuitive awareness rather than the politics of establishment, rules and dogmas, but Europe was being snared by science, industry, the pride of intellect and the vanities of topicality. Books mirrored self-centred lives and property games of middle classes and the rich.

The religious organisations sponsored the education of poor people long before the politicians, and in the face of much hostile propaganda from the middle classes.

In the early part of the eighteenth century, the Society for

CHEAP REPOSITORY.

T H E
STORY of SINFUL SALLY.
TOLD BY HERSELF.

SHEWING

How from being SALLY of the GREEN she was firſt led to become SINFUL SALLY, and afterwards DRUNKEN SAL, and how at laſt ſhe came to a moſt melancholy and almoſt hopeleſs End; being therein a Warning to all young Women both in Town and Country.

Sold by J. MARSHALL,

(PRINTER to the CHEAP REPOSITORY for Religious and Moral Tracts) No. 17, Queen-Street, Cheapſide, and No. 4, Alder-mary Church-Yard; and R. WHITE, Piccadilly, LONDON; By S. HAZARD, at BATH; and by all Bookſellers, Newſmen, and Hawkers, in Town and Country.—*Great Allowance to Shopkeepers and Hawkers*

PRICE ONE HALFPENNY,
Or, 2s. 3d. per 100.—1s. 3d. for 50.—9d. for 25.

[*Entered at Stationers Hall.*]

A Cheap Repository Tract written by Sally, sister of Hannah More

Promoting Christian Knowledge set up charity schools, and in 1723 claimed some 23,421 scholars. With the rise of Methodism, John Wesley travelled all over the country preaching and distributing cheap religious literature. Wesley had an abiding faith in the impact of the printed page and insisted on his preachers being colporteurs or book agents. They travelled on horseback with a saddle-bag filled with Wesley's publications.

Sunday Schools and Charity Schools tried to supplant broadsides and chapbooks by moral reading-matter, in order to hold back the materialistic and political trend of the times.

When the French Revolution stirred up currents of popular revolt, fanned by the radical pamphlets of Tom Paine, the religious organisations countered with religious chapbooks and broadsides. Hannah More, one of the pioneers of the Sunday School movement, was a pious well-to-do lady who regarded chapbooks and broadsides as idle, sinful and depraved, but she recognised their enormous popularity and modelled her own Cheap Repository tracts and broadsides on the productions of the broadside presses, skilfully imitating their format, style, paper and quaint little woodcuts, even employing ballad and chapbook printers like John Evans and John Marshall and distributing through the hard-bitten broadside pedlars. The new popular literature sold like hot cakes, and revolution was averted.

What made the tracts popular, as much as anything, was their simple honest style without condescension, and the integrity with which they discussed religious problems in a contemporary context. Moreover many of the tracts, especially those by Hannah More herself, were well written, witty, and fair-minded. Hannah More, an associate of Dr Johnson and David Garrick, had a considerable literary talent. But eventually her success led to an over-inflation of the form she had created. Officialdom tried to cash in on it and the market became flooded with prosy, sententious tracts, a routine affair of sincere but humdrum clergymen without vision, playing safe.

An amusing offshoot of the success of the Cheap Repository Tract movement was that for quite a while the printers found the tracts very profitable and some publishers started their own moral tracts in imitation of Hannah More's. A new demand was created for cheap literature.

In the early years of the nineteenth century, John Pitts, previously

A Lift of the Tracts publifhed during the Year 1796.

HISTORIES.

Mary Wood the Houfemaid.
Shoemakers. Part II. III. and IV.
Charles Jones the Footman.
The Cheapfide Apprentice.
The Gamefter.
Betty Brown, the St. Giles's Orange Girl.
Farmers. Part III. IV. and V.
Black Giles the Poacher. Part I, and II.

SUNDAY READINGS.

Some New Thoughts for the New Year.
The Touchftone.
Onefimus.
The Converfion of St. Paul.
The General Refurrection.
On Carrying Religion into Bufinefs.
Look at Home.
The Grand Affizes.
Explanation of the Nature of Baptifm.
Prayers.
The Valley of Tears.

POETRY.

Robert and Richard.
Sinful Sally.
The Shopkeeper turned Sailor. Part I. II. and III.
The Hackney Coachman.
The Election.
Turn the Carpet.
A Hymn of Praife.
King Dionyfius and Squire Damocles.
The Hampfhire Tragedy.

Some publications of the Cheap Repository Tract movement

working for John Marshall, printer to the Cheap Repository Tracts, set up on his own account in Seven Dials, and found just the right mixture of topicality and tradition to revive the whole broadside and chapbook trade on a vast scale.

His rival James Catnach, on whom much has been written, merely cashed in on a going concern. Between them, Pitts and Catnach generated that final tremendous expansion of street literature that lived on into the end of the nineteenth century, before it was finally killed off by Gothic novels, penny dreadfuls, cheap newspapers, magazines and books. That fantastic, riotous, nostalgic and some-times lunatic explosion of cheap street literature of Pitts, Catnach, and their imitators, has been charted in the books of Charles Hindley, and there is a choice representative selection in Hindley's *Curiosities of Street Literature*, first published London, 1871 and reprinted in 1966 by John Foreman, 'The Broadsheet King' of modern London, a present-day revivalist of street literature some-times described as the twentieth century Catnach.

Broadsides and chapbooks grew up in the early sixteenth century, flourished in the seventeenth, died down in the eighteenth, and flared up again in the nineteenth century. In the twentieth century they became dead letters, but their influence survives in the popular newspaper press, the music of Tin Pan Alley, in radio and television, the modern revival of folk music, and in the development of pop culture. Those four centuries of street literature were a great melting-pot of tradition and topicality, and symbolise the whole story of mankind, its ideals and achievements, its sins and follies.

Street literature became the one great composite form for the traditionalist, the reactionary, the agitator, the journalist, the hack writer, and the back-street entrepreneur. It covered every known aspect of conventional literature and even invented new categories (like 'cocks', 'catchpennies', and 'long-song sheets'). It kept alive beautiful old folk songs and ballads in the squalor of the industrial revolution, it gloated over crimes and executions, it gave up-to-the-minute news (sometimes before it happened), it circulated lies and rumours, it strengthened conservative loyalties and patriotism, it fomented riots and radicalism. It created an urban folklore, and printed non-books for poor people.

With all its contradictions it became the voice of the crowd, and its energies are still alive in modern society.

3: Printers and Publishers

Printers and Publishers

FROM THE BEGINNING OF THE PRINTING TRADE IN THE FIFTEENTH
century, the story of popular literature is one of progressive struggle
to free printed matter from the shackles of restrictive trade practice
and the censorship of religious and political domination.

Much of the first century of printing in Britain, from 1457 to
1557, was a period of consolidation of the book trade from foreign
competition. Many fine books were printed in this period. It was a
time of great names like Caxton, Wynkyn de Worde, Pynson, Richard
Bankes, Thomas Berthelet and John Day. Printing was centralised
in London, Westminster and Southwark, and the majority of
publications were solid, expensive items for privileged and well-
to-do readers.

Not surprisingly, the general literacy rate appears to have been
low in the early period, for during the Middle Ages books had been
costly and rare manuscripts, and teaching confined mainly to those
taking up the religious life. After the dissolution of the monasteries,
new schools grew up and printing was able to fill an expanding
demand for text-books. In addition to grammar schools and uni-
versities, the sixteenth century saw the growth of primary schools
which served apprentices and the sons of tradesmen. In the country
districts, ABC schools taught the rudiments of reading.

Only a handful of broadside ballads have survived from this
period. These were mostly political and religious items, of which
there are typical specimens preserved in the Library of the Society
of Antiquaries, London.

In 1540, William Gray and Thomas Smyth published broadside
invectives against each other and their political positions. Gray was
a Reading poet, at one time in the service of Thomas, Lord
Cromwell, and ungratefully traduced his late master in a broadside
entitled *A Balade Agvnst Malycyous Schlaunderers*. Thomas Smyth,
a Clerk to the Council to the Queen, replied to Gray in an attack
entitled *A Lytell Treatyse Agavnst Sedicyous Persons*. Gray
responded with *An Aunswere to maister Smyth, seruaunt to the kynges
most royall maiestye, And clerk of the Queenes graces counsell thou
most vnworthy*. Some seven broadsides of Gray and Smyth have

survived, and an eighth sheet from a certain 'G.L.' who intervened to reprove both antagonists in this ballad warfare.

Soon afterwards, Gray and Smyth, together with the printers of their broadsides, were summoned by the Privy Council. Gray's printer successfully laid the blame on another printer and a deceased associate, but Gray, Smyth and the second printer were imprisoned for a few weeks in the Fleet Prison. Later on, Gray was taken into the King's service, doubtless in return for his anti-Popery propaganda; he held important posts and was well rewarded with money and lands.

It was clear that broadside ballads could have a powerful influence on public opinion, and legislation was regularly invoked to control this new mass medium. As mentioned earlier, an Act was passed in 1543 'for the advancement of true religion and for the abolishment of the contrary'. It claimed that 'froward and malicious minds, intending to subvert the true exposition of scripture, have taken upon them, by printed ballads, rhymes, etc., subtilly and craftily to instruct his highness' people, and specially the youth of this his realm, untruly'. In that year, thirty printers and booksellers were summoned by the Privy Council and obliged to submit lists of their books or ballads printed over the preceding three years.

Whilst the Government determined to prevent printing from being used for seditious purposes, the printers desired to restrict their craft from competition. In 1557 the Guild of Stationers in London (which included printers, publishers, bookbinders, and retailers) petitioned for a Royal Charter and a virtual monopoly of printing. This Charter, granted 4 May 1557 (3–4 Philip & Mary), restricted all printing to members of the Company of Stationers, and empowered their Master and Wardens to search shops and houses for illegal printing, to seize and destroy books and type, and have offenders imprisoned.

Books and broadsides printed by members of the company were entered in a register, giving printer's name, title of the item, and the registration fee, initially fourpence for a broadside and sixpence for a book. Interestingly enough the first entry is a ballad: 'To William perkeryng a ballett called *a Ryse and wake*. iij^d'. Sometimes a ballad was entered as a 'book' or 'copy'. These registers are a marvellous record of authorised printing over the centuries. They list all the great books and plays of early English literature, in addition to ballads sold in the streets.

Individual printers secured the privilege to specialise in certain classes of publications such as law books, almanacs, prayer books, ABCs and primers, and this early form of copyright law gave sole rights to printers instead of authors. Later on, the exclusive rights of individual printers were transferred to the Company of Stationers itself. The value of certain publications was held in shares by printers within the company, and the money raised bought out the earlier patent rights of individual printers. Certain profitable items were grouped as the 'English Stock'. There was an 'Irish Stock', a 'Latin Stock' and a 'Ballad Stock'. Perhaps the most important book involved in royal patent was the Bible, first printed in Zurich in 1535 for British publishers. For nearly a century afterwards, the various versions of the Bible became the focus of complex schemes and intrigues between rival printers, much as the book itself became the centre of political and religious strife. In 1645 the Puritan John Lilburne bitterly condemned the Bible monopoly as wicked and intolerable, for depriving the poor people of instruction 'in the way to heaven and happiness'.

The result of official censorship and monopolist printing was the creation of illegal presses, both for private profit, and in support of an underground protest literature of politics and religion. Spies and informers were set to detect private presses or report authorised printers who dabbled in seditious printing on the side. Sometimes official printers were fined for nothing worse than printing 'undecent' ballads. In view of the outspoken ribaldry of the time, it is more likely that these were sacrilegious rather than sexual ballads, since many items of cheerful uninhibited bawdry were printed without harassment. Religion and politics were the really dangerous topics in the power games of Catholics and Protestants from the sixteenth century onwards.

In the reign of Queen Mary, an Act was passed to suppress 'dyvers heynous, sedicious and schlanderous Writinges, Rimes, Ballades, Letters, Papers, and Bookes'. Those convicted under the Act were to be placed in the pillory and have their ears cut off, or pay a fine of £100. In addition, anyone writing or printing a book, rhyme, or ballad against the King and Queen, might have his right hand cut off. This Act remained in force during the reign of Queen Elizabeth, who invoked it to punish printers who had published a libel against her.

Nearly three hundred Protestant martyrs died for their faith in three years of Queen Mary's reign, and in the forty-five years of Queen Elizabeth's reign some one hundred and twenty-four Catholic priests and laymen and women perished similarly in the name of doctrinaire religion. It is not surprising that there was much sycophantic propaganda in ballads and pamphlets, while many broadsides gloated at the sufferings and death of sincerely religious people. But it is also clear that there were many protest ballads printed and circulated, in spite of the most determined repression.

Meanwhile throughout the sixteenth century there were many other topics in books and broadsides. In the Elizabethan period the broadside ballad became firmly established as a literary and journalistic form, covering 'Strange and Wonderful News' of all the topical events, as well as satires, social criticism, merry love songs, and an occasional revival or recasting of older traditional minstrelsy. Some broadsides gave the words of jigs—a kind of miniature dance drama in dialogue form, often bawdy.

The flowering of Elizabethan theatre took drama from the streets on to the stage in new tragedies and comedies that appealed equally to sophisticated audiences and the groundlings. Shakespeare's plays have many allusions to ballads, which were appreciated by all levels of society.

Plays must have been advertised in the streets in much the same way as new books or ballads. In 1624 Francis Wambus set up a bill at Norwich, announcing that the Lady Elizabeth's Men would act 'an excellent new comedy called the Spanische Contract'. Townsend, the leader of the company, was summonsed for putting up a playbill. In 1649 at Salisbury, Richard Heton was granted a patent to act 'comedyes, tragedyes, &c., wᵗʰ the tymes they are to be acted, to proclame in such places as afores'd with drums, trumpetts, and by publike bills as they thinke fit'. The posting of playbills is mentioned in *The Obstinate Lady* by Sir Aston Cockayn, entered in the Stationers' Registers 29 September 1656:

'I'll challenge him by such sure circumstances, and set the papers
On public places by the play-bills.'

Robert Heath, in a verse entitled 'To my Book-seller' in *Clarastella* (1650) begs the dealer not to advertise his book—

. . . nor poast it on each wall

And corner poast underneath the Play
That must be acted at Black-friers that day.

From the Elizabethan period onwards, plays, books and ballads
on the same themes sold side by side. In 1594 the printer John
Danter registered a copy of Shakespeare's play *Titus Andronicus*
and 'the ballad thereof' on the same day. Both Robert Wilson's
story of *Three Ladies of London* (1584) and the broadside ballad of
'A new Song, shewing the crueltie of Gernutus a Jew, who lending
to a Marchant a hundred Crownes, would haue a pound of his Flesh,
because he could not pay him at the day appoynted' deal with a
theme found in Shakespeare's *The Merchant of Venice*. The theme of
the pound of flesh is of even greater antiquity, for it is found in the
story of King Sivi and the Dove in the old Indian religious epic
the *Mahabharata*.

Thomas Deloney's story of *Jack of Newbury, called the Clothier of
England,* which continued for a couple of centuries as a favourite
chapbook theme, was first licensed in 1595; a ballad version was
registered two years later. A ballad about a monstrous fish, composed
by Martin Parker in 1635, ends with a puff 'There is a book to
satisfie such as desire a larger description hereof'.

Two hundred and fifty printers of ballads during the seventeenth
century have been identified, but many of them printed books and
pamphlets too, and the tide of popular literature ebbed and flowed
with changes in government and new regulations relating to the
printing trade.

In the long warfare between authorities and hidden presses,
nothing stands out so boldly as the audacious 'Martin Marprelate'
tracts of the secret Puritans. The first item was *The Epistle*,
published in November 1588, after which the secret press was
removed in turn to East Molesey, Fawsley, Coventry and Wolston,
in a thrilling story of spies, informers, and midnight journeys with
smuggled type. Because Robert Waldegrave, a London printer, was
concerned in earlier Puritan tracts, his press was destroyed and his
family impoverished. But Waldegrave escaped with a box of type
under his cloak and his wife carried other bits and pieces of the
press. In August 1589, the secret press, type and accessories were
hidden in a haycart and carried from Wolston to Warrington. Here
some of the type was accidentally dropped, and found its way into
the hands of the authorities. The secret printers again moved on, to

Newton Lane, near Manchester, where they were tracked and arrested with sheets of a new Marprelate tract actually set up. Henry Hodgkins, one of the printers, was sent to London and tortured in the Tower of London. But no one ever discovered the secret of the identity of the author of the Marprelate tracts.

Between 1586 and 1641, the number of master printers had been regulated by decrees of the Star Chamber at Westminster. This court was originally established by Henry VIII as a tribunal which enforced judgement without a jury, cancelling the right of a prisoner to be tried by his peers. When this Court was abolished in 1641, some of the restrictions on the printing trade were lifted, although new problems also arose. From this time onwards, jobbing printing began to expand, and a flourishing street literature developed in the form of news pamphlets or sheets. These grew out of the 'corantos' (currents of news) printed on the Continent (chiefly in Amsterdam) from 1620 onwards, before London became the centre of a large trade.

Censorship was not immediately relaxed. In March 1643 the House of Commons issued an order authorising the Committee of Examination to appoint persons to search for scandalous pamphlets and to seize presses or printers. It was this order that provoked poet John Milton to publish his famous *Areopagitica, or Appeal for the Liberty of Unlicensed Printing*, 1644.

The suppression of all unofficial news pamphlets in 1649 effectively prevented publication of any full discussion of the appalling butcheries of Cromwell in Ireland at the taking of Drogheda and Wexford. These outrages were over by May 1650, when licensed news books reappeared.

Throughout the Civil War and Commonwealth period, the illegal underground presses became more influential than the official printers, whose trade was often impeded by official censorship. Parliament had appointed committees to purge the Book of Common Prayer and other religious best-sellers from any hint of popery; the Primer was suppressed altogether in 1651.

Ballad writers were increasingly in demand to supply the unlicensed presses. Martin Parker headed a syndicate of some twenty-four ballad poets, while established writers like John Cleveland, John Taylor, Sir John Birkenhead, and others wrote ballads as political weapons against Parliament.

The prose news pamphlets became popular because they offered

Numb. 9.

A Continuation of the true Diurnall
of Proceedings in PARLIAMENT,
from *March* 7. to the 14 of the same.
1641.

Containing the great affaires of this Kingdome: as also for repelling of such grievances as have beene formerly a perturbance to this his Majesties Dominions.

Monday, 7. March.

His day there were divers petitions delivered unto the house of Commons, from severall petitions, whose husbands, wives and children were taken prisoners by the Turkes, and committed to Argier in slavery, whose daily cries humbly supplicate a deliverance, wher- upon the house of Com. were pleased to move the Lords with it, who together assented for the sending of speedy sup- ply of shipping, either to receive the said prisoners back a- gaine upon demand, or to proceed against it in open vie- lence.

In the house of Commons they likewise held a debate concerning his Majesties answer to their last Petition, con- cerning ordering the Militia of the Kingdome, which an- fwer they received on Friday before, importing that it was a matter of such great weight and consequence, in re- spect his Queene and daughter being now in Holland, and
the
I

---

(721)   *Numb. 79.*

Mercurius Britanicus,
Communicating the affaires of great
BRITAINE:

For the better Information of the People.

From *Monday* the 14. of *April*, to *Monday* the 21. of *April.* 1645.

FET upon! Here's a deale of waiting for an *Aulicus*; a little *Aulicus* Oxford forgery called *Court-Intelligence*: Is it possible their never *Affaires* should not afford a *Sheete* in three *Weekes*? But I told you thrived what his *Scotish bragg* would come to: Now they are all thunder- yet by strucke with the *Newes* from *Scotland*; nay, the *Rowing* reach't to bragging their very *Counsells*, and put a *demurre* to his *Majesties* advance. Now they Begin to curse all *Jugling* in the *Treaty* at *Uxbridge*, when they might have had *Peace* if they would: Now they leave altogether upon that *bruised Reed, Ireland*; nothing left to uphold this *unnaturall Conspiracie*, but that *unparallel'd Rebellion*: only All their they hope well of their *Westerne Stragglers*; whose valour may in hope in time recruite *Aulicus* again to the credit of a *Pamphlet*. Till then Ireland. you must not expect him; but never looke to see him prosper long, for

We have recieved excellent *Intelligence* of our *successe* in *Scot- land* against their *Montrosse*, obtained under the auspicious Con- A gallant duct of Generall *Urrey*: No lesse than 500 of those *Rebels* slaine Victory upon the place, the rest disperst, I aving many and much taken. It over Mon- *Knights* so gallant a *Commander*: One such another *Bone* will de- the best *Honour* then, that every His *Majesty* bestowed, to trode. serve a *Lordship*, and in time procure it; for how can the *King* do lesse hereafter, when his *Service* shall be considered in the *prefer- vation*
Dddd

Two early news pamphlets. Diurnall's reported Parliamentary proceedings. Mercurius Brtanicus lashes out scornfully at other periodicals

a more flexible form for satire and journalistic propaganda [see page 59]. They circulated a broader view of home and foreign news than the ballads, but were not simple reading for the man in the street. The biting satire, inflated language and invective of politics were often turgid, and there were dangers in being associated with seditious literature. After the Restoration there was a spate of loyal popular literature, but the pressure of official restriction did not relax. In 1662 came the Licensing Act, and Sir Roger L'Estrange became Surveyor of the Press, with power to suppress unlicensed publications. Since he had been granted a monopoly of news publications he had something of a vested interest in suppression. Even ballads had to be licensed, and those which bear the initials 'R.L.S.' can be assigned to 1662–85, the period he held office. Those signed 'R.P.' relate to the period 1685–8 when Richard Pocock succeeded L'Estrange. It was a time of much scurrilous religious propaganda in periodicals.

With the new freedoms of Restoration drama, however, many bawdy ballads circulated. Between 1698 and 1706 was published Tom D'Urfey's *Wit and Mirth: or Pills to Purge Melancholy*, a remarkable mixture of beauty and bawdy. It included sophisticated songs and popular street ballads.

Meanwhile, playbills had developed into elaborate programmes, detailing the cast and the plot of plays. Orange girls inside and outside the theatres offered a bill of the play to customers who bought their fruit. Pepys records meeting that most famous orange-seller Nell Gwynne, after she became an actress and captured the favour of Charles II. Pepys visited Drury Lane Theatre on 8 April 1663 and recorded that Nell was 'a most pretty woman, who acted the great part Coelia to-day very fine, and did it pretty well'. At a much later date Hogarth's engraving 'The Laughing Audience', published in 1733, showed a couple of handsome orange girls offering fruit and a playbill to the beaux in the boxes [see page 63].

In the early seventeenth century there had been great competition within the Company of Stationers for printing rights in 'items printed on one side of paper or parchment', including briefs, indentures, playbills, proclamations and ballads. These were profitable items for the master printers of the Stationers' Company, and there was a struggle to establish the rights of 'poore Masters and Journey-men Printers' rather than with the 'few riche Printers'. The story of

Vol.3. THE **Numb.6**

OBSERVATOR.

of Otes'es Cafe, Character, Perfon, and Plot: His laying of Things together. The Obfervator's Declaration, and Confeffion. His Opinion of the Papifts, as well as of the Popifh Plot.

Saturday, February 21. 168⅘

TRIM. SO that You are upon a *Sure Ground*, I per-*MER.* ceive, for what you do in *Mr Otes'es Bus'nefs.*

OBSERVATOR. I am upon a *Great* many *fure Grounds, Trimmer:* The *Sure Grounds* of *Authority, Law, Reafon, Juftice, Truth, Honour,* and *Confcience.*

Trim. And yet he *Bears-up,* you fee, like Another *Athanafius.* *Titus* againft *the World,* and *the World againft Titus.*

Obf. He'd have taken it better, to have been Coupled with *Judas,* then with *Athanafius:* For *They Two* have formerly had fome *Hard Words,* you muft know; and *Otes* call'd him **a Creed-making Rafcall** for his *Pains:* But the *Guinneys,* and the *Bottles* come in *ftill,* they fay.

Trim. Ay, And he has his *Friends* about him too; and *Betts* ye his *Mony* at *Nine-Pins* as Free as an *Emperor.* 'Twould do a man Good, to fee how *Heartily* he'le *Laugh* at an Unlucky *Tip:* But **Peace within,** is a Great Matter. This could never be, *Nobs,* if All were not *Well at home:* And then for fo many *Difhes of Meat,* the *King Himfelf Eats* no *Better.*

Obf. From whence does All This come I prethee?

Trim. Why whence came the *Prophets Afcat* in the *Wildernefs.*

Obf. From *Providence,* No doubt on't: But the *Prophets Meat* in the **Cage,** I'm afraid, comes from *Another Quarter;* and we have a *Roguy Proverb* too, in favour of that Opinion, *i.e. The Devill helps his Servants;* Though what he **does,** 'tis True, with *One* hand, he **Undoes** with *'tother;* for as faft as the *Ravens* **Bring** in *Ven'fon Paftys,* the *Rooks* **Fly away** with 'em.

Trim. Such Another *Quibble,* turns my Stomack: But this is enough to fhew ye, that *Otes,* and *Otes'es Plot,* are not fo low yet in the *Reputation* of the *World,* as you *Think* for.

Obf. As to *Otes'es Perfonal Credit,* thou canft not fhew me *One Action,* or *Circumftance,* in the whole Tract of his *Life,* fo much as to *Colour* for't: Nay, He has Employ'd his *Talent,* from the very *Cradle,* in *Lyes, Scandals, Treachery, Malice, Revenge;* and in the *Love,* and *Practice* of *Wickednefs,* even for *Wickednefs fake.* [*Give me the Bible* (fays he in *Cambridge,* upon his Taylors bringing a Bill for a *Gown*) *and you fhall have my Oath upon't, that I never had any fuch Gown of him in my Life*] Though the *Having* of it, and the *Difpofing* of it, was *Prov'd Undeniably* againft him. His *Oath* againft *Parker* in *Suffex,* was not only *Prov'd* to be **falfe;** but fo *Ridiculoufly put Together,* that in Four, or Five Particulars, even of the *Tale it felf,* it was *Morally Impoffible* to be *True.* His *Endeavouring* to *Suborn* a *Perjury* againft the *Father* of That *Parker,* when he Charg'd him before the King and Council, is upon *Oath* likewife: To fay nothing of his *Tampering* againft *Coll. Diggs,* and feveral Others, in the Same Manner. Whenever he had a *Pique* to any body, [**I'le have the Hearts Bloud**

of him,] was the very *Form* of the *Menace.* [*I'le Blow Bellafis's Bellows for him,* **I'le have his Hearts Bloud.**] [*I'le have the Hearts Bloud* of Thimbleby, and of Strange, and of Whitebread,] becaufe they would not Admit him into the *Society.* As to his *Treachery,* I cannot call to mind above *One Perfon,* that ever he was *Beholden* to; and the *Charity* that put *Bread* in the Mouth of This *Indigent Varlet,* was Emprov'd into an *Evidence* againft the *Benefactor:* And for the *Cleannefs* of his *Manners* now, there are fo many *Witneffes* of his *Pollutions* that way, that he has fcarce had a *Servant,* upon whom he has not *Attempted* the *Vileft* of *Abominations.* And he has made as bold with **God,** in his *Holy Sacraments;* and in the *Mockerys* that he has put (with Fore-thought, Counsel, and Deliberation) upon the moft *Tremendous Myfteries* of the *Chriftian Religion;* as he has upon **Man,** in the *Violation* of All the *Duties* of *Reafonable Nature.* And for the *Credit* of his **Plot** now; I will be Anfwerable to fhew ye **Forty Paffages,** wherein he **himfelf** does as good as **Swear** that is **Forfworn.** But to Conclude; Set the *Paffages* that we know *Certainly,* and *Infallibly* to be *Falfe,* againft *Thofe* **Other Paffages,** for which we have *Otes'es Oath,* againft *Reafon* and *Common Senfe,* and *True;* and *'faith* tell me your felf then, upon the *Main,* **What do you think of** *Otes'sPlot?* Keep your Tongue in your Mouth, *Trimmer,* or fpeak according to your *Confcience.*

Trim. Why *Otes* may be an *Ill* **Man,** and the *Plot* yet, *a very Good* **Plot,** for all *That.*

Obf. Well! But if it be neither *Credible* for the *Witnefs* fake, nor for the *Matter,* or *Coherence* of it: What is't, I befeech ye that you'l *Bottom* your *Credit* upon : Or what if I fhould Ask ye now, which *Part* of it you *Believe?* The *Narrative* was *Old Tonges:* *Young Tong* tells ye long fince, that the *Whole Contrivance* was a *Juggle; Part* of it Written in the *Barbican, Part* at *Fox-Hall;* that the *Original Defign* of it was to *Remove* the *Queen,* and to *Deftroy* the *Duke* of York; that *Otes* was *Advis'd* by *Tong* to go beyond-*Seas,* to get *Materials* toward the *Framing* of it; and I have *Papers* in my hand of *Old Tonges Writing,* at this Inftant, to *Confirm* All This to a *Syllable.* I have *Proofs* from feveral of *Tong's Parifhioners,* of his Offering *fo much a Man,* per week, to thofe that would go over to the Church of *Rome,* before the *Plot Brakeout;* which could be with *No Other Defign,* then to find *Mercenary Rogues* that would come back again for *Half a Crown a Week* **More,** perhaps, and make **Evidences.** The *Five Windfor Letters,* no body *Denies* to be a *Cheat;* Pickerings *Screw'd-Gun,* and *Silver Bullets,* is fo *Ridiculous,* and *Impracticable* a *Sham,* that every-body fees thorough it that does but know a *Carabin,* from a *Glifter-Pipe;* the *Story* of the *Ruffians,* got a *Knock* in the *Cradle,* and came the Wrong way into the World, under the *Curfe* of *Doubling,* and *Contradictions; Wakeman's Poyfon,* and *Conyers'es Dagger,* lay too *Open* and *Barefac'd,* to do any *Exe-*

A periodical started by Sir Roger L'Estrange. It presented propaganda in dialogue form, and continued until the eve of the Revolution

rights in ballad titles is a complex one.

By the latter part of the seventeenth century the ballad market was dominated by partnerships involving the names of Francis Coles, Thomas Vere, John Wright, John Clarke, William Thackeray, Thomas Passinger, William Onley, and various subsidiary partners in a descent of ballad stock between 1655 and 1692. In the Bagford Collection at the British Museum is a Trade List of 'small Books, Ballads and Histories' sold by William Thackeray 'at the Angel in Duck-lane, London; where any Chapman may be furnished with them or any other Books at Reasonable Rates'; the list is undated but is probably circa 1689. It gives the titles of 301 broadside ballads, many of which remained favourites long afterwards, as well as various 'Broad Sheets, Small Godly Books, Small Merry Books, Double Books, and Histories'. These 'books' would have been of a chapbook kind.

Such ballads and chapbooks were a profitable line, but after 1695, when the Licensing Act expired, restrictions on printing were withdrawn. As the monopolist power of the Company of Stationers was broken, the trade began to expand, and soon the Stationers' Registers were no longer representative of exclusive rights in old ballads or books. In 1709 the Copyright Act of Queen Anne gave rights to authors, as opposed to printers.

On 20 September 1712, there was a large entry in the Registers to Charles Brown and Thomas Norris, covering 71 Ballads, 6 Broadsides (some of which may have been ballads), and various 'Sheets', 'Sheet Books', 'Small Books' and 'Sticht Histories', as well as 'Bound Books'; many were chapbook titles. This entry seems to have been a belated attempt to stake a claim in the old favourites from the ballad stock of Coles, Vere, Wright, Clarke, Thackeray and others, for many of the titles are the same. But during the eighteenth century most of these titles were widely reprinted by scores of provincial presses.

There is strong presumptive evidence that the old ballad stock descended through Brown, Norris and others to the great ballad and chapbook warehouse of Dicey and Marshall at Bow Church Yard and Aldemary Church Yard, London, thence to Marshall's son, and afterwards to his successor John Pitts, the first nineteenth century revivalist of the ballad and chapbook trade.

Throughout the eighteenth century, the Dicey and Marshall

e Laughing Audience', from an engraving by William Hogarth

warehouse dominated the ballad and chapbook trade, in spite of growing competition from the provinces. William Dicey had printed chapbooks at Northampton, and he and his son Cluer Dicey supplied a provincial trade based at Bow Church Yard. During the century, many cities like Newcastle-upon-Tyne, York, Tewkesbury, White-haven, and Bath also became centres of chapbook publishing and sales.

In the country areas there was still a strong feeling for tradition, and farm labourers sang old ballads and folk songs. In London, the demand for traditional style broadsides must have been a shrinking one, for the emphasis was now on sophisticated music—opera, concerts, theatrical songs, glee clubs, and professional singing. The beauty and extravagance of the fashionable entertainments at pleasure gardens like Vauxhall, Ranelagh and Marylebone estab-lished the concept of classical music as a cultured phenomenon far removed from the songs of the streets. Books and single sheets of elaborately engraved music were published. Many of the eighteenth century street broadsides featured songs sung in the theatres. Ballads and penny histories must have become more of a sideline at the Dicey warehouse, where beautifully engraved maps, prints, copy books, and drawing books brought in more money.

For the man in the street in city and country, the world of literature remained largely a closed book. Working men dreamed of the beauty and wisdom locked away in the printed pages, and literacy seemed the key to a magic world as wonderful as the joys of heaven which religious leaders had preached lay beyond the harsh everyday toil and poverty. Even newspapers were dull, over-clever, or pompous, and with a tax rising from 1d to $3\frac{1}{2}$d at the end of the century, a broadside ballad was the only sheet most poor people could afford. A few ingenious periodicals evaded the tax from time to time, and there were some 'Farthing Posts'. These halfpenny and farthing news-sheets were vended in the streets without stamp duty, in defiance of the law. A typical title is: *All-Alive and Merry: or, the London Daily Post; London, printed for A. Merryman and sold by the Hawkers*. This was a small folio half-sheet with three columns of letterpress on each side. Plate IV of Hogarth's *The Rake's Progress* shows a boy intently reading a newspaper which is titled 'The Farthing Post'.

To tell the truth, there was probably more romance and magic in

Theatre Royal, English Opera House, Strand.

LAST NIGHTS!

This Evening, 18th inst. Last Night of The TRIP TO AMERICA and ALL *WELL* AT NATCHITOCHES.

Thursday, 21st, ,, The HOME CIRCUIT & THEATRICAL GALLERY,

Positively the Last Night of Mr. M.'s Performances.

The Publick are respectfully informed, that they will find

Mr. MATHEWS

AT HOME

This Evening, **MONDAY,** June 18th, 1827,

With his Lecture on Peculiarities, Character and Manners, founded on Observations and Adventures during his

TRIP

TO

AMERICA!

PART I. Exordium—Tourists—Embarking on board the *William Thompson*—Speaking trumpet—Whimsical coincidence of names—Yellow fever—In sight of New York—New Brunswick—English importation—Jack Topham and his Cousin Bray—Waterloo Hotel, Liverpool, contrasted with Jack Bowers's hotel at Elizabeth Town—American phrases expounded—Cool landlord, hot wine—Arrival at Bristol (in America)—First Appearance at Baltimore—Philadelphia—Steam boat and stage coach characters—Arrival at New York—

Song—" Mrs. BRADISH's BOARDING-HOUSE."

More characters—American fun—Mr. Raventop, the American jester—Major Grimstone ; " Very well!"—Mr. Pennington—American strictures on English tourists—Jack Topham's fancies—Native Indians—War—Publick dinner—General Jackson—French Poet Laureat—

Song—" ODE TO GENERAL JACKSON."

American army—Irregular regulars—Muskets and umbrellas—Swords and fishing rods—

Song—" MILITIA MUSTER FOLK."

PART II. Birth Tragedian : " To be or not to be ?"—

Song—" OPOSSUM UP A GUM TREE."—(Real Negro Melody.)

Definition of the word Yankee—Jack Topham on the natives—Arrival at Boston—Bunker's Hill—A real YANKEE, Jonathan W. Doubikins, and his Uncle Ben—John and Jonathan, on " I guess" and " You know"—Monsieur Mallet—Election—

Song—" BOSTON POST OFFICE."

Providence—Enticements for Mr. Mathews to perform—Court of Justice—Charge to the Jury—Emigration discouraged by a British Farmer—Disabled goods and chattels—

Song—" ILLINOIS INVENTORY."

Preparations to depart—

FAREWELL FINALE.

PART III. A *Monopolylogue,* called

All WELL at Natchitoches.

COLONEL HIRAM PEGLER,	-	a Kentucky Shoe Maker.
AGAMEMNON,	-	a poor runaway Negro.
JONATHAN W. DOUBIKINS,	-	a real YANKEE, (his Master.)
MONSIEUR CAPOT,	-	a French Emigrant Tailor.
Mr. O'SULLIVIN,	-	an Irish improver of his fortunes.

☞ The Songs will be accompanied on the Piano Forte by Mr. JAMES T. HARRIS, who will play favorite Rondos between the Parts.

The SUMMER SEASON of the ENGLISH OPERA commences *Monday, July 2.*

Boxes 5s. *Pit* 3s. *Lower Gallery* 2s. *Upper Gallery* 1s. Doors open at HALF-PAST SEVEN, commences at EIGHT

PLACES cannot possibly be kept after HALF-PAST EIGHT o'clock.

Boxes, Family Boxes, and Places, to be had at the Box-Office, from 10 till 4.

[S. G. Fairbrother, Lyceum Printing Office, 1, Exeter Court, Strand.

A nineteenth-century theatre playbill, with versatile layout and typefaces

the simple broadsides and chapbooks than in all the expensively bound books of Pope, Swift, Addison, Johnson, Shenstone, Tickell, Grainger, Wolcot, and other heroes of the middle classes and aristocracy.

In the 1790s came that extraordinary confrontation between religion and politics in the mass medium of cheap pamphlets. The middle classes had already opposed the teaching of reading by Charity Schools and Sunday Schools, even although the fare offered was soberly religious and morally improving. In 1792 Paine's *Rights of Man* was published in a sixpenny edition, admittedly still a lot of money for a labourer, but within the capacity of groups of workmen, or the radical societies that were springing up all over the country. In 1802 Paine himself claimed that the number of copies circulated in England, Scotland and Ireland, besides translation into foreign languages, was between *four and five hundred thousand*.

A Royal Proclamation of 21 May 1792 was directed against 'wicked and seditious writings'. There were arrests and trials of radical authors and publishers, but this could not touch the thousands of ordinary people captivated by Paine's fluent arguments. Meanwhile, the reactionary critics of the Sunday Schools renewed their attacks on the awful consequences of teaching reading to poor children and adults.

The Cheap Repository Tract movement was not only designed to answer what the religious authorities considered to be the shallow, materialistic and seditious arguments of the radicals, but also as a justification of teaching poor people to read.

Hannah More was then a brilliant but pious bluestocking in the circle of Johnson and other literary lions. Bishop Porteus appealed to her to write a popular pamphlet to answer the propaganda of the radicals. The result was a modest tract called *Village Politics, by Will Chip, a Country Carpenter* [see page 69]. It was shrewdly written with great sincerity and simplicity, and became the model for more than a hundred Cheap Repository Tracts which followed, written by Hannah More, her sisters and associates. Two printers were involved in the beginning: Samuel Hazard, at Bath, and John Marshall, publishing simultaneously in London. Marshall was later supplanted by John Evans, London, a printer friendly with the Marshall family. Marshall was a well-known publisher of books for children in the John Newbery style, and as successor to the Dicey

Bow Church

St Mary Aldermary

VILLAGE POLITICS.

ADDRESSED

TO ALL THE MECHANICS, JOURNEYMEN,

A N D

DAY LABOURERS,

IN GREAT BRITAIN.

By W I L L C H I P,

A COUNTRY CARPENTER.

E I G H T H E D I T I O N.

L O N D O N:

PRINTED FOR AND SOLD BY F. AND C. RIVINGTON,
NO. 62, ST. PAUL'S CHURCH-YARD,
1793.
[Price 2d. or 25 for 3s.]

Hannah More's first tract

warehouse at Aldemary Church Yard was well qualified to organise
the hawkers who sold the old-fashioned broadsides and chapbooks.

The retail price of the tracts was ½d, 1d and 1½d. Chapmen were
allowed their usual trade discount terms, working out at about 25
tracts for 10d. The scheme was subsidised by contributions from
religious bodies and sympathisers, and well-to-do people could also
buy tracts at a favourable rate for free distribution.

The enormous success of this flood of religious propaganda
encouraged John Marshall and other printers to bring out imitations
of the tracts, and soon the market became flooded with religious
literature.

John Pitts, successor to Marshall in the ballad and chapbook
stock, utilised this renaissance of popular cheap literature to revive
the traditional ballad and chapbook trade at the opening of the
nineteenth century. In 1802, John Pitts was established at No 14
Great St Andrew Street, in the squalid Seven Dials area of London,
scene of John Gay's *The Beggars Opera*. Seven Dials was one of the
city's largest slums, crowded with Irish immigrants, old-clothes

dealers, gin sellers, beggars and criminals. In 1819 Pitts moved to No 6 Great St Andrew Street, where his 'Toy and Marble Warehouse' became famous for old and new ballads.

The importance of Pitts lies in his claim to represent a continuous tradition of stock since the old ballad houses of the sixteenth and seventeenth centuries. Pitts once stated that his business had descended from the great ballad factors Coles, Vere and Wright, through the Diceys to his predecessor John Marshall.

Pitts was a traditionalist, and reissued many of the old favourite ballads that had been popular nearly two centuries earlier, often reproducing the same old woodcut illustrations. He collected folk songs and ballads from the Irish immigrants of Seven Dials, and it seems that he also introduced the long-song sheet of 'Three Yards a Penny', often credited to his rivals. In fact, the sheet was barely a yard long, but the street seller could tell you that there were three columns on it!

Pitts was certainly a remarkable man. In his later years he went blind, but it is said that his sense of feeling was so acute that he could detect counterfeit coins or notes, and serve his customers without difficulty. He died in 1844. His friend and executor Robert Harrild was a famous figure in printing history whose invention of a composition roller revolutionised newspaper production. A detailed study of the life and output of Pitts will be found in my earlier book *John Pitts, Ballad Printer of Seven Dials, London 1765–1844, with a short account of his predecessors in the Ballad and Chapbook Trade* (1969).

There is something extraordinarily romantic about the old broadsides reissued by Pitts throughout the first decades of the nineteenth century, ballads like:

A Famous Sea Fight Between Captain Ward and the Rainbow

The Faithless Captain, Or Betrayed Virgin

The Children In The Wood, Or the Norfolk Gentleman's Last Will and Testament

A Tragical Ballad of the Unfortunate Loves Lord Thomas and Fair Eleanor

An Excellent New Ballad entitled The Cripple of Cornwall, Wherein is shewn his dissolate Life and deserved Death.

The last-named ballad was 'new' when it was first registered on 14 December 1624, nearly two centuries earlier.

A Famous Sea Fight

BETWEEN

CAPTAIN WARD

AND THE

RAINBOW,

STRIKE up ye lusty gallants,
With musicks sound of drum;
For there is such a rover,
Upon the sea is come;
His name is Captain Ward,
Full well it doth appear,
There has not been such a rover,
Found out these thousand years.

For he hath sent unto the king;
The sixth of January,
Desiring that he might come in,
With all his company,

And if the king will let me come,
Till I my tale have told,
I will bestow for my ransom,
Full thirty ton of gold.

O nay, O nay, then said the king,
O nay that must not be,
To yield to such a rover,
Myself will not agree,
He hath deceiv'd the Frenchmen,
Likewise the king of Spain,
Then how can he be true to me,
Who has been false to twain.

With that the king grew vexed,
A ship of worthy fame,
The Rainbow she is call'd;
If you would know her name,
And now the gallant rainbow,
She rolls upon the sea,
Five hundred gallant seamen,
To keep her company.

The Dutchmen and the Spaniards,
She made them for to flee,
Also the bonny Frenchmen,
As she met on the seas,
When as the gallant Rainbow,
Did come where Ward did lie,
Where is the Captain of that ship,
The rainbow she did cry.

O that I am, says Captain Ward,
There's no one bids me lie,
And if thou art the king's fair ship,
Thou art welcome unto me,
I'll tell thee what I said the rainbow,
Our king is in great grief,
That thou shouldst lie upon the seas,
And play the errant thief.

You will not let your merchantmen,
Pass as they did before,
Such tidings to our king is come,
Which grieves his heart full sore,
With that the gallant Rainbow,
She shot out of her pride,
Full fifty good brass pieces,
Charged on every side.

And yet these gallant shooters,
Prevailed not a pin,
Though they were brass on the outside,
Brave Ward was steel within.

Shoot on, shoot on, said Captain Ward,
Your sport well pleaseth me,
And he that first gives over,
Shall yield unto the sea.

I never wronged an English ship,
But Turk and king of Spain,
Likewise the blackguard Dutchmen,
As I met on the main,
If I had known your king,
But two or three days before,
I would have fav'd Lord Essex's life,
Whose death doth grieve me sore,

Go tell the king of England,
Go tell him thus from me,
If he reigns king of all the land,
I will reign king at sea.
With that the gallant Rainbow,
She fired and shot amain,
Then left the rovers company,
And home return'd again.

Our royal king of England,
Your ship's return'd again,
For Captain Ward he is so strong,
He never will be taken.
O everlasting said the king,
I have lost jewels three,
Which would have gone unto the sea,
And brought proud Ward to me.

The first was Lord Clifford,
Great Earl of Cumberland,
The second was Lord Mountjoy,
As you shall understand,
The third was brave Lord Essex,
From field would never flee,
Who was lately gone unto the sea,
And brought proud Ward to me.

Printed and Sold by J. Pitts, 14, Great St. andrew street, Seven Dials.
Price One Penny.

An old ballad issued by John Pitts

From 1813 onwards, Pitts suffered intense competition from his great rival James Catnach, about whom much has been written because of his flamboyant style and roughshod methods. Catnach was the son of a Scottish printer who had been established at Alnwick, Northumberland, before moving to London. 'Jemmy Catnach' was described by an old pressman who knew him as a 'plodding ignorant, dirty, successful individual', an eccentric and a hard drinker. Although he also printed many traditional songs, he specialised in topical items, giving the news in verse. He published hundreds of crudely written ballads that became the poor man's newspapers, dealing with politics, sport, fashions, murders, dying speeches and confessions. Catnach became famous for his 'cocks' and 'catchpennies', fictitious narratives printed up when real news was scarce. In *London Labour and the London Poor* (1861–2), Henry Mayhew describes how these sheets were sold:

Few of the residents in London—but chiefly those in the quieter streets—have not been aroused, and most frequently in the evening, by a hurly-burly on each side of the street. An attentive listening will not lead any one to an accurate knowledge of what the clamour is about. It is from a 'mob' or 'school' of the running patterers (for both those words are used), and consists of two, three or four men. All these men state that the greater the noise they make, the better is the chance of sale, and better still when the noise is on each side of a street, for it appears as if the vendors were proclaiming such interesting or important intelligence, that they were vieing with one another who should supply the demand which must ensue. It is not possible to ascertain with any certitude *what* the patterers are so anxious to sell, for only a few leading words are audible. One of the cleverest of running patterers repeated to me, in a subdued tone, his announcements of murders. The words 'Murder', 'Horrible', 'Barbarous', 'Love', 'Mysterious', 'Former Crimes', and the like, could only be caught by the ear, but there was no announcement of anything like 'particulars'. If, however, the 'paper' relate to any well-known criminal such as Rush, the name is given distinctly enough, and so is any new or pretended fact. The running patterers describe, or profess to describe, the contents of their papers as they go rapidly along, and they seldom or ever stand still. They usually deal in murders, seductions, crim.-cons., explosions, alarming accidents, 'assassina-

From Mayhew's London Labour and the London Poor

tions', deaths of public characters, duels, and love-letters. But popular, or notorious, murders are the 'great goes'. The running patterer cares less than other street-sellers for bad weather, for if he 'work' on a wet and gloomy evening, and if the work be 'a cock', which is a fictitious statement or even a pretended fictitious statement, there is the less chance of any detecting the *ruse*. But of late years no new 'cocks' have been printed, except for temporary purposes. . . . Among the old stereotyped 'cocks' are love-letters. One is well known as 'The Husband caught in a Trap', and being in an epistolary form subserves any purpose: whether it be the patterer's aim to sell the 'Love Letters' of any well-known person, such as Lola Montes, or to fit them for a local (pretended) scandal, as the 'Letters from a Lady in this neighbourhood to a Gentleman not 100 miles off.'

I have found no authoritative distinction between the terms 'cock' and 'catchpenny', which many people regard as synonymous. There is an often repeated story that the latter term arose after Catnach had cleared £500 from selling no less than 250,000 copies of a sheet on the murder of Mr Weare by John Thurtell in 1824. A fortnight after the execution Jemmy brought out a startling sheet headed 'WE ARE ALIVE AGAIN!' but with so little space between the words 'WE' and 'ARE' that it looked as if the hanged criminal had been miraculously resuscitated. Thousands of sheets were sold, but, says Charles Hindley, Catnach's biographer, 'those who did not like the trick called it a "catch penny", and this gave rise to this peculiar term, which ever afterwards stuck to the issues of the "Seven Dials' Press", though they sold as well as ever'.

The term 'catchpenny' was actually in use as early as 1759, and it was also used by Edmond Malone in a letter to the great balladist Bishop Percy, describing an incorrect and hasty biography got up for quick sale as 'a mere catchpenny'. My own view is that 'catchpenny' is a generic term for all deceptive narratives, and a 'cock' is a timeless story which might be made to crow at any date.

Murder and execution sheets were best-sellers, and Henry Mayhew estimated that no less than two-and-a-half million copies were sold on the execution of James Bloomfield Rush (1849). Mayhew also gave the following information on trade prices of the sheets:

The paper now published for the streets is classed as quarter sheets, which cost (wholesale) 1*s.* a gross; half sheets, which cost

2s.; and whole or broad sheets (such as for executions), which cost 3s. 6d. a gross the first day, and 3s. the next day or two, and afterwards, but only if a ream be taken, 5s. 6d.; a ream contains forty dozen. When 'illustrated', the charge is from 3d. to 1s. per ream extra. The books, for such cases as the Sloanes, or the murder of Jael Denny, are given in books—which are best adapted for the suburban and country trade, when London is 'worked' sufficiently—are the 'whole sheet' printed so as to fold into eight pages, each side of the paper being then, of course, printed upon. A book is charged from 6d. to 1s. extra (to a whole sheet) per gross, and afterwards the same extra per ream.

The average profit per week to a running stationer selling execution sheets was about 9s, sometimes as high as 12s 6d.

Another profitable line for Catnach and his rivals was children's literature, and many old nursery favourites were reprinted, things like: *Jack the Giant Killer, The Babes in the Wood, Tom Hickathrift*, and other fairy tales and nursery rhymes. There were 'battledores' too, not the bats used by children in playing with shuttlecocks, but folding alphabet cards, with words, phrases and woodcut illustrations. They developed from the ancient horn-books, which were the first convenient means by which children learned their letters. At Christmas time another great attraction was the carol sheets— broadsides with dozens of strange old woodcuts, sometimes hand-coloured, and verses of carols, some of them very old.

There are many well-worn stories about Catnach. At one time he used to take the hundreds of dirty pennies from his customers to the Bank of England, carrying the large bags in a hackney coach, and exchanging the pennies for silver. There was a story that one might easily catch fever from handling the coins from hawkers and beggars. On other occasions, Catnach boiled all his pennies in potash and vinegar, so they were clean and sterile. For all that he had so many bad pennies that he was able to pave a small back kitchen with them, embedding the coins in plaster of Paris.

Pitts and Catnach were deadly enemies. They copied each other's best sheets and circulated ribald lampoons against each other. Their rivalry, as well as the colourful life of the beggars and hawkers of Seven Dials, has been amusingly described by Charles Hindley in his book *The Life and Times of James Catnach (Late of Seven Dials), Ballad Monger* (1878). Catnach died in 1841, and was succeeded by his sister Anne Ryle and James Paul, formerly employed by Catnach. Throughout the nineteenth century a score of other London printers and many more in the provinces followed the lead of Pitts and Catnach in the street literature trade. The most notable names were Disley, Seven Dials, who specialised in gallows literature, and Henry Parker Such, whose family business continued from 1849 right through the music-hall period until as late as 1917. In the later years, the sheets from the Such Press were small hand-bills, with the words of music-hall songs printed on coloured paper.

It was curiously appropriate that the rivalries of Pitts and Catnach were finally resolved in the eventual succession of William S. Fortey, who inherited the stock of both of them and reissued many of their best items. After his death in 1901, his great accumulation of Pitts and Catnach items was sold at Sotheby's, and in due course a substantial selection came into the hands of Mr George F. Wilson of the Advance Foundry Ltd, who placed them on permanent loan at the Printing Library of the St Bride Foundation, London.

It was a strange chance that the choice remains of popular street literature should find their last resting place in a building dedicated to a more dignified history of printing! Here, at St Bride's, the traditional and the topical, the solid books and the stray sheets of street literature, finally found common ground.

Towards the end of the nineteenth century, ballads and chapbooks were supplanted by cheaply priced books for the mass reading public. Popular penny newspapers told the same stories as broadsides in the greater freedom of prose, and with colourful incidental detail. After a profitable phase of improving miscellanies and old Gothic novels trimmed down to pamphlet size, publishers began to churn out novels for mass circulation through the newly formed libraries and railway-station bookstalls. The same literature became available to all classes in society. Literature had become one common stream.

There were gains and losses in all this. Wise and beautiful books became freely available; the greatest talents and techniques perfected books to the highest standards. But the old ballads and romances disappeared, except for scholarly study, and the richness of the old myths was finally secularised into everyday fiction.

Gradually publishing came to depend more and more upon mass circulation, and to lose much of its independence and idealism in the desire to please the crowd. In a curious way, this fusion of sophisticated with street literature has revived the attitudes and techniques of the catchpenny printers like Old Jemmy Catnach. For better or for worse, the book industry, the newspaper empires, and the newer mass media of radio and television have become a more highly polished version of the street literature trade, in a world hypnotised by money, power, egoism and pop culture.

Yet without the struggles of printers and publishers in the street trade there could have been no medium for the ideas and emotions of the masses over nearly four centuries. Many individuals were in this business for power and money too, but at various times in history they also followed political or religious ideals, sometimes at great risk. And they identified themselves with the under-privileged masses who were striving to find social equality, justice, religious freedom, or merely entertainment in their drab lives. Street literature also provided a new outlet for popular writers. As early as 1600, the poet Nicholas Breton wrote:

> Goe tell the Poets that their pidling rimes
> Begin apace to grow out of request. . . .
> And tell poore Writers, stories are so stale,
> That penny ballads make a better sale.

Parallel with the history of the publication of street literature is the story of the thousands of ballad and chapbook hawkers who were the link between printer and public, the often anonymous pioneers who laid the foundations of the successful book industry of modern society.

4: Pedlars and Patterers

Pedlars and Patterers

IN THE EARLY DAYS OF PRINTING, BOOKS, PAMPHLETS AND BALLADS were sold from stalls in churchyards in London. St Paul's Churchyard was one of the great centres for literature. In addition to the printing establishments in the houses around the churchyard, there were also small booths or shops which displayed books, as well as many stalls in the churchyard itself. These were open at 7 o'clock in the morning. Many printers with offices in other parts of the city would also display and sell their work in the churchyard.

Books and ballads were advertised by fixing titles in cleft sticks or on the posts that served for advertising; sometimes they were stuck on the church doors. Some stationers served from their stalls (the name 'stationer' derives from one with a station or shop); others employed apprentices who would bawl out to the crowd, just as in any modern street market. Many pious people were offended by the raucous cries of 'What lack ye? Fine ballads! New ballads! Come along and buy!' Some booksellers even tried to sell their wares on Sundays, for which they were prosecuted.

Ballad-sellers roamed through the city streets, calling the titles of their latest items until they could get together a crowd of tradespeople, apprentices, porters and housewives. 'Ballads! my masters, ballads! Will ye ha' any ballads o' the newest and truest matter in London? Here be your story-ballads, your love-ballads, and your ballads of good life; fit for your gallant, your nice maiden, your grave senior, and all sorts of men beside. Ballads! my masters, rare ballads! Take a fine new Ballad, Sir, with a picture to't.'

Many broadsides carried the title 'A New Ballad of—' and that heading carried conviction, for few could doubt the truth of the printed word. Newness was the great attraction in the trade, although a wise ballad-seller also kept a few old favourites like 'Chevy Chase' or 'The Lord of Lorne'.

Once a crowd had formed, the ballad-seller would sing his ballads lustily, to teach the tune to the purchaser of the halfpenny or penny sheets. Many of the standard melodies were old dance tunes. It was not difficult for anyone to pick up a new tune, for the Elizabethan age was a musical one. As William Chappell commented in his

Popular Music of the Olden Time (1855–9), 'Tinkers sang catches; milkmaids sang ballads; carters whistled; each trade, and even the beggars, had their special songs; the base-viol hung in the drawing-room for the amusement of waiting visitors; and the lute, cittern, and virginals, for the amusement of waiting customers, were the necessary furniture of the barber's shop. They had music at dinner; music at supper; music at weddings; music at funerals; music at night; music at dawn; music at work; and music at play.'

The rise of the balladmongers coincided with the decline of the old minstrels, who were now classed as rogues and vagabonds. No doubt some of them took to composing or selling ballads. In his *Arte of English Poesie*, published in 1589, Puttenham referred to: 'Ballads and small popular musickes sung by these cantabanqui upon benches and barrels heads, where they have none other audience than boyes or countrye fellowes that passe by them in the street, or else by blind harpers, or such like taverne minstrels that give a fit of mirth for a groat; and their matters being for the most part stories of old time, as the tale of Sir Topas, Bevis of Southampton, Guy of Warwick, Adam Bell and Clymme of the Clough, and such other old romances or historical rhimes, made purposely for the recreation of the common people at Christmas dinners and bride ales, and in taverns and alehouses, and such other places of base resort.'

Some ballad-sellers were sturdy rogues, others blind, lame or deformed. Sometimes they were in league with the pickpockets who robbed their spellbound audiences, as Ben Jonson described so amusingly in *Bartholomew Fair* (1614). [See page 83.]

Selling ballads was a profitable trade, and a balladmonger might take as much as twenty shillings on a very good day—a small fortune when you consider that in the seventeenth century a halfpenny might buy a quarter of a pound of meat.

By the mid-seventeenth century, hawkers called 'mercuries' were selling their pamphlets of domestic news. A news book usually cost one penny, but the style was more difficult than a ballad, and the mixture of satire, abuse and propaganda was bewildering to a working man. Mounting interest in the excitement of politics enlarged the journalistic market, culminating in a thirst for news with the outbreak of the Great Rebellion. The national convulsions of politics soon flooded the market with thousands of news

Picking a pocket at Bartholomew Fair. While the victim is engaged by the balladmonger, a confederate tickles his ear with a straw and picks his pocket

pamphlets and made many of the ballads seem old-fashioned. The issues were now too complex for simple verses. Many writers switched over from ballads to prose pamphlets. Martin Parker, prince of ballad-writers and author of the famous 'When the King enjoys his own again', became a pamphleteer for the Royalist cause.

Today it seems incredible that anyone could have found his way through the tangle of reasonable reporting, downright lies, special pleading, involved rhetoric, satire and sarcasm that passed for news in the twenty eventful years between 1640 and 1660.

During this period, sophisticated literature was dominated by heavy and dull books of sermons and religious exhortations. Of course, there were notable exceptions, like Herrick's *Hesperides* (1647–8), poems by Richard Lovelace (1649), and Walton's immortal *Compleat Angler* (1653), but these were not for working people. Another important, but solid, work was the great *Polyglott Bible*, in six volumes, 1657. There was little light relief during the Civil War, for the theatres were closed most of the time. In general the genius of Milton overshadowed other writers, but for the most part books were remote from the course of history.

For the ordinary people, literature was on the streets in ballads and news pamphlets that were in intimate contact with the spirit of the times. The most severe legislation failed to stem the flood of illegal pamphlets and ballads, although it sometimes put up the price. Penny pamphlets were sold for twopence or even sixpence when they were highly seditious and there were great risks in open sale. In 1649, *Mercurius Pragmaticus*, a Royalist weekly, was peddled secretly for twopence. The Government employed spies, one of the most famous being Elizabeth Alkin, nicknamed 'Parliament Joan'. She posed as a mercury woman, even publishing and selling her own news book in order to trap Royalist mercuries. She was paid as much as ten pounds a time for the editors captured through her spying.

With the death of Cromwell on 3 September 1658, there was an outburst of spiteful ballads, and when Charles II entered London on 29 May 1660 there were many congratulatory verses. In spite of the Licensing Act two years later, there was now little real need for fly-by-night propaganda pamphlets.

In 1665, *The Oxford Gazette* was licensed by the Secretary of State. From its 24th issue (5 February 1665–6) it became *The London*

Londons Gazette here

Nouvelle Gazette
Chi Compra gl'auisi di Londra

M.auron delin:

P.Tempest exc:
Cum Privilegio

Gazette, the first true newspaper as distinct from the news pamphlets. It was a half sheet printed on both sides. Samuel Pepys commented that it was 'very pretty, full of news, and no folly in it'. It has survived into modern times, and still appears.

From the Restoration onwards, for more than a century, newspapers now became slanted to the taste of gentlemen and merchants rather than ordinary people, for whom chapbooks took the place of news pamphlets. For the man in the street there seems to have been a romantic swing back to the old penny histories of Tom Thumb, Dr Faustus, Guy of Warwick, Robin Hood, and all the old folk and fairy tales. The older traditional ballads were still printed.

In 1666, the London stationers suffered the catastrophic destruction of the Great Fire. Samuel Pepys, lover of both books and ballads, recorded a graphic first-hand account of the calamity in his diary for 2 September. On the 7th, he visited the melancholy ruins of the booksellers at St Paul's Churchyard, where he had often bought books. The damage has been estimated at a million pounds. One of the earliest ballads added by Pepys to his Selden Collection was:

London mourning in Ashes;

OR, Lamentable Narrative lively expressing the Ruine of that Royal City by fire which began in *Pudding-Lane* on *September* the second, 1666, at one of the clock in the morning being *Sunday*, and continuing until *Thursday* night following, being the sixth day, with the great care the King, and the Duke of York took in their own Persons, day and night to quench it.

The tune, *In sad and ashy weeds*.

It was a great loss for both popular and sophisticated literature. In 1667, Thomas Rookes, who was luckier than most other booksellers, issued a catalogue with the following comments:

The late conflagration consumed my own, together with the Stock of Books (as it were) of the Company of Stationers, London. Since that lamentable disaster, next my own loss, this doth trouble me, That when any of those few ingenious persons who desire books, inquire after them; they are often answered (by such as have them not), That they are all burnt, Which discourageth any further inquiry, not only to the Learned, but even of country Chapmen. Wherefore to let all men know, notwithstanding that late dreadful calamity, that there are books yet to be had; and for the convenience of ingenious buyers: I publish the ensuing catalogue.

Buy a new Almanack
Almanachs Nouveaux
Lunarÿ dell Anno Nuovo

'Country chapmen' now constituted a growing industry as the book trade got on its feet again. Many of the London-printed ballads and chapbooks circulated throughout the countryside, carried by pedlars with ribbons, pins, garters, lace, and other cheap merchandise.

London booksellers like Charles Bates, 'at the Sun and Bible in Guiltspur-street', and John Foster, 'at the Golden Ball in Pye-corner', advertised 'where any country chapmen or others may be furnished with all sorts of historys, small books, and ballads, at reasonable rates'. Road-books were also published in London, and in 1686 *The City and Countrey Chapman's Almanack for the Year of Our Lord 1687* listed dates and places of fairs and markets, as well as routes and post roads.

At the great country fairs, pedlars of the type of Shakespeare's Autolycus in *The Winter's Tale* sold ballads, chapbooks, and almanacs with their small wares, side by side with mummers, tumblers, jugglers, beggars and quack mountebanks. Country girls would enliven their work with songs, or sit in the shade singing old traditional ballads. Farmers would remind themselves of the important events of the calendar year in almanacs which also gave mysterious prognostications.

A broadside ballad circa 1686 entitled 'The Sorrowful Lamentation of the Pedlars, and petty Chapmen, for the hardness of the times, and the decay of Trade' enumerated all the items in a chapman's pack, and included a verse:

> We have choice of Songs and merry books too,
> All pleasant, and witty, delightful, and new,
> Which every young swain may whistle at Plough,
> And every fair Milk-maid may sing to her Cow
>> *Then Maidens and Men, come see what you lack,*
>> *Come buy my fine Toys that I have in my Pack*

Pedlars might well complain of their trade, for they were often bedevilled by licensing or by regulations which classed them as beggars and rogues. One old by-law referred to 'Hawkers, Vendors, Pedlars, petty Chapmen, and unruly people'. Often the chapmen *were* rogues, with inferior and over-priced goods, and there is evidence that they drank and debauched, and sometimes seduced young women. But in country districts they were the only real connection with the outside world, bringing news, essential knick-knacks and novelties.

The tradition of chapbook pedlars was an extraordinarily conservative one, for it continued with little change for more than three centuries until well into the nineteenth century. Throughout this period, seventeenth century chapbook and ballad titles continued to be popular.

During the eighteenth century there was no effective copyright in the old favourites, and the same titles were printed or distributed by dozens of provincial presses. The widespread distribution of Dicey chapbooks may be seen from this imprint on a chapbook of *Faithful friendship or, Alphonso and Ganselo*: 'sold by William Peachey, near St. Benet's Church, in Cambridge, at Burnham's snuff-shop in Aylesbury; Mrs. Margaret Ward, in Sun Lane, Reading; Paul Stevens in Bicester; Tho. Williams in Tring; Anthony Thorpe in St. Albans; John Timbs and Henry Potter, in Stony Stratford; and by Churrude Brady in St. Ives. At all which places, chapmen, travellers, &c., may be furnish'd with all sorts of old and new ballads, broadsheets, histories, &c.'

This widespread supply network was a by-product of William Dicey's enterprising distribution of the *Northampton Mercury* newspaper, which he founded in partnership with Robert Raikes, father of the famous founder of the Sunday School movement. A catalogue issued by Cluer Dicey and Richard Marshall at the Printing Office in Aldemary Church Yard in 1764 listed one hundred and fifty chapbooks, and spoke of 'near three thousand different sorts of ballads'. Trade prices were as follows: old ballads, collections of songs, and eight-page patters '48 to the Quire, and 20 Quires to the Ream, per Ream 4 shillings'; Penny History Books '104 at 2s. 6d.'; 'Small Histories or Books of Amusements for Children on various subjects, adorned with a Variety of Cuts, 100 at 6s., ditto stitch'd on embossed paper, 13 for 9d'. *Robin Hood's Garland*, a special chapbook retailing at 6d net, was sold wholesale at 16s per hundred.

During this period the cheapest books available cost from 2s 6d to 6s for an octavo volume, and 10s to 13s for a quarto or folio. In the countryside, a book might represent more than a week's wages. Moreover, ordinary people had little time for reading, and would have found the majority of books difficult to understand. The simple old stories of chapbooks and ballad-sheets stirred the imagination in the drudgery of everyday life, and preserved scraps of traditional lore. Here is a typical sampling of the classics of a chapman, taken from a Dicey catalogue:

CHAPBOOKS
Argalus and Parthenia
Bateman's Tragedy
Bevis of Southampton
Blind Beggar of Bednal Green
Children in the Wood
Dorastus and Fawnia
Doctor Faustus
Esop's Fables
Fair Rosamond
Fryer Bacon
Fortunatus
Guy of Warwick
Groats-Worth of Wit
George Barnwell
Hero and Leander
Jane Shore
King and Cobler
Mad Men of Gotham
Partridge and Flamsted [Almanac]
Patient Grizel
Parismus of Bohemia
Reynard the Fox
Saint George
Seven Champions
Thomas Hickathrift
Titus Andronicus
Valentine and Orson
BALLADS
Barbara Allen's Cruelty
Captain Ward and the Rainbow
Catskin: Or, the Wandering Young Gentlewoman
Chevy-Chase
David and Bathsheba
Fair Rosamond and King Henry II
Great Boobie
Golden Bull: Or, the Garland of Love's Craftiness

Johnny Armstrong
King Henry II and the Miller of Mansfield
Lord Thomas and fair Eleanor
Little Musgrove and Lady Barnet
Maudlin, the Merchant's Daughter of Bristol
Noble Riddles wisely expounded
Pleasant Ballad of Tobias
Patient Grizzel
Queen Eleanor's Confession
Robin Hood and Little John
Sir Eglamore
Sir Andrew Barton
St. George and the King of Ægypt's Daughter
Thomas Stukeley
Wandering Jew: Or, The Shoemaker of Jerusalem
William Grismond's Downfall

Most of these best-sellers for more than two centuries have an appeal and inspiration missing from the more solid books of their time. The themes of old chivalry, romance, tragedy and true love brought an idealism to simple lives, lacking in the sophisticates of town and city.

We have few records of the half-world of the travelling chapmen and their customers. Much of their story is a lost unwritten history of hardworking traders, rogues and cheapjacks, of lonely places wrapped in a timeless spell of labour through the seasons, of echoes of medieval religion, folk customs and songs, and ancient romances, the saga of simple people who lived, loved and died with no record other than a church register. Chapmen were explorers in a strange world, and if they sometimes cheated and lived rough, at least they left dreams, hopes, new ideas, entertainment, and the rudiments of literary education.

In addition to the popular old chapbooks, there were also newer titles composed by local writers, or even by the pedlars themselves, drawing upon the folklore of their travels.

One of the most famous chapman-authors was Dougal Graham, in his later years appointed 'skellat bellman' or town crier of Glasgow. Graham was born in a Stirling village about the year 1724. As a young man he was a farm worker, but in 1745 he became attached to the Highland army during the Jacobite Rebellion. Soon after the battle of Culloden he published a rhymed *History of the Rebellion.* Priced at fourpence it was more substantial than most chapbooks, but it became immensely popular, carried all over Scotland by the chapmen. Graham went on to compose and sell a score of chapbooks, full of pawky humour and shrewd wit. Some of the most famous titles were: *Jockey and Maggy's Courtship, The Coalman's Courtship, The Comical Sayings of Paddy from Cork, The Witty and Entertaining Exploits of George Buchanan, The History of Haverel Wives, Leper the Tailor* and *John Cheap the Chapman.* These were reprinted over and over again for more than a hundred years, and passed into the folklore of Scotland. *John Cheap the Chapman* is probably autobiographical:

John Cheap the chapman, was a very comical short thick fellow, with a broad face and a long nose; both lame and lazy, and something leacherous among the lasses; he chused rather to sit idle than work at any time, as he was a hater of hard labour. No man needed to offer him cheese and bread after he cursed he would not have it; for he would blush at bread and milk, when hungry, as a beggar doth at a bawbee. He got the name of John Cheap the chapman by his selling twenty needles for a penny, and twa leather laces for a farthing.

The bookseller and chapbook printer George Caldwell, of Paisley, knew Graham as well as any man and said of him: 'Dougald was an unco glib body at the pen, and could screed aff a bit penny history in less than nae time. A' his warks took weel—they were level to the meanest capacity, and had plenty of coarse jokes to season them. I never kent a history of Dougald's that stack in the sale yet, and we were aye fain to get a haud of some new piece frae him.'

The way of the chapman was a hard one, particularly in the wilds of Scotland. Roads were often little more than rough tracks. As late as 1763 there was only one monthly stage-coach between Scotland and London, which took from fifteen to eighteen days to make the journey. Apart from the rigours of travelling hundreds of miles on foot, there were the hazards of robbers both on the highways and in the underworld of the towns and cities. Some chapmen banded together to form a 'Fraternity', a kind of trade union, with rules of government and penalties for misbehaviour. Once a year they would hold a gala day. The Fraternities of Chapmen of Stirling, Fife and Perth even kept minute books, dating from the opening of the eighteenth century.

A well-known chapman who left his reminiscences was David Love of Nottingham. Born at Torriburn, near Edinburgh, in 1750, he became in turn farm labourer, collier, soldier, shopkeeper and chapman. In *The Life, Adventures and Experience of David Love* (1825) he tells the story of a romantic and eventful life. He travelled all over England from Edinburgh to the Isle of Wight, was married three times, imprisoned on one occasion, almost hanged, and finally passed away in Nottingham in 1824. He wrote many of his own sheets, and the quaintly stilted verses have an ancient ring to them:

> I have composed many rhymes,
> On various subjects, and the times,
> And call'd the trials of prisoners' Crimes
> > The cash to bring;
> When old I grew, composed hymns,
> > And them did sing.

David Love, of Nottingham,

Aged 74, A. D. 1824.

> " Here's David's likeness for his book,
> All those who buy may at it look,
> As he is in his present state,
> Now printed from a copper-plate."

Here is a sample of David Love's patter, in selling his compositions at country fairs:

Good people, here are two excellent new songs, never before printed, composed by myself, your humble servant. One is the 'Pride and Vanity of Young Women, with advice to Young Men that they may take care who they marry.' And, that the young women may not be offended, I have another which may serve as an answer, the 'Pride and Vanity of Young Men, with advice to the Maids to beware of being ensnared by their flatteries and enticing words'.

After singing a verse or two from these simple homely pieces, he would sell copies as fast as ever he could hand them out, 'the men', as he said, 'buying the song concerning the women, and the women that of the men'.

Another great wandering chapman who left autobiographical notes was William Cameron, better known throughout Scotland as 'Hawkie'. Street orator, hawker of chapbooks, beggar and wit, his biting sarcasm and lively humour became treasured folklore north of the border, and much of it passed into books of Scottish stories. His reminiscences present a picaresque rogue's tour of Scotland during the nineteenth century, with graphic descriptions of all the vagrants, beggars, rogues and criminals of the time. Hawkie was on lodging-house terms with the kind of colourful characters described in Burns's 'The Jolly Beggars'. Hawkie was born in Stirling about 1785, and spent some years as a journeyman tailor and a field-preacher, before eventually taking to the road. He fell in with gypsies and learned their secret slang. Around 1815 he was selling chapbooks in Glasgow and Paisley, pattering the stories through the streets. He had no compunction about crying witty stories quite unconnected with the chapbooks he sold. One day, when his chapbook supplier was out of materials, Hawkie obtained some newspapers from his house, and, as he says:

I went out into the street, told a long tale, and sold the papers. Times were good then; I drew upwards of 4s. None challenged me that night, but on the Monday following when I was at the 'Cross', a young woman came to me and said, 'You rascal, you cheated me on Saturday night; you sold me a newspaper instead of a book.' I asked her 'What she gave for it?' She said, 'A halfpenny.' And I told her she could never be cheated with a newspaper for a halfpenny.

Hawkie stayed in the lowest lodging-houses, lousy with bugs, and once saw rats eating a companion who had died in his sleep. Although he would pull every trick of the trade to earn a few shillings for drink, he had his own peculiar principles. When he found that a lodging-house family of cheats he had known earlier was now established in a smart expensive shop, he lashed them sharply: 'When I looked at their rise and their present splendour, in the very place where people knew they were beggars, and their conscience told them they had imposed on the public, I then considered that I, in the street with a halfpenny paper in my hand, was a better man than they in the shop.'

Hawkie gives a vivid picture of the fuddled drinking and rivalry of other chapbook sellers and rogues, in and out of jail:

William Cameron, better known as 'Hawkie', chapman, beggar and street orator

When I got to Renfrew there were two 'patterers' there before me; when I saw them I was aware they were for Greenock also. A dram was proposed. They were as 'kittle' neighbours as Glasgow could produce. One of them, William Anderson, had been three times transported for seven years; he and the other man, James Johnston, could never meet without a fight.

We got to Paisley and went into a public house. After drinking 'half-mutchkins' [half an English pint] each, Johnston and Anderson quarrelled, and fought with their staves; they broke a number of articles in the room. Anderson got Johnston down, and when down, put Johnston's books in the fire, and held him till they were burned. Johnston got an opportunity, and burned Anderson's books.

The house was in danger of being burned, and the landlord sent us to the black hole; they kept us there till next day, and put us out of the town. I still had my books, and promised to divide them when we were half-way from Paisley, at a place called 'The Whiskey Well,' where we proposed a gill, and went in; before we came out, my books were also burned, and we were all without a book. I was still in possession of a few shillings, and I was aware they were determined to make me spend the last farthing.

We came again to Paisley, and my two old boys cast out in the street, and were both taken to the Police Office. I was then rid of my neighbours, with whom I never thought to part till I had got a broken head.

I went to the house of George Caldwell, senr., a bookseller, who had retired from business, and was living privately at the head of 'Dyer's Wynd;' but still kept a few small books to serve hawkers. He had a copy of an eight-paged book of which he had some reams. It was called 'The Life and Transactions with the Trial and Burning of Maggie Lang, the Cardonald Witch,' who suffered in Paisley, this being the last that suffered in Scotland as a witch.

This book had a great sale; I cleaned his shop of every copy, and got another book called 'The Life and Transactions with the Trial and Burning of Maggie Osborne, the Ayrshire Witch.' Of this book I sold a ream in one day; one half in the butter Market in Ayr and the other at the Cross of Ayr, in front of the house where she lived.

A chapman could do well if he did not waste his earnings in gin r whisky. Hawkie tells how he bought eight-page ballads at twopence dozen, and with an initial capital of only twopence made six hillings in about three hours. Another of his catchpenny exploits vas 'straw selling', making a great mystery of a quite ordinary hapbook:

My next effort was 'STRAW' selling, and giving the book into the bargain, saying, 'This is a most particular book, but I daurna' cry the book, 'deed I daurna' either name the book, nor sell the book, but I will sell ony o' ye a *straw*, an' gie ye the book into the bargain.' This 'system' was new in Edinburgh, and I took money fast; the book I sold in this way was entitled, 'Gilderoy, the Scotch Robber', of which I sold nearly twenty reams.

The practice of 'strawing' persisted in mid-nineteenth century London, and the same patter was even used by ballad-sellers in Ireland. It seems to have arisen from the sale of radical literature, and about 1820 leaves from Richard Carlile's *Republican* were sold in this way. Carlile, publisher of Thomas Paine, was one of many radical publishers threatened by the newspaper tax of 1819, designed to cut off seditious reading from the masses.

Of the many hundreds of chapmen and balladmongers of the eighteenth and nineteenth centuries, a few have achieved fame in scattered anecdotes or in folk legend.

James Rankin, born blind in 1770 in Aberdeenshire, became a beggar on the death of his father, and travelled through Scotland singing old songs and ballads. Around 1828 he was employed by the publisher Peter Buchan, to whom he supplied many ballads, some of which found their way eventually into the great ballad corpus of Professor F. J. Child's *English & Scottish Popular Ballads* (1882–98).

'Mussel-mou'd Charlie', born Charles Leslie, was known to Sir Walter Scott as 'an old Aberdeenshire minstrel, the very last, probably of the race'. He was a devoted Jacobite, singing and selling the ballads which he carried in a large bag slung over his shoulder. He died in 1782 at the ripe age of one hundred and five years.

Some characters were not above the most impudent cheating, and more than once chapmen sold credulous crowds *blank paper* for chapbooks or broadsides. Old 'General' Mayo of Nottingham, in the early nineteenth century, once walked through the streets calling 'Here's the grand and noble speech as the Duke of York made yesterday'. A purchaser who found himself in possession of a blank sheet for his penny stared at it and complained 'General, here nothing on it!' 'No, sir,' retorted Mayo, 'the Duke of York sai *nowt!*'

Perhaps the most affectionately remembered eccentric was th cantankerous old blind 'Zozimus', pre-eminent minstrel of the Dubli streets during the first half of the nineteenth century. Born Micha Moran, about 1794, he became a reciter and composer of ballads sacred and profane, whose style and patter have been minutel recorded. His name derived from a favourite recitation of an ol piece by Bishop Coyle about St Mary of Egypt and the hermi Zozimus. Tall, attenuated, dressed in a heavy coarse long-taile coat and a worn hat, Zozimus stumped in measured stride throug the Dublin streets with his stout blackthorn stick fastened to hi wrist by a leather thong. The stick was his weapon against th unruly. Then, with upturned face and deeply guttural voice, h would commence an oration:

'Gather 'round me boys, gather 'round poor Zozimus, yer friend. Boys, am I standin' in puddle, am I standin' in wet?'

(*Voices:* 'Ah no, yer not, yer in a nice dry place. Go on with St. Mary.')

'Awl me buzzum friends are turned backbiters. Now, me dead-knowledge coves, if yez don't drop yer coddin' an' devasion, I'll lave sum av yez a kase.'

Before commencing, he would pause, absorbed in deep reverie, as if waiting for inspiration, then pronounce:

'This is the full, true, and particular account of the sufferings and hardships, the severe penance and privations, with the pious, holy life and miraculous conversion of Saint Mary of Egypt, blessed be her holy name. . . .'

His most famous composition, *The Finding of Moses*, has descended in Dublin street lore in the following (probably adapted) form:

> In Agypt's land contaygious to the Nile,
> Old Pharao's daughter went to bathe in style,
> She tuk her dip and came unto the land,
> And for to dry her royal pelt she ran along the strand:
> A bull-rush tripped her, whereupon she saw
> A smiling babby in a wad of straw,
> She tuk it up and said in accents mild,
> 'Tare-an-ages, girls, which o' yees own the child?'

Around the end of the eighteenth century and the early years of the nineteenth, many writers of miscellaneous reminiscences remembered the pedlars and chapbook sellers of their youth. In *Random Recollections* (1905), the publisher William Tinsley recalled his boyhood days in a Hertfordshire village some sixty years earlier. Ballad-sellers often visited the village, which was relatively near to London, selling their murder broadsides. Tinsley commented dryly:

The news of the last dying speeches and confessions of murderers reached our village very early as a rule; in fact, now and then, before the execution had taken place. . . . Of course, when the news of a reprieve did overtake Master Jimmy Catnach's men in the country, they soon made their way back to Seven Dials with their useless stock of false reports, and I suppose Catnach made them some allowance, for he was a shrewd business man, and made a fair fortune out of the printing and sales of Newgate literature, ballads, and other kinds of penny broadsides.

Tinsley also described the attractions of broadside ballads to a young farm labourer:

I remember a farmer's boy, named James Turner, who I think should and would have been a good rustic poet had he had a better education, more books, and fairly intellectual society. In fact, could he have had even less chance than myself of seeing the world, men, and books, I think there might have been one more poet to name with Bloomfield. Turner and myself worked on the same farm for some few months, and his mania was for songs and ballads of all kinds. Every penny, and indeed every halfpenny he had to spend, went to an old ballad hawker, who came our way once a week, and was Turner's adviser in song and literary matters, giving him a sort of cue to the tunes of the new songs, either by humming or whistling them. Perhaps Turner's strongest point was whistling; he would whistle faint resemblances of the airs of numerous songs one after the other, and it was almost wonderful what a retentive memory he had, for he could in his way sing or recite song after song word for word without the slightest prompting. Some weeks Turner's purchases from the old song merchant amounted to as much as three pence, and as he carried all his library about with him, as a rule his pockets were stuffed with the little tissue paper broadsides. I cannot now remember that the old hawker ever sold or tried to sell Turner any songs beyond those of a fairly interesting

domestic nature, even if he carried them, but perhaps he did no
Turner had scores of songs and ballads that I have forgotten a
about, but he was letter perfect in 'Home, Sweet Home,' 'Th
Mistletoe hung in the Castle Hall,' 'The Deeds of Young Napoleo
shall sting the Bonny Bunch of Roses,' 'Lord Bateman was
noble Lord,' 'Verlin down bray,' 'On yonder high mountain a wil
fowl doth fly, and there is one amongst them that soars very high
Some of those old songs had fairly long lives fifty or sixty years ago

The ballad-sheets printed by the Seven Dials press and oth
London printers were mostly thin quarto sheets, roughly $7'' \times 10$
with two songs in adjacent columns. A sheet could be cut down t
middle and each song sold for a halfpenny. Many of the executic
sheets, carol sheets, and other specialties were large broadside
anything from $14\frac{3}{4}'' \times 20''$ to $19\frac{3}{4}'' \times 29\frac{1}{2}''$. The old-fashioned balla
printed by John Pitts on blue or green tinted rough paper varie
from approximately $7'' \times 10''$ quartos to larger folios about $14\frac{1}{2}'' \times 10$

By the middle of the nineteenth century there were sever
hundred ballad-sellers still at work in London, many specialising
particular types of sale.

About two hundred men were general 'chaunters' or ballad singer
selling miscellaneous sheets. 'Ballads on a subject' might be politica
criminal, or relating to any event or topic of the day—'The Marriag
of the Queen', 'When we get Johnny's Reform', 'The Fenians ar
Coming', 'A New Song on the Bloomer Costume', 'Sayers & Heenan
Great Fight for the Championship', 'The Great Agricultural Show
'The Windham Lunacy Case', 'Death of H.R.H. the Duke c
Cambridge', 'Funny Doings in the Convent', 'The Naughty Lord &
The Gay Young Lady, damages, £10,000', 'The Funny He-Sh
Ladies!', 'Terrible Accident on the Ice in Regent's Park', and so on
The payment to street authors for these effusions was usually
shilling, with perhaps 'a penny or two over' if the printers like
them. But there were also many old traditional favourites lik
'The Children in the Wood', 'Death and the Lady', 'Chevy Chase'
and the deathless 'Barbara Allen'.

The 'standing patterer' attracted attention by his pictorial board
supported on a pole, with crude gaudy illustrations such as the
flogging of the nuns of Minsk, in gory detail, Calcraft the hangman
or simply vaguely menacing but irrelevant cartoons of skeletons
coffins, and other mysteries. These boards were as specialised an

rt as painting inn signs. The patterers would recite the verses or
ialogues printed on the sheets. A few patterers specialised in
itanies' without a board, giving difficult street elocution of complex
rose sheets in character, sometimes in sketchy costume. Popular
:ems were 'The Rent Day', 'The Drunkard's Catechism', 'A Pack
f Cards turned into a Bible, a Prayer-book and an Almanack',
Good Advice to Young Men on Choosing their Wives', 'Rich Man
nd his Wife Quarrelling because they have no Family' and 'What
s Happiness?'. In effect the standing patterer gave a one-man
heatrical performance, selling the text afterwards. It cost about
leven shillings to set up in this trade—5s 6d for the board and
ole, painting 3s 6d to the specialist artist, and about 2s for ballad
:tock.

The 'running patterers' numbered nearly a hundred, and were
mostly concerned with news ballads, especially murders and 'cocks'.
A 'good' murder yielded a sequence of sheets. First, a normal
quarter-sheet (about $9\frac{1}{2}'' \times 7\frac{1}{2}''$) with the earliest report of the crime,
next half-sheets (twice the size) with 'later particulars or discoveries'
(often copied from newspapers), then the great broadsheets with
grisly woodcuts, containing Sorrowful Lamentations and Last
Farewells, and the alleged last moments at the scaffold (usually
written up the day before). One informant frankly admitted to
Henry Mayhew that the sheets 'invented every lie likely to go
down'. ' "Here you have also an exact likeness," they say, "of the
murderer, taken at the bar of the Old Bailey!" when all the time it is
an old wood-cut that's been used for every criminal for the last
forty years.' We have many first-hand accounts of the grim scenes
of public execution, from contemporary writers who knew all the
details—the dense crowds of sweating men, women and children,
joking or jeering as they waited in one huge mass, drinking in the
spectacle, rich spectators vieing for position with the poor, the
erection of the gallows, the appearance of the wretched criminal,
hooted, cheered, or pelted with rubbish, the chaplain's brief words,
the drop, and the dangling corpse. Sometimes the Smithfield
butchers, overalls soaked in blood, would surge forward to the
gallows to get a close view just before the end. Afterwards the
ballad-sellers sold their melancholy sheets. Some patterers carried
real or invented details to the country trade, travelling through
Hertfordshire, Cambridgeshire and Suffolk. One patterer claimed

USEFUL SUNDAY LITERATURE FOR THE MASSES;

OR, MURDER MADE FAMILIAR.

Father of a Family (reads). "The wretched Murderer is supposed to have cut the throats of his three eldest Children, and then to have killed the Baby by beating it repeatedly with a Poker. * * * * * In person he is of a rather bloated appearance, with a bull neck, small eyes, broad large nose, and coarse vulgar mouth. His dress was a light blue coat, with brass buttons, elegant yellow summer vest, and pepper-and-salt trowsers. When at the Station House he expressed himself as being rather 'peckish,' and said he should like a **Black Pudding**, which, with a Cup of Coffee, was immediately procured for him."

hat he covered 800 to 1,000 miles with one big murder. In the large
owns, printers who were not on the Catnach or Disley circuit would
opy particulars on to their own sheets.

It is one thing to condemn the crudities of the dying-
speechmongers, but popular and cultured literary interests came
together on the gruesome details of Horrible Murders and Executions. The *Illustrated London News* had graphic woodcuts of any
leading crime, and Sunday newspapers gave special coverage to
important executions. The *Lady's Newspaper* sent a special artist to
Paris to make drawings of the scene of the murder by the Duc de
Praslin, illustrating the bloodstains in the bedchamber.

All this gallows literature represented the last dishonourable
descent of the old tradition of dignified farewells from the execution
block in former centuries, when noble speeches were made by martyrs
and political victims.

In addition to such best-selling literature, there were ballad-sheets
on an enormous range of subjects. One Seven Dials printer alone
claimed to stock more than five thousand different titles. Some of
these have been mentioned already. There were also many fine old
country songs, as well as unauthorised reprints of established writers
like Burns, Byron, Moore, Dickens and Eliza Cook, and bits and
pieces of Herrick, Suckling and Shakespeare. One of the most
colourful of the ballad-selling trades was the 'pinner-up', who
created something of a poor man's picture gallery or library at any
suitable street site. A writer in *Chambers' Journal* (No 130, 28 June
1856) described this picturesque activity:

Besides the chanters, who sing the songs through the streets of
every city, town, village, and hamlet in the kingdom—the long-
song seller, who shouts their titles on the kerb-stone . . . is the
Pinner-up, who takes his stand against a dead-wall or a long range
of iron-railing, and, first festooning it liberally with twine, pins
up one or two thousand ballads for public perusal and selection.
Time was when this was a thriving trade; and we are old enough
to remember the day when a good half-mile of wall fluttered with
the minstrelsy of war and love, under the guardianship of a
scattered file of pinners-up, along the south side of Oxford Street
alone. Twenty years ago, the dead-walls gave place to shop-fronts,
and the pinners-up departed to their long homes.

Much of street balladry passed into the more theatrical art of the music-hall. One line of broadsides descended by way of sheet music to Tin Pan Alley and, much later, the gramophone record industry of popular music that preceded today's boom in pop groups.

Another stream of street literature passed into cheap books, for many nineteenth century pioneers of cheap printing began with pamphlets which grew into paper-backs of popular novels. Organisations like the Religious Tract Society, founded in 1799, continued the chapbook tradition with their colporteurs, travelling through the country with a pack of cheap bibles, prayer books and improving tracts. In the last decade of the century some of these latter-day chapmen even travelled on bicycles.

Perhaps the most enterprising adaptation of the chapbook pedlar tradition was the cheap literature of William Milner of Halifax, who founded the 'Cottage Library' of sturdy little sixpenny and shilling books for poor people. In 1836, while chapbooks were still circulating, Milner set up with a hand-press as a jobbing printer. He was something of a Socialist of the Owenite type, and published political tracts and handbills before broadening his views. In 1837 he determined to bring the best and most attractive titles of available English literature within the reach of the poor. The Cottage Library series consisted of royal 32mo volumes, approx. $3'' \times 5''$, well produced, many of a 'strictly moral and religious tendency', covering classics of Burns, Byron, Bloomfield, Keats, Milton, Pope, Shelley, Scott and others [see page 105]. They included a pleasing engraved frontispiece. Milner's business prospered, and from one hand-press he graduated to sixteen, and after his death in 1850, the business continued to grow under the imprint of 'Milner and Sowerby'. In 1864 extensive new premises were built, and the business became a limited liability company in which some of the oldest workmen were admitted as shareholders and directors. A Branch was opened at Paternoster Row, London. In the final period, several hundred different titles were listed, including dictionaries, spelling books, arithmetic books, novels, and a juvenile series. Many of the titles are reminiscent of the 'small godly books' and 'small merry books' of the seventeenth century.

Milner began by combining the functions of printer, wholesaler and retailer, carrying his books in a van to the most remote villages, like a gypsy chapman. He set up his stall at any country fair or market, and in larger towns would rent a small shop for a week or

A LIST OF CHEAP BOOKS,
SOLD BY ALL BOOKSELLERS:
PUBLISHED BY MILNER AND SOWERBY,
CHEAPSIDE, HALIFAX.

THE COTTAGE LIBRARY,—(HALIFAX.)
ROYAL 32MO. CLOTH. LETTERED. UNIFORMLY BOUND.

A book that will Suit You
Æsop's Fables
Anna Lee; or, The Maiden, The Wife, and The Mother
Arabian Night's Entertainments
American Receipt Book
Anecdotes of Napoleon
Avondale Priory
Basket of Flowers
Baxter's Saints' Rest
Benevolent Jew
Berquin's Children's Friend
Bogatzky's Golden Treasury
Brown's Concordance
Bruce's Travels in Abyssinia
Buchan's Domestic Medicine
Buffon's Natural History
Bunyan's Pilgrim's Progress
Bunyan's Choice Works—First Series
Bunyan's Choice Works—Second Series
Bunyan's Holy War
Burns' Poetical Works
Byron's Select Works
Byron's Choice Works
Caleb Williams, by Godwin
Captain Cannot, the African Slaver
Castle of Wolfenbach
Canse and Cure of Infidelity
Children of the Abbey
Christian's Every Day Book
Christ's Famous Titles
Christmas Eve & other Tales
Coleridge's Poetical Works
Cowper's Poetical Works
Cook's Voyages
Cooper's Last of the Mohicans
Cooper's Pilot
Cooper's Sea Lions
Cooper's Spy
Cooper's Deerslayer
Cottage Gardener
Culpeper's Complete Herbal
Culpeper's Doctor
Daily Comforter
Death-bed Triumphs
Dialogues between a Pilgrim, Adam, Noah, &c.
Dialogues of Devils, by Defoe
Domestic Cookery, by a Lady
Dodd's Beauties of Shakspeare
Dodd's Beauties of History
Dodd's Discourses to Young Men
Doddridge's Rise & Progress
Christian Warrior (The), &c.
Evenings at Home
Farmer of Inglewood Forest
Fashion and Famine
Fatherless Fanny
Fern Leaves, by Fanny Fern
Finney's Revivals of Religion
Glory through Faith—Life of Billing
Little Hermit, (The), &c.
Good Time Coming, (The)
Gulliver's Travels
Henry Earl of Moreland
Hervey's Meditations
History of the Russian War
House of the Seven Gables
Kirke White's Remains

MILNER AND SOWERBY'S CHEAP LIST. 2

Lamplighter (The)
Language & Poetry of Flowers
Law of Kindness, &c.
Lena Rivers, By M.J.Holmes
Life of Christ, by Bromley
Life of Joseph, & Death of Abel
Life of Wellington
Life of Cromwell
Life of Baron Trenck
Life of Napoleon Bonaparte
Life of the Rev. J. Fletcher
Life of Mrs. Fletcher
Life of the Rev. John Wesley
Life of Dr. Adam Clarke
Longfellow's Poetical Works
Memoirs of Mrs. Huntington
Milton's Poetical Works
More's Practical Piety
Entertaining Anecdotes
Newsfrom the Invisible World
Nick of the Woods
Paley's Horæ Paulinæ
Pleasing Instructor
Poe's Tales of Mystery, &c.
Pope's Poetical Works
Pope's Homer's Iliad
Pope's Homer's Odyssey
Pamela, or Virtue Rewarded
Quarle's Divine Emblems
Quechy, by Miss Wetherell
Reciter for the Million
Records of Good Men
Religious Courtship
Robinson Crusoe
Romance of the Forest
Ross Clark, & other Sketches
Sabbath Musings,&c. by Bond
Sacred Garland—1st Series
Sacred Garland—2nd Series
Sandford and Merton
Scarlet Letter
Scottish Chiefs
Scott's Lady of the Lake
Scott's Lord of the Isles
Shady Side, by a Pastor's Wife
Shipwrecks and Disasters at Sea
Simpson's Plea for Religion
Simpson's Key to the Prophecies
Smith's Bread from Heaven
Smith's Early and Latter Rain
Smith's Good Seed for the Lord's Field
Smith's Light for Dark Days
Stephen's Travels in Egypt,&c
St. Clair of the Isles
Sunny Memories of Foreign Lands. By Mrs. Stowe
Tales and Stories of Ireland
Tales of Fairy Land
Thomsons Poetical Works
Todd's Student's Manual
Todd's Sunday School Teacher
Tregortha's Bank of Faith
Two Years before the Mast
Twice-Told Tales, by Hawthorne
Uncle Tom's Cabin
Wallsend Miner, by J.Everett
Watts' on the Mind
Watts' World to Come
Watts' Scripture History
Wesley's Choice Sermons
White Slave
Wide, Wide World
Wilson's Wonderful Characters
Wit of the World
Wonders of Nature and Art
Wordsworth's Excursion, &c.
Wordsworth's Select Poems
Young's Poetical Works
Young Man's Own Book
Young Man's Book of Amusement
Young Man's Best Companion
Young Woman's Companion

UNIFORM WITH THE ABOVE.
Comic Album & Comic Minstrel
Crotchet
Don Juan
Every Man his Own Farrier
Lives of Pirates & Sea Robbers
Lives of Highwaymen
Popular Song Book

5   MILNER AND SOWERBY'S CHEAP LIST.
BY THE AUTHOR OF "THE BASKET OF FLOWERS." ROYAL 32MO. CLOTH. LETTERED. GILT EDGES.

Basket of Flowers
Christmas Eve
Christian Warrior, (The)
Countess of Toggenbourg
Easter Eggs
Godfrey, the Little Hermit
Garland of Hope (The)
Henry of Eichenfels
Lewis, the Little Emigrant
Rose of Tannenbourg
Two Brothers, &c.
Timothy and Philemon
The Pet Lamb
The Good Fridolin and The Wicked Thierry
100 Pretty Tales
100 New Pretty Tales
200 Pretty Tales

ABBOTT'S WORKS. ROYAL 32MO. CLOTH. LETTERED. GILT.

Caleb in Town
Caleb in the Country
Child at Home
China and English
Corner Stone
Every Day Duty
Fireside
Hoary Head
Little Philosopher
Mc Donner
Mother at Home
Path of Peace
School Boy
Teacher
Way to do Good
Way of Salvation
Young Christian

DEMY 32MO. UNIFORMLY BOUND. COLOURED PLATE. GILT SIDES AND EDGES.

Ball-room Manual
Etiquette of Love
Etiquette of Courtship
Etiquette of Marriage
Etiquette for Gentlemen
Etiquette for Ladies
Elixir of Beauty
Golden Wedding Ring
Forget-me-not and Blue-bell
Language of Flowers
Language of Love
Primrose and Violet
Rose and Lily
Snowdrop and Daisy
Hints on the Flower Garden

DEMY 32MO. CLOTH. GILT EDGES.

A Full Christ for Empty Sinners
A Kiss for a Blow
Baxter's Now or Never
Baxter's Call
Brook's Apples of Gold
Chesterfield's Advice
Dairyman's Daughter (The)
Fawcett's Advice
Fenelon's Pious Thoughts
Hand Book of Maxims
Hill's Deep Things of God
Hill's It is Well
History of Jesus (The)
Hussey's Glory of Christ
Janeway's Token for Children
Law of Kindness
Mason's Crumbs
Pure Gold
Rowe's Devout Exercises
Young Cottager (the)

Nearly the whole of the above are done up in neat Illuminated Paper Covers.

MILNER AND SOWERBY'S CHEAP LIST. 6
DEMY 48MO. GILT EDGES.

Affection's Gift
Comic Album
Comic Minstrel
Gems of Wit and Humour
Kisses of Joannes Secundus and Jean Bonnefous
Little's Poems
Ovid's Art of Love
Shakspeare's Poems
Toast-Master
Semi-Quaver; or, Gems of Song and Melody

MISCELLANEOUS.

Arabian Nights' Entertainments. 12mo.
Basket of Flowers, and other Tales. 12mo.
Buchan's Domestic Medicine, 12mo., Do. Imp. 32mo.
Bunyan's Pilgrim's Progress Three Parts, Complete, Eight Steel Plates. Plain and Gilt Edges. 12mo.
Burns' Complete Works, 8vo.
Beautiful Thoughts, 18mo.
Byron's Poetical Works. Demy 12mo. Beautiful new Edition, Eight Steel Plates. Gilt Edges
Cope's Natural History, 250 Engravings, 8vo.
Culpeper's Complete Herbal, coloured plates, 12mo.
Domestic Cookery, 12mo.
Dupin's Mathematics, 8vo.
Edgeworth's Juvenile Stories, 12mo.
Elisha, 12mo.
Every Man his own Farrier.
Ferguson's History of the Roman Republic, Imp. 32mo.
Franklin's Works, Imp.32mo
Fleetwood's Life of Christ, Imp. 32mo.
Gibbon's Decline and Fall of the Roman Empire, 12 vols, in 4., 8vo.
Goldsmith's England, 12mo.
Josephus (The Works of Flavius,) 8vo.
More's (Mrs. H.) Poetical Works, Imp. 32mo.
Paley's Natural Theology
Paley's View of the Evidences of Christianity, Imp 32mo
Pearls of Great Price. Crown 8vo.
Reciter (General), 18mo.
Robertson's America. Imp. 32mo.
Robertson's History of the Reign of Charles V. Sacred Garland. Crown 8vo.
Songs of the Seasons.
Sturm's Reflections.
Taylor's Holy Living and Dying. Imp. 32mo.
Walker and Johnson's Pronouncing Dictionary, 8vo
Walkingame's Arithmetic.
Wordsworths Poetical Works. 12mo. Complete Edition

Cottage Library publications of Milner and Sowerby, Halifax

so. He also employed travellers to sell his books, just like the cheapjack pedlars. His circulation was tremendous. In 1837 he sold 10,000 copies of the poems of Burns, and in the following two years another 30,000. In 1840 he sold another 7,000, and thereafter editions of several thousand a year, until by 1869 the total was *a hundred thousand*. In 1852 the enterprising Milner and Sowerby editions of *Uncle Tom's Cabin* at one shilling net reached 25,000 in a few months, and by the end of 1895 some 133,000 copies had been sold. Other well-loved titles were *Arabian Nights' Entertainments*, Bunyan's *Pilgrim's Progress, Robinson Crusoe, The Seven Champions of Christendom* (always a good chapbook title), and *Life and Ballads of Robin Hood*.

These humble low-priced little volumes must have had a profound effect in thousands of homes, particularly in the countryside, transporting poor people into a new world of education and literary culture.

The chapbooks and ballad-sheets had grown up.

5: The Influence
of Street Literature

The Influence
of Street Literature

THE STORY OF STREET LITERATURE IS NOT A FORMAL HISTORY, WITH precise dates and leading figures. There were, of course, characteristic phases, but many of the pioneers were anonymous, and street literature was involved in so many different areas—social, political and literary—that it could not follow one consecutive line. The strands leading from ancient myth to the mass media arts, from minstrelsy to Fleet Street, and from popular propaganda to contemporary politics, were intertwined and doubled back in a complex pattern. If there are overall themes, they are largely the age-old conflicts of religion and politics, of tradition and topicality. The history of street literature, its forerunners and successors, is as amorphous and contradictory as man himself, a history of impulses, emotions, ideas and trends, as metaphysical as a myth in which some dark truth of the soul flashes up in allegory.

People ask whether this or that broadside or pamphlet achieved some given effect at a certain time and place. It is not so simple. Every scrap of traditional and printed lore found its way into the psyche of the masses, and the consequent action was sometimes immediate, often like the reverberations of an echo. Sometimes a political paper might sway a crowd; at other times a religious pamphlet might subdue radicalism. One of Hannah More's ballads, 'The Riot', is said to have stopped a riot near Bath, when mills and private houses were threatened. The local colliers were on strike and had inflamed other workmen until a bloody riot was imminent. Hundreds of copies of the ballad were distributed in the district, and the verses sung by schoolchildren and by people in public houses, and peace was miraculously restored. 'A fresh proof by what weak instruments evils are, now and then, prevented!' was Hannah More's comment.

But the propaganda which gave some people comfort and hope changed others into social revolutionaries. Until the culminating mass syndrome of manufacture, marketing and social stereotyping of the twentieth century, the effects of both popular and sophisticated literature were largely unco-ordinated and haphazard. But there are certain discernible effects of street literature which should be specified.

In the first place, there can be no doubt that the chapbooks and ballad-sheets taught under-privileged people to read, and sustained the practice of literacy in people too poor to buy books. They also created a hunger for books.

We have no precise information on the literacy rate of the first centuries of print. In *A History of the English Language* (1935), Albert C. Baugh estimated that in Shakespeare's London between a third and a half of the people were literate. Shakespeare's references to Autolycus in *The Winter's Tale* make it clear that even simple country people read ballads. Thereafter, the rise of the middle classes increasingly emphasised divisions in society, and privilege in education and culture, reinforced by narrow Puritanism after the Civil War. In the eighteenth century, the charity school movement of the Society for the Propagation of Christian Knowledge made a good beginning in teaching poor children, but this and subsequent religious educational movements encountered heavy opposition and many setbacks. Towards the end of the eighteenth century, the material preoccupations of property, urbanisation and depression of farm labour culminated in the industrial revolution and the autocracy of power and wealth. During the first half of the nineteenth century, there was a startling increase in population and thousands of country people were drawn into the industrial squalor of the big cities and the wage slavery of daily toil. The intricacies of this social and political development in relation to mass literacy are too complex for discussion here, but they are brilliantly examined by Richard D. Altick in *The English Common Reader* (1957). In general, books of any kind appear to have had a more positive and socially valuable effect upon poor readers than upon the genteel, for if they moved the emotions of sophisticated readers they did not transform the overall movement of society. What is significant, however, is the part played by the cheap literature of ballads and chapbooks in propagating and supporting literacy, long before the Education Act of 1870, and in stimulating creativity. A few brief sketches will illustrate the effect of these humble materials in helping a poor man to rise in the world of culture.

THOMAS HOLCROFT (1745–1809) was the son of a shoemaker. He learned to read from his father's Bible. Another apprentice presented him with two chapbooks—the *History of Parismus and Parismenes*, and *The Seven Champions of Christendom*. In his

Memoirs Holcroft recorded 'It was scarcely possible for anything to have been more grateful to me than this present. Parismus and Parismenes, with all the adventures detailed in the Seven Champions of Christendom, were soon as familiar to me as my catechism, or the daily prayers I repeated kneeling before my father.' His family became wanderers, the boy travelling with them as his mother peddled pins, needles, tape, and garters through country villages. Young Thomas learned the old ballad of 'Chevy Chase' by heart. For several years he did not see a book, but refreshed his reading from stray leaves. As he wrote: 'Even the walls of cottages and little alehouses would do something; for many of them had old English ballads, such as Death and the Lady, and Margaret's Ghost, with lamentable tragedies, or King Charles's golden rules, occasionally pasted on them.' In spite of many obstacles in his adventurous life, Holcroft became an actor, playwright, and also published comic operas, novels, and translations.

WILLIAM GIFFORD (1756–1826) was the son of a man who had descended from a well-to-do family to become in turn a beggar, apprentice to a plumber, and a sailor. William was sent to a schoolmistress to learn to read, but as he himself recorded: 'I cannot boast much of my acquisitions at this school; they consisted merely of the contents of the Child's Spelling Book; but from my mother, who had stored up the literature of a country town, which, about half a century ago, amounted to little more than what was disseminated by itinerant ballad-singers, or rather readers, I had acquired much curious knowledge of "Catskin, and the Golden Bull," and "the Bloody Gardener," and many other histories equally instructive and amusing.' Orphaned before he was thirteen, he had many ups and downs, was a sailor briefly, then apprenticed at the age of fifteen to a Presbyterian shoemaker whose reading was confined to religious tracts. Gifford's reading included the favourite black-letter romance of *Parismus and Parismenes*, a few odd numbers of magazines, Thomas à Kempis and the Bible. He studied a treatise on Arithmetic in secret. Being without money to buy pen, ink or paper, he beat out scraps of leather until they were smooth, and wrote his problems on them with a blunted awl. Gifford became first editor of the *Quarterly Review*, edited Juvenal, and wrote poetry.

ALEXANDER WILSON (1766–1813), apprenticed to a weaver, became a pedlar and wrote poetry. He composed the famous 'Watty and Meg, or the Wife Reformed' in 1792, and 'The Loss of the Pack', two of the most popular chapbooks in Scotland, reprinted until the end of the nineteenth century. Wilson emigrated to America, became a rural schoolmaster, and took up the study of ornithology. In 1806 he became assistant editor of the American edition of *Ree's Encyclopaedia*, and his great work *American Ornithology*, seven volumes in all, was completed by 1813.

DR ALEXANDER MURRAY (1775–1813) began life as the son of a Scottish shepherd. He learned to read from his father's *A BC With the Catechism* at the age of six, and surreptitiously borrowed Bible leaves. At the age of seven or eight he was set to minding sheep, but had no ability as a shepherd. He preferred reading, and in the absence of pen or paper spent time writing on boards with coal. Later he was boarded at a school, but fell ill and had to return home to become a shepherd boy once more. He recalled: 'I was still, however, attached to reading, printing of words, and getting by heart ballads, of which I had procured several. . . . About this time, and for years after, I spent every sixpence that friends or strangers gave me, on ballads and penny histories. I carried bundles of these in my pockets, and read them when sent to look for cattle. . . .' Later, Murray was able to get more schooling, and learned Hebrew, Latin, French and Greek. He graduated at Edinburgh University, and became Professor of Oriental Languages, and author of *History of European Languages*.

JOHN CLARE (1793–1864), greatest of the peasant-poets, grew up with parents who sang folk songs and ballads like 'Peggy Band', 'Barbara Allen', and 'Lord Randal'. His father boasted that he could sing or recite more than a hundred popular pieces. Clare himself was greatly influenced by this background. He confessed: 'I made many things before I ventured to commit them to writing . . . imitations of some popular songs floating among the vulgar at the markets and fairs till they were common to all.'

These are a few of the recorded instances of humble people whose lives were influenced by street literature and traditional balladry. There must have been thousands more who did not rise to fame, but enlarged their cultural horizons and enriched their lives.

The line of literacy has several strands, leading from the mere skill itself to art and culture, or to social and political consciousness. On the cultural side, broadsides and chapbooks had a great influence on sophisticated literature ever since Addison's half-jocular ballad papers in *The Spectator* in 1711, and the 1723 *A Collection of Old Ballads*.

The impact of Bishop Percy's *Reliques* has already been mentioned. Percy, who had taken twenty-two songs from D'Urfey's *Pills to Purge Melancholy* into his own work, also included broadside ballads from the Dicey warehouse. In a letter to Shenstone on 19 July 1761, Percy wrote:

Perhaps I shall derive greater assistance from an acquaintance I have made of a much lower stamp, and that is with Dicey of the Printing-Office in Bow Church Yard, the greatest printer of ballads in the kingdom; he has promised me copies of all his old Stock Ballads, and engaged to rommage into his Warehouse for everything curious that it contains: as a specimen only I have already rec^d above four-score pieces from him some of which I never saw before.

The Dicey warehouse became a legendary source of romantic popular literature. A three-volume collection of 83 chapbooks formed by James Boswell (now in Harvard College Library) bears a charming manuscript note on the fly-leaf of the first volume, curiously echoing Percy's respect for old street literature:

James Boswell, Inner Temple 1763. Having when a boy, been much entertained with Jack the Giant-Killer, and such little Store Books, I have always retained a kind of affection for them, as they recall my early days. I went to the Printing Office in Bow Churchyard, and bought this collection and had it bound up with the Title of Curious Productions. I shall certainly, some time or other, write a little Story Book in the stile of these. It will not be a very easy task for me; it will require much nature and simplicity, and a great acquaintance with the humours and traditions of the English common people. I shall be happy to succeed for He who pleases the children will be remembered with pleasure by the men.

So many sophisticated writers were stimulated by the *Reliques* that it only emphasised the staleness, artificiality or mere cleverness of so many eighteenth century books. Broadside ballads began to circulate at all levels in society—in the books of middle-class and antiquarian readers, and on the penny sheets of the man in the street. The growing split between the common people and the socially and politically privileged classes was not entirely impassable for the isolated individual, but it became a chasm for the masses. There was, however, much cross-fertilisation of popular and sophisticated literature, with a nostalgic nod to tradition.

Sir Walter Scott (born 1770 or 1771), grew up with a genuine and intense love of balladry and chapbook histories. He listened to traditional tales and songs from his grandmother and his Aunt Jenny. Even as a boy he made manuscript collections of ballads and had a library of chapbooks. Amongst these were titles like *Rosewal and Lilian, Valentine and Orson, The Seven Sages of Rome, The Oxfordshire Tragedy, The Bride's Burial,* and *The Whole Proceedings of Jockey and Maggie.* In 1810 he had 114 chapbooks, which he bound in six volumes, mostly items bought before the age of ten. These were equally popular with his servants. Such simple literature, and the often-quoted inspiration of the *Reliques,* lay behind not only Scott's *Minstrelsy of the Scottish Border,* but the whole romantic impulse in his successful novels.

Wordsworth was familiar with chapbooks and broadsides, and in the *Lyrical Ballads* both he and Coleridge deliberately set out to rationalise the techniques and style of the broadside ballad. In *The Prelude,* V, 290–363 (1805–6 version), Wordsworth referred nostalgically to the chapbooks of his youth:

Oh! give us once again the Wishing-Cap
Of Fortunatus, and the invisible Coat
Of Jack the Giant-killer, Robin Hood,
And Sabra in the forest with St. George!
The child, whose love is here, at least, doth reap
One precious gain, that he forgets himself.

It was a cry from the heart for a lost innocence, simplicity, and sense of meaning that had been largely extinguished in the Augustan age of literature.

Wordsworth had also studied *A Collection of Old Ballads,* and claimed that he had been 'absolutely redeemed' by Percy's *Reliques.* Many later poets like William Morris and Swinburne were similarly inspired. Other poets who experimented in the ballad idiom or adapted its commonplaces include Keats, Rossetti, Tennyson, John Davidson, Walter de la Mare, W. H. Auden and W. B. Yeats.

In addition to regenerating literary form and content, the broadside ballads also exercised a very great influence on printing history in purely aesthetic aspects of typography and layout.

Modern cheap newspapers derived their attractive format of illustrations alternating with text, of forceful headlining, and even of journalistic style from the nineteenth century broadsides, for the official taxed newspapers of the eighteenth and nineteenth centuries were dull and unadventurous in format. Moreover the pioneers of cheap newspapers graduated from street literature. Edward Lloyd, founder of the enormously successful *Lloyd's Newspaper*, had previously published cheap thrillers, romances, and 'penny dreadfuls'. From an early period he campaigned to abolish the stamp duty, which did not finally disappear until 1855, after which date cheap newspapers began to displace topical ballad-sheets.

Newspaper advertising also owes its origin to the news pamphleteers of the early seventeenth century. In 1611 there had been a scheme for erecting an office to be called 'the Publicke Register for Generall Commerce', at which there would be given 'generall notice and publique intelligence' of buying and selling. The idea was premature, although revived from time to time. But in 1648, advertisements were inserted in 'mercuries' for a fee of sixpence. These were called 'advices', the term 'advertisement' not being used until about 1660. Advertisements using the opening formula 'If any one . . .' were known as 'Siquis' (If any's). In May 1660, after the Restoration, *Mercurius Publicus* ran this astonishingly modern toothpaste ad:

. . . most excellent Dentifrices to scour and cleanse the Teeth, making them white as Ivory: Preserves from the Toothach, fastens the Teeth, and sweetens the Breath, and preserves the Gums from Cankers and Imposthumes . . .

Some of the most nostalgic periodical advertisements are those for patent medicines and specifics, like 'Dr Bateman's Pectoral Drops', 'The True Antidote Against Buggs', 'Hungary Water', and Daffey's Elixir Salutis'. Such famous items were also a profitable line with the ballad and chapbook warehouse of the Dicey family in the eighteenth century.

Election bills were another form of advertising, and from the late eighteenth century onwards these street notices became progressively adventurous in their typography and layout, as well as style. The satire, abuse and sarcasm displayed was as unrestrained as in the unlicensed news pamphlets from the previous century [see page 116]. Many of the jobbing printers of these bills also published broadsides

A FEW

W O R D S

TO

A FREEMAN, and TRUE BLUE.

Mr. Brazen Face,

THE moment I saw your address this morning, it brought to my mind the old saying, " Great words often come from a weak Stomach." What a clever, penetrating fellow you must be, to assert, that " no one blue has deserted his colours," &c. This is *True Blue assurance*, with a witness. I suppose you are some compound creature, made up of the *Hawk* and *Owl*; the one would destroy its own species, and the other chuses the dark to seek its prey: yet I am much mistaken if the *Crocodile* does not make a part of your composition.

It is true, that the *Independent Freemen* of *Coventry* are now struggling against " *undue influence, threats, and tampering of the common enemy.*" They are not tame enough yet, to be sold like cattle at Smithfield Market. It is in character for an Indian Nabob to say the people may do *without a King*, and wish to govern *us* himself. Let him purchase *slaves*, and sell them again ; but FREEMEN value their liberty, and will stedfastly resist every mean attempt to enslave them. Support

JEFFERYS AND BARLOW,

the true sons of freedom ; and tyranny will never again attempt to raise its hydra head in this City. It is NOW, or NEVER. The Issue of the present contest will determine, whether Coventry is to continue a *free City* or an *enslaved borough.* It is not the downfal of *Corporation Tyranny,* but *Independence* you are attempting to destroy. Freemen, rally round the standard of those who are the defenders of your privileges, and victory will be yours.---JEFFERYS and BARLOW for ever !

JULY 14, 1802.   A real Independent Freeman.

MERRIDEW'S Office, Coventry.

A typical discourteous election bill from the Coventry Election of 1802

and chapbooks, and had a flair for street propaganda.

The history of the development of democratic elections lies outside the scope of the present work, but much of it is reflected in the street bills. Election ballads were common in the Stuart period, and there is a group circa 1679–80 in the Bagford Collection at the British Museum. A great many ballads of party warfare between Whigs and Tories were written by highly placed poets rather than street balladists. As elections began to be increasingly concerned with the man in the street, election squibs and placards became more numerous.

The Great Westminster Election of 1784 involving Fox, Wray and Hood, produced a whirlwind of propaganda at all levels—street notices, handbills, ballads and satirical prints. There were accusations of bribery, intimidations, riots and counter-riots. Servants, workmen, craftsmen, merchants, peers, duchesses, beggars and ballad singers thought and talked of little but the election, and emotions ran high. The Duchess of Devonshire was reported to have solicited a vote for Fox by kissing a butcher, and this led to an

THE DUCHESS CANVASSING FOR HER FAVOURITE MEMBER

A coarse lampoon from the Westminster Election of 1784

eruption of coarse satirical prints and lampoons [see page 117]. A collection of many of the street papers was published as *History of the Westminster Election*, 1784; it runs to over 500 pages.

In addition to election material, thousands of broadsides were published on other issues of the times—'Proposals Humbly Offer'd', 'Cases', 'Reasons', 'Addresses', and 'Notices' on all aspects of trade, economics, local disputes, and every conceivable grievance and controversy. Publishing a broadside was something between writing to your MP or engaging a public relations man in modern times. The broadside of *The East-India Company's Case with Relation to the Separate Traders to the East-Indies* (1713) competes with *The Case and Petition of the Licensed Hackney Chair-men, and the Widows of Such*, or *Reasons Humbly Offer'd Against Opening a Trade with France for Wines*. The jobbing printers were also busy with Lost and Found notices, Trade Announcements and advertising handbills. Such ephemeral papers are indispensable material for historical study. There is a splendid collection of diverse broadsides, dating from 1641 to 1868, in the Goldsmiths' Library of Economic Literature, University of London. There is a useful published catalogue.

One other curious kind of advertising broadside deserves passing mention—the traditional sheet of 'Bellman's Verses' that persisted into the early nineteenth century. The Bellman's trade was an ancient one, and in 1608 Thomas Dekker described him as 'the child

of darkness; a common night-walker; a man that had no man to wait upon him but only a dog; one that was a disordered person, and at midnight would beat at men's doors, bidding them (in mere mockery) to look to their candles, when they themselves were in their dread sleeps'. This reassuring watchman would produce 'A Copy of Verses' every Christmas, which he would offer to each householder for a small gratuity. A typical broadside dated 1683–4 is entitled: 'A Copy of Verses presented by Isaac Ragg, Bellman, to

A COPY OF VERSES,

HUMBLY PRESENTED TO ALL MY WORTHY

MASTERS and MISTRESSES,

OF STAMFORD, LINCOLNSHIRE,

BY JOHN MEWSE, BELLMAN.

1814.

THE ADVENT OF THE MESSIAH.

But see! what sudden glories from the sky,
To my benighted soul appear,
And all the gloomy prospects cheer,
What awful form approaches nigh?
Awful yet mild, as is the southern wind,
That gently bids the forest nod :
Hark! thunder breaks the air, and angels speak,
Behold the SAVIOUR of the World, behold the Lamb
of God!
Ye sons of men behold his aspect meek,
The tear of pity on his cheek,
See in his train appear
Humility and patience sweet,
Repentance prostrate at his sacred feet,
Bedew'd with tears and wipes them with his flowing hair.
No more repine, my coward soul,
The sorrows of mankind to share,
Which he who could the world controul,
Did not disdain to bear.
Check not the flow of sweet fraternal love,
By Heav'ns high King in bounty given;
Thy stubborn heart to soften and improve,
Thy earth-clad spirit to redeem,
And gradual raise to love divine,
And wing its soaring flight to heaven!

WINTER.

Though slow and pensive now the moments roll,
Successive months shall from our torpid soul
Hurry these scenes again : the laughing hours,
Advancing swift, shall strew spontaneous flow'rs;
The early-peeping snowdrop, crocus mild,
And modest violet, grace the secret wild :
Pale primrose, daisy, maypole-decking sweet,
And purple hyacinth together meet :
All nature's sweets in joyous circles move,
And wake the frozen soul again to love !

UNIVERSAL PEACE.

Ah! when shall reason's intellectual ray,
Shed o'er the world more perfect day?
When shall that gloomy world appear no more
A waste where desolating tempests roar?—
When savage discord howls in threat'ning form,
And wild ambition lends the madd'ning storm,
Where hideous carnage marks his dangerous way,
And where the screaming vulture scents his prey?
Ah! come blest concord! close with smile serene,
The hostile passions from the human scene!
May glory's lofty path be found afar
From agonizing groans and crimson war;
And may the ardent mind that seeks renown
Claim not the martial but the civic crown.

WINTER SONG.

Dear boy, throw that icicle down,
And swoop the deep snow from the door :
Old Winter comes on with a frown;
A terrible frown from the poor.
In a season so rude and forlorn,
How can age, how can infancy, bear
The silent neglect and the scorn,
Of those who have plenty to spare?

Fresh broach'd is my cask of old ale,
Well tim'd now the frost is set in :
Here's Job glad to tell us a tale,
We'll make him at home to a pin.
While my wife and I bask o'er the fire,
The roll of the seasons will prove,
That time may diminish desire,
But cannot extinguish true love.

O the pleasures of neighbourly chat,
If we can but keep scandal away,
To learn what the world has been at,
And what the great orators say :
Though the wind through the crevices sing,
And hail down the chimney rebound ;
I'm happier than many a king,
While the bellows blow bass to the sound.

Abundance was never my lot ;
But out of the trifle that's given,
That no curse may alight in my cot,
I'll distribute the bounty of heaven.
The fool and the slave gather wealth ;
But if I add nought to the store,
Yet while I keep conscience in health,
I've a mine that will never grow poor.

HOME.

How oft with transport was my bosom fired,
When near this happy seat of peace I drew ;
When of the faithless forms of friendship tired,
The abode of solid pleasures met my view :

How was I pleas'd to re: the smoke ascend
In many a rolling volume light and blue ;
How pleas'd to see you grove's thick branches bend,
And hide my mansion from the public view :

When the last streaks of slow receding light
Above the dusky hills were faintly seen,
When the pale glow-worm shone serenely bright,
And gradual darkness veil'd the rural scene:

When nature's softness harmonis'd the mind,
How was I charm'd my pleasing home to seek,
How charm'd congratulating love to find,
With sweetness unaffected, soft and meek.

How pleased amidst the dark tempestuous night
When in the howling storm returning late,
To see my windows shed the taper's light,
And hear the watch-dog barking at the gate.

Pleas'd to anticipate with fond desire,
(Whilst all around was dreary, cold, and wild,)
The circling pleasures of an evening fire,
Where friendship met and love connubial smil'd.

CHARITY.

Oh Charity! our helpless nature's pride,
Thou friend to him who knows no friend beside,
Is there in morning's breath, or the sweet gale
That steals o'er the tir'd pilgrim of the vale,
Cheering with fragrance fresh, his weary frame,
Aught like the incense of thy holy flame?
Is aught, in all the beauties that adorn
The azure heav'n, or purple lights of morn,—
Is aught so fair in evening's ling'ring gleam,
As from thy eye the meek and pensive beam,
That falls like saddest moonlight on the hill,
And distant grove, when the wide world is still?
Thine are the ample views, that uncontrol'd,
Stretch to the utmost walks of human kind
Thine is the spirit, that with widest plan,
Brother to brother binds, and man to man!

SHARARD, PRINTER, STAMFORD.

the Masters and Mistresses of Holbourne Division, in the Parish of
St. Gile's-in-the-Fields'. One verse runs:

> Time Masters, calls your bellman to his task,
> To see your doors and windows are as fast,
> And that no villany or foul crime be done
> To you or yours in absence of the sun.
> If any base lurker I do meet,
> In private alley or in open street,
> You shall have warning by my timely call,
> And so God bless you and give rest to all.

Although the cheap presses churned out crude sheets and
pamphlets for profit, there was still a kind of folk art, an unconscious
good taste or daring experiment in the use of woodcut decorations,
borders, spirited typefaces and layout. True, so far as broadside
printers were concerned, this arose from the sheer limitations of
having to buy secondhand type founts, or wood blocks left over from
other people's books, and the typesetting standards were bizarre.
Economical publishers like Catnach, grinding out the last farthing
of value, would simply invert a 'u' if short for an 'n', filling out
missing roman letters with italics, or even by 'x' or anything else
to hand.

Yet for all that, this was the 'pop art' of the printing of its time,
and there were stimulating elements which more cultured publishers
have not hesitated to copy.

Broadsides and chapbooks profoundly influenced many individuals
concerned with pictorial art and book production. Joseph Crawhall,

senior (1821–96), manufacturer, sportsman,
and artist, grew up in Newcastle-upon-Tyne,
a great provincial centre for the chapbook
and broadside trade. Crawhall was equally
impressed with the woodcuts of Thomas
Bewick and the quaint illustrations of
broadsides. Around 1859 he cut many
blocks himself in a deliberately affected
ancient style, based on broadside illustrations with the addition of his own unique
humour. He was friendly with Andrew Tuer
of the Leadenhall Press, London, who

specialised in quaint 'antique' typefaces and unusual books. Together they collaborated on reissuing old ballad and chapbook tales, illustrated by Crawhall's characteristic woodcuts, many of them hand-coloured. Two collections of these charming items in book form were: *Old Tayles Newlye Relayted* (1883), and *Chap-book Chaplets* (1883-4). Tuer's highly individual use of type and his antiquarian interests (he published a masterly study on *The History of the Horn Book*, 1897) stimulated other publishers of unusual books.

Crawhall's use of broadside prototypes for his illustrations, and his popularisation of old chapbook tales, also influenced the twentieth century artists William Nicholson, Gordon Craig and Claude Lovat Fraser. Early in the century, Haldane Macfall wrote an appreciation of Crawhall, published in *The Page* and reissued in chapbook format as *The Cornhill Booklet*. This article, *Some Thoughts Suggested by the Art of Joseph Crawhall*, attracted Fraser to both street literature and the technique of Crawhall. It was Macfall who suggested to Fraser that he should publish *modern* broadsheets and chapbooks. In January 1913 Fraser bought a collection of broadsides from a little general shop in Endell Street, London, and these profoundly affected his later work, in both style and subject-matter. This collection of 1,580 sheets in twenty volumes is now in the Beinecke Rare Book and Manuscript Library at Yale University.

Towards the end of 1912, Fraser had proposed a collaboration with poet Ralph Hodgson and Holbrook Jackson, to further a chapbook project. Later, Walter de la Mare and James Stephens also participated. In May 1913, 'The Sign of Flying Fame', established at 45 Roland Gardens, London, S.W.7, issued its first broadsides and chapbooks, decorated by Fraser [see page 141]. The first broadside was *SONG* by Ralph Hodgson, and the Flying Fame announcement adapted the old toy theatre sheet tag of 'Penny plain, Twopence coloured' to read: '2 Pence Plain, 4 Pence Coloured'. The chapbooks were sixpence each. Some fifty broadsides and chapbooks followed, some with Hodgson poems, others by Walter de la Mare, and James Stephens. Later, Harold Monro issued a further series from his famous Poetry Bookshop. All these productions are delightful collector's items. Their style and charm influenced other artists and typographers engaged in publicity work.

The influence of street literature has been a widespread and important one in many areas of life. Much of the early history of street songs was heavily involved in the politics of church and state.

Before the development of printing, minstrels were employed to sing the praises of political leaders, or to satirise the opposition. The printed sheets made such propaganda more efficient. Street poets could be hired to write libels and satires to order. In the seventeenth century, when James, Duke of York, visited Scotland, he hired a ballad writer to overcome his unpopularity there. Ironically enough it was a ballad ('Lilliburlero') which celebrated his unpopularity as James II during the Irish campaign!

In *An Account of a Conversation Concerning a Right Regulation of Government* (1704), Andrew Fletcher of Saltoun published the often quoted aphorism: 'I said, I knew a very wise man . . . he believed if a man were permitted to make all the ballads, he need not care who should make the laws of a nation.' He added: 'And we find, that most of the ancient legislators thought they could not well reform the manners of any city without the help of a lyric, and sometimes of a dramatic, poet.' In another expression of the same sentiment, Steele wrote in *The Spectator*, Monday 6 October 1712:

I have heard that a Minister of State in the Reign of Queen *Elizabeth* had all manner of Books and Ballads brought to him, of what kind soever, and took great Notice how much they took with the People; upon which he would, and most certainly might, very well judge of their present Dispositions, and the most proper way of applying them according to his own purposes.

It is known that in the sixteenth century, foreign embassies in London studied ballads and even reported back on them to their governments. Often a street ballad was a better indicator of public sentiment than a State Paper. However, early historians were inclined to be over-credulous about the factual content of ballads.

The first historian to evaluate systematically the place of broadside ballads, proclamations, and other street ephemera as historical materials, was Thomas Babington Macaulay. In his great *History of England* (1849–55) he cited various ballads in relation to historical events. In discussing the state of England in 1685 (Chapter III), he commented:

Other evidence is extant which proves that a shilling a day was the pay to which the English manufacturer [factory hand] then thought himself entitled, but that he was often forced to work for less. The common people of that age were not in the habit of meeting for public discussion, of haranguing, or of petitioning Parliament. No newspaper pleaded their cause. It was in a rude rhyme that their love and hatred, their exultation and their distress found utterance. A great part of their history is to be learned only from their ballads.

Much careful analysis of street literature lay behind Macaulay's *History*. He consulted ballads in the Pepys Collection and, as his nephew Sir G. O. Trevelyan commented in his *Life and Letters of Lord Macaulay* (1908):

He bought every halfpenny song on which he could lay his hands; if only it was decent, and a genuine, undoubted poem of the people. He has left a scrap-book containing about eighty ballads; for the most part vigorous and picturesque enough, however, defective they may be in rhyme and grammar; printed on flimsy discoloured paper, and headed with coarsely executed vignettes, seldom bearing even the most remote reference to the subject which they are supposed to illustrate.

There is an amusing anecdote that Macaulay was once followed by a crowd of street urchins after he bought a batch of ballads; the children took him for a street hawker, and were overheard discussing when he would start singing! [See page 124]

Macaulay had a strong link with Hannah More, for his father was a member of the Clapham Sect which brought together William Wilberforce, Henry Thornton and other 'Evangelicals'. Hannah More guided the early education of Macaulay and provided guineas for him to buy books at Hatchards. When he was six years old she wrote:

Though you are a little boy now, you will one day, if it please God, be a man, but long before you are a man I hope you will be a scholar. I, therefore, wish you to purchase such books as will be useful and agreeable to you *then*, and that you employ this very small sum in laying a tiny corner-stone for your future Library.

A couple of years later she was suggesting Johnson's *Hebrides*, Walton's *Lives*, Cowper's *Poems*, and Milton's *Paradise Lost* to this precocious scholar.

Macaulay's *History* ended at 1701. Had he been able to extend it, he would have found a rewarding field for research in the thousands of broadsides, handbills and placards circulated during the summer

A RECOLLECTION OF LORD MACAULAY.

LORD MACAULAY, after his elevation to the peerage, desirous to acquaint himself with the ballad literature of the day, bought a handful of songs from a street patterer in Seven Dials. It is said that, proceeding on his way home, he was astonished, on suddenly stopping, to find himself surrounded by half a score of urchins, their faces beaming with expectation.

"Now then," said the historian, "what is it?"

"Oh! that is a good un," replied the boys, "after we've a-come all this way."

"But what are you waiting for?" said he, astonished at the lads' familiarity.

"Waiting for? why, to hear you sing, to be sure!"

and autumn of 1803, with the threat of invasion from Napoleon's forces. These ephemeral papers included all kinds of street ballads, political tracts, pamphlets, and caricatures, designed for circulation in the streets or for posting up. In addition to this street literature, the great caricaturists Gillray, Rowlandson and Isaac Cruikshank published some of their most stirring and extravagant coloured sheets, available at book and print shops for middle-class purchasers. The broadsides were sold for a halfpenny or a penny, but were also available in quantity at reduced prices for patriotic and well-to-do patrons to buy for general distribution. For example, *Victorious Englishmen* published by James Asperne, dated 8 August 1803, bears the note: 'Noblemen, Magistrates, and Gentlemen would do well by ordering a few dozen of the above Tracts of their different Booksellers, and causing them to be stuck up in the respective Villages where they reside, that the Inhabitants may be convinced of the Cruelty of the Corsican Usurper.' Such patriotic notices undoubtedly sustained public morale and also, regretfully, diverted attention from political and social problems nearer at hand.

During the nineteenth century, broadsides recorded the tragic impoverishment of farm labourers and city workers, and the sharp repression of popular revolt. There was a ballad-sheet on the Peterloo Massacre in 1819, when over 60,000 men, women and children had assembled to hear Henry 'Orator' Hunt call for Parliamentary reform, and mounted troops charged the crowd with drawn sabres. There were ballads on the cruel conditions in the army and navy, when a deserter might receive 500 lashes. This inhuman flogging was not abolished until 1881. There are ballads of transportation. In 1811 a man could be sentenced to seven years' transportation for stealing a watch. During the great Lancashire cotton famine of 1862, many unemployed operatives became vagrant ballad-singers, a number of them rendering their own very moving compositions.

But it should not be assumed that nineteenth century ballads necessarily provoked specific public action, as in the earlier periods of street literature. They certainly constituted a protest literature of their time, but they were only one aspect of a broad spectrum of news, topical trivia, and entertainment. Rather they created a climate of opinion and sentiment. It is true that many riots had their flashpoint in a 'paper' of some sort—a leaflet or handbill—

and many crowds chanted or sang. But generally speaking, nineteenth century broadsides about the multitudinous issues of the day merely underlined a mood that did not find a direct expression.

For example, the broadside 'The Death of Parker' gives a moving and detailed account of the unhappy story of Richard Parker and the mutiny of the Grand Fleet in 1797 [see page 127]. This ballad was composed after the event. The cause of the mutiny was the accumulation of grievances of men who had been ill fed, badly paid, and brutally treated for a long time. The ballad remained in public circulation several decades later, and was constantly reprinted. It may well have subscribed to public sentiment demanding fair play for the navy. The story was a tragic one, and the ballad has a heartrending pathos.

It is difficult to form a balanced judgment of those days unless one also studies the thousands of often contradictory ballads. As against the themes of bad conditions and press-gangs, one must set the many happy ballads of a seaman's life, such as the prolific output of Charles Dibdin, the man whose songs helped to win the Battle of Trafalgar and brought more men into the navy than all the press-gangs. Had these ballads been simply meretricious propaganda they would not have remained in public popularity all through the nineteenth century.

The transition from the eighteenth century to the nineteenth was a momentous one. Religion, long since displaced as a supreme political force, now faced virtual extinction even as a way of life, in the growing preoccupation with materialism, radicalism and freethinking. It has since become fashionable to mock the Evangelical politicians and churchmen, and the widespread literature of the tract movements, but on the whole they only underlined those simple values of kindness, honesty and justice which are also basic to proper political realism. If they had a real fault it was that they became dull after the first inspiration. At a political level, the movement generated that great tide of humanitarian reform and peaceful transformation of society that was more firmly based than all subsequent political agitation and revolt.

In the first two centuries of street literature, propaganda was specifically planned by committed publishers and writers. In the nineteenth century, street ballads were printed for money, and the propaganda was largely incidental except in so far as it was likely to

DEATH
OF
PARKER.

YE Gods above, protect the widow,
  And with pity look down on me,
Help me, help me, out of my trouble,
  And out of all calamity ;
For by the death of my brave Parker,
  Fortune has prov'd to me unkind ;
Though doom'd by law he was to suffer,
  I can't arrest him from my mind.

Parker he was my lawful husband,
  My bosom friend I lov'd so dear ;
At the awful moment he was going to suffer
  I was not allowed to come near.
In vain I strove, in vain I asked,
  Three times o'er and o'er again,
But they replied, you must be denied,
  You must return our shore again.

First time I attempted my love to see,
  I was obliged to go away,
Oppress'd with grief, and broken-hearted
  To think they harshly should me stay.
I thought I saw the yellow flag flying,
  The signal for my dear to die ;
A gun was fir'd, as they requir'd,
  As the time it did draw nigh.

The boatswain did his best endeavour,
  To get me on shore without delay,
When I stood trembling and confounded,
  Ready to take his body away.
Though his trembling hand did wave, :
  As a signal of farewell,
The grief I suffer'd at this moment,
  No heart can paint or tongue can tell.

My fleeting spirit I thought would follow
  The soul of him I lov'd so dear,
No friend or neighbour would come nigh me,
  To ease me of my grief and care,
Every moment I thought an hour,
  Till the law its course had run,
I wish'd to finish the doleful task
  That his imprudence had begun.

In the dead of the night when it is silent,
  And all the world are fast asleep,
My trembling heart that knows no comfort
  O'er his grave does often weep.
Each lingering minute that passes,
  Brings me nearer to that shore,
When we shall shine in endless glory,
  Never to be parted more.

Farewell, Parker, thou bright genius,
  That was once my only pride,
Though parted now, it won't be long
  E'er I am buried by thy side.
All you that see my tender ditty,
  Don't laugh at me, nor me disdain,
But look down with an eye of pity,
  For it is my only claim.

NEVER FLOG
OUR
SOLDIER'S

IF I was Queen of England, I would find a better
    plan,
I would never flog the soldiers who guard our native
    land,
They guard us night and day, and from danger keep
    us free,
When God defends the right, they fight for you and me,
They bid us stand at ease while fighting hand to hand,
Oh, never flog the soldiers who guard our native land.

The night my Willie 'listed we both were torn apart,
I thought I'd ne'er more see him, and that would break
    my heart,
My sorrow then began, and I was left alone—
The tortures of the army by him could not be borne !
I have heard my Willie say, the sight he ould not
    stand,
Oh, never flog the soldiers who guard our native land.

Oh, now he's gone for ever, I thought we ne'er would
    part,
I will wear this little treasure for ever next my heart,
I gaze on it so dear, it looks like his blythsome way,
He told me not to fear, he'd be back some other day.
Ah, what is that I hear ! the door open with his hand,
Oh, never flog the soldiers who guard our native land.

Now you have come to see me, you're wearing your
    red coat,
I think now that you love me, and that keeps up my
    hope,
But if you should be late, and suppose you don't get in,
They'll flog you like the rest of men that serve our
    British Queen !
But if they flog you now you have offered me your
    hand,
You shall never be a soldier to guard our native land.

Now, good night, God bless you ! for I'll be left alone,
Come let me now impress you, that I'll make you a
    home,
We'll live happy day by day, and our sorrow then set
    free,
Oh, do not longer stay, the flogging troubles me.
They will take you going back, for desertion bind your
    hands,
And flog you like the soldier who guards our native
    land.

The night my Willie 'listed, how merry he did seem,
To think he had the honour to serve our British Queen,
Never thinking of the lash that was lying in his way,
To torture him so cruel if he went astray.
If the lash it is not burnt, and banished from our land.
He shall ne'er remain a soldier to guard our native land.

Nineteenth-century broadsides

meet a public mood and sell well. Once the broadsides were released from both monopolist printing and political censorship, they lost much of their militancy and became largely entertainment with a rough edge. Had Jemmy Catnach or his rivals been social agitators they might well have created a revolution. As it is, they were in the business for the cash.

On the other hand, Hannah More and her associates were idealists,

What's Old England come to?

Tune.—" Irish Stranger. "

One cold winter's morning as the day was dawning
A voice came so hollow and shrill,   (falling,
The cold winds did whistle, the fnow faft was
As a ftranger came over the hill.
The clothing he wore was tatter'd and torn,
He feem'd all difpairing and wand'ring forlorn,
Lamenting for pleasures that ne'er will return,
Oh ! Old England, what have you come to ?

He said oh, I figh for thofe hearts fo undeferving,
On their own native land left to ftray,   (ftarving,
And in the midst of plenty fome thoufands are
Neither house, food, nor clothing have they.
I am surrounded by poverty & can't find a friend,
My cottage it is fold from me, my joys are at an end
So, like a pilgrim, my steps I onward bend,
Oh ! Old England, what have you come to ?

There once was a time I could find friends in plenty
To feed on my bounteous ftore,
But friends they are few now my portion is fcanty,
But Providence may open her door.
It nearly breaks my heart when my cottage I behold
It is claim'd by a villain with plenty of gold,
And I pafing by, and all fhivering with cold,
Oh ! Old England, what have you come to ?

The Farmer and Comedian do daily affemble,
And do try their exertion and skill,
But alas ! after all, on this land they do tremble,
For all trades are near ftanding ftill.   (call,
If the great god of war now fhould quickly on us
I would break my chains fo galling and boldly face
a ball,   (than all,
For to see my babies ftarving it grieves me worfe
Oh ! Old England, what have you come to ?

There's Manchefter and Birmingham, alas ! are fell
to ruin,
In fact all the country is at a ftand,
Our fhipping lays in harbour and is nothing doing,
While our tars are starving on the land.
'Twould break the hearts of monarch's bold,
could rise again,   (brain,
To view our defolation, would near diftract their
So pity a poor ftranger, or death may eafe my pain
Oh ! Old England, what have you come to ?
Swincoln, Printer.

THE YOUNG RECRUIT; OR Thirteen Pence A-DAY.

William Pratt, Printer, No. 82, Digbeth, Birmingham.

Come and be a soldier, lads, come lads come !
Mark ! don't you hear the fife and the drum,
Come to the battle field, march, march away ;
Come and lose your eyes and limbs for thirteen pence a day.

Come and take the shilling lads, come lads, drink !
Come and drive dull care away, but never dare to think,
Break your mammas' hearts my lads, and bid good-bye to daddy,
You shall be a general, or a private, if you'll only be a swaddy.

Come along you gaubies, come and be drilled
By a puppy of a sergeant that's not worth being killed,
You'll be made a corporal, if you're a jolly cock !
Come and be a soldier, but be in by eight o'clock.

When you are a soldier lad, if you do not limp,
You shall go recruiting, lad, then you'll be a crimp,
Perhaps a yokel takes your money, when in drink he's frisky,
But you know it's quite respectable to kidnap human flesh.

Remember we are soldiers, the bravest of the brave,
Come and be a soldier, then you'll be a slave,
Come to Colonel White my lads, but don't pretend to cry,
For if you are not happy, we can flog you till you die.

Come and learn your exercise, run lads, run.
Soon you'll know the use of bayonet and gun,
Then you'll go abroad my lads, and there you'll soon be warm,
By shooting men you never knew, who never did you harm.

If you should be killed my lads, never mind that them,
You will die with honour lads, you'll be free from care,
Never mind your wives and children, they'll soon be forgotten.
What's your wives and children to you, when you're dead and
rotten.

And if you should escape my lads, and get your lives away,
After a long servitude you will receive a pay (
Sixpence a-day for twelve months my lads you will receive,
You're filled as a pensioner, so then you need not grieve.

Did you ever think, my lads, or ever go to school,
He who would a soldier be, must surely be a fool ;
Talk of honour, that's all nonsense, 'tis an idle story ;
Live like honest men, my lads, that is the real glory.

Oh ! never be so silly as to fight for kings and queens,
For none of them is half so good as half a bunch of greens
Remember what I say, my lads, it is a serious thing,
Almighty made the human race, but never made a king.

Nineteenth-century broadsides

and their tract movement was as well planned and executed as any modern large-scale advertising campaign. The same is also true of the work of the Religious Tract Society, founded by a group of clergymen and missionaries to extend the movement started by Hannah More. Its first premises were in Stationers' Court, Ludgate Hill, then at 60 Paternoster Row. In 1820 the Society settled at 65 St Paul's Churchyard, the most historic site of London bookselling, where the early stationers and ballad-sellers had started business, and close to where the goodnatured Mr John Newbery had sold his delectable little histories for children in the days of Goldsmith.

In addition to many hundreds of tracts circulated by hawkers and colporteurs, the Religious Tract Society also published some excellent magazines during the nineteenth century, notably *The Leisure Hour, The Boy's Own Paper* and *The Girl's Own Paper*. During the twentieth century they also issued some notable books. Perhaps their best-seller amongst early writers was the Rev Legh Richmond, whose pathetic little story *The Dairyman's Daughter* (1809) sold well over a million copies in less than half a century. In *Lavengro* (1851), George Borrow related how he visited the Society's Repository in 1824 and was presented with a copy of this classic religious tract, which a publisher advised him to study for style.

Of course the tract movement has been rightly satirised, notably by Dickens in his novel *Bleak House*, in which Mrs Pardiggle forces tracts upon an unsympathetic working class. In *The Moonstone*, Wilkie Collins created Miss Drusilla Clack, a relentless giver of unwanted tracts:

I paid the cabman exactly his fare. He received it with an oath; upon which I instantly gave him a tract. If I had presented a pistol at his head, this abandoned wretch could hardly have exhibited greater consternation.

This is good fun, for there was certainly a humourless tendency to create dull tracts with titles for every eventuality, and to produce these like religious pills for all situations in life. Drusilla Clack, handing an irate blasphemer a tract called *Hush, for Heaven's Sake* is hardly a parody when a real colporteur could solemnly report with evident pride:

In the first room there were six or seven women drinking. One of them said, 'Why you have come to a public house!' I said, 'Yes, and I wish you were all teetotallers.' Looking for a suitable tract I found one entitled, 'Scotch Jim, the Drunken Ballad Singer.' A man then called me into the next room, where about twenty men sat smoking and drinking. They commenced laughing at me, one in particular, to whom I then gave a tract called 'Don't Laugh it Off.' [from C. H. Spurgeon, *Booksellers & Bookbuyers in Byeways and Highways*]

Of course, excessive piety and sententiousness brought deserved ridicule to the tract movement, but against this it must be admitted that working-class drunkenness and squalor were no laughing matter. Moreover the very real kindness and religious inspiration of the best of the tract writers, the genuine joy and consolation which this literature brought to many poor people, and the courage and generosity of so many missionaries in darkest London, make interesting comparison with the sick decadence of today's 'liberated' affluent society and its literature.

It was appropriate that chapbooks and broadsides should compete with religious tracts in the nineteenth century, for this was surely the last major encounter between the concepts of the religious life and the political life. Radicalism may have begun as a dream of social justice for poor men, but it has finished up as a decadent and violent power game in modern society. The religious position emphasised a respect for basic human values, the patience to endure, responsibility for constant reform by peaceful means, and a deeper view of life than the gains and losses of history. This was the distant echo of tradition in a topical world as the old pedlars, cheapjacks and chapmen vanished from the scene.

Yet perhaps the pedlars and rogues had a better understanding of the human situation than the more sophisticated writers, for they had learned the hard way to see through the illusions of property, wealth, power and ambition. It was Hawkie, the lame chapbook seller and vagrant, who spoke this sonorous patter:

> This is the end of all,
> High and low, great and small;
> This finishes the poor vain show,
> And the King, with all his pride,
> In his life-time deified—
> With the beggar is at last laid low.

6: Survivals

Survivals

I WILL GO DOWN TO SOME LONELY VALLEY
Where no man on earth shall me find,
Where the pretty little small birds
   do change their voices
And, every evening, blow boist'rous winds.

So sang the country folk singer a century ago as progress closed in around him, blotting out his familiar world with industrialisation, education and mass culture. At the dawn of the twentieth century even the penny broadsides of a *Horrible and Barbarous Murder* had disappeared, while the countryman had little enough to sing about. Both traditional and printed songs became museum relics, of interest to scholars, country parsons and antiquarians.

We owe much to the collectors of country songs and street literature, who preserved those ephemeral fragments from which we construct a history which would otherwise be lost. It is now possible to see how much the traditional folk music of the countryside depended upon the printed broadsides. It was Lucy E. Broadwood, a perceptive collector, who stressed in her book *English Traditional Songs and Carols* (1908):

The words of many country ballads are derived, directly or indirectly, from broadsides. The invention of printing early gave birth to these, which recorded both the orally-traditional and newly-made ballads of the strolling minstrel and tavern-bard. Before the days of cheap literature, the broadside, indeed, took the place of the newspaper, political pamphlet, history, novel, poetry-book, and hymnal of our times; and upon the ballad-sheets—largely circulated by pedlars, themselves often singers— the country folk relied for fresh information, amusement, and moral instruction, the more easily assimilated when in homely verse.

It is often by the most slender chance that street literature has been saved for study. We do not know how the respectable Mr Pepys acquired Selden's collection of ballads, but we can be grateful to him for preserving and adding to it, a preoccupation which many of his friends would have regarded as vulgar and disreputable. We know that some great collections have been filled with stolen sheets.

Others were acquired at grave risk at critical points in history. When the bookseller George Thomason began to assemble over twenty-two thousand items, he had them bound in volumes and buried in boxes, but as the collection grew, there were dangers that it would be discovered and Thomason persecuted for harbouring seditious literature. He contrived the daring expedient of putting the volumes in his warehouse in the form of tables round the room, covered with canvas. Thomason was actually imprisoned for seven weeks on one occasion, but in twenty years' hazardous collection his volumes remained undiscovered, and after many vicissitudes finally found their way to the British Museum. We do not know how many other items of street literature may have been destroyed over the centuries. One collection of ballad-sheets and chapbooks that would have been fascinating to study was that formed by Hannah More, concerning which Bishop Porteus wrote in 1794:

I should be much gratified with the sight of those invaluable original productions both in prose and verse which you have collected from your friends the village hawkers and pedlars. They would form the best sans-culotte library in Europe, and will, I daresay, some day or other, be visited by travellers as we now do the Vatican or the Museum.

Centuries pass between one's fingers in a bundle of old ballads or a pile of chapbooks, and life itself becomes a pile of stray papers. There is a certain melancholy in the disappearance of old traditions. Ballads, folk songs and chapbooks may have been a very distant echo of the myths and mysteries of an ancient past, yet even a dying echo is a precious reminder of the human situation.

I recently walked down the Whitechapel Road, in London's East End, where I had first started work as a youngster. In those days it was a romantic European ghetto, full of legends, in which one half expected to catch a glimpse of another Golem, like that created by the good Rabbi Loewe of Prague in former times. I looked for the old shop of Mazin's, the great centre for Hebrew literature, where they sold broadside song-sheets in Yiddish and English for refugees from European pogroms. These included songs of religious hope, in the infancy of the Zionist movement, and ballads about America as 'The Golden Land' [see page 135]. But the shop had closed down, and the East End had become a wilderness of unromantic housing estates.

JERUSALEM.

מיט מיוזיק 6 פענס.

פרייז 1 פעננ׳

ירושלים.

1.

Ich lieg auf mein geleger,
  Un mir shtelt sich for a traum,
Ich seh dos alte Zion nei,
  Un ach, mir gloibt sich kaum,
Ich her a geisst-reich englen chor,
  Mein hertz wert frei fun bang,
Un her, in harmonien-reich } biss
  A heilig siss gesang

1.

איך ליעג איף מיין געלעגער,
אין מיר שטעלט זיך פאר א טרוים,
איך זעה דאס אלטע ציון ניי,
און אך, מיר גלויבט זיך קוים,
איך זעה א גייסטרייך ענגלין כאהר,
מיין הערץ ווערט פריי פון באנג,
אין הער, אין הארמאניעןרייך, } ביס
א הייליג זים געזאנג!

Chorus :

Yerusholayim ! Yerusholayim !
Hoib auf deine oigen un blik,
Dein ume, o die frume,
Sie kehrt zu dir zurick.

כאהר :

ירושלים! ירושלים!
הייב אויף דיינע אויגען און בליק,
דיין אומה, א, די פרומע,
זי קעהרט צו דיר צוריק,

2.

Ich lieg un traum, doch seh ich klohr
  Die alte shtodt erwacht,
Es kumt der heller morgen,
  Un feryogt die tunkele nacht
Auf Zion's alte wegen dort,
  Hert sich a shwerer gang,
Dort kumt dos folk yisroel, } biss
  Mit musik un gesang.

2.

איך ליעג אין טרוים, דאך זעה איך קלאהר,
די אלטע שטאהרט ערוואכם,
עס קומט דער העללער מארגען,
און פעריאגט די טונקעלע נאכט,
אויף ציון'ס אלטע וועגען דארם,
הערט זיך א שווערער גאנג,
דארם קומט דאם פאלק ישראל } ביס
מים מוזיק און געזאנג,

Chorus :

Yerusholayim..... &c.

כאהר:

ירושלים......א,ן וו.

3.

Do wert dos bild fershwunden,
  Un a neies bild kumt on,
Ich seh auf Zion's moieren,
  Flatert shtoltz die alte fohn,
Un Yerusholayim glentzt,
  Ihr groisskeit wie amoll,
Mit groisse pracht; bekrentzt
  Is yeder berg un tol,
Un arum dem neiem tempel dort,
  Wos bleibt auf leben lang,
Dort shtcht dos folk yisroel,
  Un singt a loib gesang.

3.

דא ווערם דאם בילד פערשוואונדען,
און א נייעם בילד קומם אן
איך זעה אויף ציון'ס מויערען,
פלאטערם שטאלץ די אלטע פאהן,
און ירושלים גרענצט
איהר' גרויסקייט וויא אמאהל,
מים גרויסע פראכם; בעקרענצט
איז יעדער בערג און טאהל,
און ארום דעם נייעם טעמפעל דארם,
וואם בלייבט אויף לעבען לאנג,
דארם שטעהט דאם פאלק פערוואמעלם,
און זינגם א לויב געזאנג,

Chorus :

Yerusholayim ! Yerusholayim !
Hoib auf deine oigen un blik,
Dein ume, o die frume,
Sie kehrt zu dir zurick.

כאהר :

ירושלים! ירושלים!
הייב אויף דיינע אויגען און בליק,
דיין אומה, א די פרומע,
זי קעהרם צו דיר צוריק.

A broadside published by R. Mazin & Co Ltd in London's East End, probably early twentieth century

The folk song and broadside ballad tradition lingered longest in Ireland, where ballad-sheets were sold at country fairs into the twentieth century, as writers like J. M. Synge and Padraic Colum have recorded. The beautiful poetry of W. B. Yeats owes much to a background of Irish ballads. His 'Down by the salley gardens' is a rewriting of a song which was printed on broadsides as 'The Rambling Boys of Pleasure'; the original line is 'Down by yon valley gardens' [see page 137]. In July 1908 appeared the first issue ('June') of A BROADSIDE from the Dun Emer Press founded by Elizabeth Corbet Yeats in 1903, part of a William Morris style project 'to find work for Irish hands in the making of beautiful things'. From the second number onwards the imprint was The Cuala Press, associated with the books of great Irish writers like AE, Douglas Hyde, Lady Gregory, W. B. Yeats, and many others. A BROADSIDE was published from 1908 to 1916, each number containing ballad poetry, traditional and modern, some with drawings by Jack B. Yeats, many of them hand-coloured [see page 138]. This publication, which ran to eighty-four numbers, was the most beautiful fusion between folklore, broadside and chapbook traditions ever contrived. In 1935 and 1937 two later series, each of twelve parts, were published. It is good to report that the work of The Cuala Press is continuing in modern times. When I was last in Lower Baggot Street, Dublin, I was delighted to see that the original Albion hand-press was still in use, and the old blocks being reprinted.

But the tradition of selling broadside verses in the streets of Dublin died out a long time ago. In other parts of the world one or two old men carried on.

In the 1960s, Jim Smith was a familiar figure in Oxford Street, London, with his tray of original songs and patters printed on one side of small cards. When he was a young man he used to travel around the country fairs. His songs were on topical political subjects. Today, Mr Smith has moved on, although *Old Moore's Almanac*, last of the ephemeral pamphlets, is still sold in the streets of London in several editions, each claiming to be the 'Original and Genuine' one. In 1963 there was an old man in Puerto Rico selling the local verse broadsides called 'décimas'.

There are other fragments of a tradition in Europe, where there had been a street literature movement similar to that in Britain. In Épinal, France, much of the old 'imagerie populaire' is still being

THE RAMBLING
Boys of Pleasure.

Printed, and Sold Wholesale and Retail, by G .
Jacques, Oldham Road Library, Manchester.

You rambling boys of pleasure,
Give hear unto these lines I write,
It's true I am a rover,
And in roving I take great delight;
I placed my mind on a handsome girl,
Who oftentimes did me slight,
But my mind was never easy,
But when my love was in my sight.

The first time that I saw my love,
I really thought her heart was mine,
Her graceful and her handsome face,
I thought that she was quite divine :
Curst gold is the root of evil
Altho' it shines with a glittering hue,
It causes many a lad and lass to part,
Let their hearts and minds be ere so true.

Down by yon valley gardens,
One evening as I chanced to stray,
It's their I saw my darling,
I took her to be the queen of May,
She told me to take love easy,
nst as the leaves grow on the trees,
J But I being young and foolish,
er then I did not agree,

There is one thing more that grieves me,
That to be called a runaway,
To leave where I was bred and born,
O, Cupid won't you set me free,
To leave my love behind me
Alack and alas what shall I do'
Must I become a rover into
The land I never knew.

When I am sitting o'er my quart,
And no one around me but strangers all,
I will think upon my own true love,
When I am boosing far away,
Where I could have sweethearts plenty,
And flowing bowls on every side
Let fortune never daunt you love,
For we are young and the world is wide.

I wish it was in Dublin,
And my own true love along with me,
And money to support us,
And keep us in good company ;
Where I could have sweethearts plenty,
And flowing bowls on every side,
Let fortune never daunt you love,
For we are young and the world is wide.

(No. 59.)

The broadside ballad that inspired W. B. Yeats's 'Down by the salley gardens'

NO. 9 (NEW SERIES) SEPTEMBER 1935.

A BROADSIDE

EDITORS: W. B. YEATS AND F. R. HIGGINS; MUSICAL EDITOR,
ARTHUR DUFF. PUBLISHED MONTHLY AT THE CUALA PRESS,
ONE HUNDRED AND THIRTY THREE LOWER BAGGOT STREET,
DUBLIN.

AN OLD AIR

As I was walking I met a woman
And she side-saddled on a horse,
Most proudly riding the road to Moyrus
On a stallion worthy of a fine race-course.

The horse it sidled; I asked her kindly,
With a timid hand on the jolting rein,
"Now are you Niamh or Grace O'Maille,
Or a female grandee from the fields of Spain?"

She merely fondled those bridled fingers
And little fearing sweetly replied,
"Among my people you'd grow so noble
That none would know you did here abide;

Then live with me, man, and I will give you
The run of twelve hills with a still in each."
Her eyes were craving that rainy evening
While a gentle air was in her speech.

300 copies only.

A Cuala Press broadsheet

reprinted. In Switzerland, satirical broadsides are issued during the Basle Fastnacht Carnival. These are long slips of coloured paper with little cartoons and verses in a ribald tradition. I recently received some cheaply printed paper-covered booklets from Greece; these had folk tales in a true chapbook tradition.

Something rather like the nineteenth century explosion of Seven Dials printing occurred in Nigeria before the Biafran war. In the 1940s a number of cheap Indian novelettes were imported there. With growing education and an emphasis on the English language, there was a demand for locally printed cheap literature, and in the 1960s over 250 titles were on sale in the Onitsha Market. Here are some typical titles: *Beware of Harlots and Many Friends, How to Write Love Letters, Why Maria Killed Her Husband, Money Hard But Some Women Don't Know, My Seven Daughters Are After Young Boys*. This is, in every sense, an ephemeral literature, since readers use the books as waste paper afterwards, often tearing up the pages for paper to roll cigarettes.

In many parts of the world there are stray survivals of a dying tradition, a challenge to the modern collector and social historian. The old broadsides and chapbooks are now hard to come by, and prices are inflated. Twenty years ago I paid sixpence a sheet for penny Victorian broadsides; today the price is upwards of one pound. Nineteenth-century penny chapbooks may cost several pounds each.

In recent times there has been a widespread movement to revive the whole field of traditional and printed folk music. In the mid-twentieth century came a sudden nostalgia for tradition, and the banner of 'folk' began to be flourished equally by the romantic and the social revolutionary. The stimulus came from the USA, where the old British ballads had been transplanted by early settlers and nineteenth century broadsides. America had a continuing evolution of urban and country folk music in the inter-war years, much of it commandeered by left-wing radicalism. In Britain, many young people were drawn to the serious study of Jazz and its sociological background of negro blues singing. The remains of Anglo-American folk song, admirably preserved by the recordings of the Library of Congress Folk Music Division and by dedicated folk scholars, were popularised by singers like Burl Ives and Harry Belafonte through mass media. There was a scramble to copyright folk tradition.

Out of a melting-pot of jazz, folk blues, and Anglo-American folk song came 'Skiffle'—a British development involving folk song with jazz undertones and simple instrumentation. Lonnie Donegan became famous singing the songs of the late Huddie Ledbetter, negro ex-convict protégé of American folklorists John and Alan Lomax. While commercialisation of skiffle helped to shape teenage taste in rock-and-roll and pop singing, the amateur skiffle movement resulted in a British folk song revival which spread like wildfire. Cecil Sharp House in London, headquarters of the English Folk Dance and Song Society, was ransacked for texts, tunes and recordings; guitars hung like Christmas turkeys in the music shops; folk clubs sprang up overnight in cellars, coffee bars and pubs. Some groups played on the streets.

Revivalists split into two main groups—traditionalists, who wanted to sing country songs and ballads in the same way as the old singers, often unaccompanied; and modernists, who set new topical verses to old or new tunes and used a guitar or other instrumental backing. Even the choice of songs led to local chauvinism, some holding that British singers should sing only British style and not attempt the American accent.

All agreed on the need to spread the words and music of new and old songs, and printed broadsides and song books began to appear once more. Although the balladmongers of the past sang and sold their sheets and pamphlets in the streets or at country fairs, the revivalists mostly keep to their own little magazines, or to gramophone records, radio or television programmes. But some modern broadside sheets have been sold and sung in the streets.

The pioneer revivalist is John Foreman, 'The Broadsheet King', who reprinted many sheets by Catnach and other printers, as well as publishing new broadsides and chapbooks in traditional style [see page 142]. His sheet on *The Smithfield Market Fire* was on sale in the street at Petticoat Lane, London, soon after the event. John Foreman is also a versatile entertainer, and sings music-hall songs in the old style at folk clubs. As mentioned earlier, he was responsible for the first British reprint of Charles Hindley's classic collection *Curiosities of Street Literature*, originally published 1871. This new edition is in two volumes, each broadside being printed on one side only of differently coloured sheets, altogether a magnificent piece of work. Other broadside and chapbook editions by The

At the Sign of Flying Fame.

LIST OF PUBLICATIONS.

BROADSIDES.
2 PENCE PLAIN,
4 PENCE COLOURED.

1. **SONG.** *By Ralph Hodgson.*
2. **FEBRUARY.** *By Ralph Hodgson.*
3. **THE ROBIN'S SONG.** *By Richard Honeywood.*
4. **A PARABLE.** *By Lovat Fraser.* Uncoloured.
5. **CAPTAIN MACHEATH.** *by Lovat Fraser.* Drawing, uncoloured.

AT 4 PENCE.

6. **THE LONELY HOUSE.** *By Lovat Fraser.* Drawing in colours.

CHAP-BOOKS.
AT 6 PENCE.

1. **EVE, and Other Poems.** *By Ralph Hodgson.*
2. **TOWN.** *An Essay.* **By Holbrook Jackson.**
3. **THE TWO WIZARDS, and Other Songs.** *By Richard Honeywood.*

AT 3 PENCE.

4. **SIX ESSAYS in the XVIIIth Century. By Richard Honeywood.**

Postage on above, 1 Penny.

In the Press, other Chap-books, Broadsides, and Drawings, by James Stephens, Holbrook Jackson, Walter de la Mare, Ralph Hodgson, Richard Honeywood, and Lovat Fraser.
All publications decorated throughout by Lovat Fraser.

PRINTED BY *A. T. STEVENS,* OF 55 ST. MARTIN'S LANE, IN THE CITY OF WESTMINSTER, FOR *R.H., L.F.* AND *H.J.,* AT THE S. N OF *FLYING FAME,* 45 ROLAND GARDENS, LONDON, S.W. WHERE COPIES MAY BE HAD.

1 9 1 3 .

Broadside publisher's list for Lovat Fraser broadsides and chapbooks

TIM EVANS

Ewan MacColl

Tim Evans was a prisoner,
Fast in his prison cell.
And those who read about his crimes,
They damned his soul to hell.
    Saying, go down, you murderer, go down!

For the murder of his own true wife,
And the killing of his own child.
The jury found him guilty
And the hanging judge he smiled.

Now Evans pleaded innocent
And swore by him on high,
That he never killed his own dear wife
Nor caused his child to die.

They moved him out at nine o'clock
To his final flowery-dell.
And day and night two screws were there
And never left his cell.

Sometimes they played draughts with him
And solo and pontoon,
To stop him brooding on the rope
That was to be his doom.

They brought his grub in on a tray,
There was eggs and meat and ham,
And all the snout that he could smoke
Was there at his command.

The governor came in one day,
The chaplain by his side;
Says, "Your appeal has been turned down,
Prepare yourself to die."

So Evans walked in the prison yard
And the screws they walked behind,
And he saw the sky above the wall
And he knew no peace of mind.

They came for him at eight o'clock
And the chaplain read a prayer.
And then they walked him to that place
Where the hangman did prepare.

The rope was fixed around his neck,
And the buckle behind his ear;
And the prison bell was tolling
But Tim Evans did not hear.

A thousand lags were cursing
And a banging on the doors.
Tim Evans could not hear them,
He was deaf for evermore.

They sent Tim Evans to the drop
For a crime he didn't do.
It was Christy was the murderer
And the judge and jury too.

B K

A modern broadside, published by John Foreman, 'The Broadsheet King'. Verses by Ewan MacColl

Broadsheet King are as likely to become collector's items as those by Claude Lovat Fraser. Many other folk enthusiasts have also put out modern broadsides, notably Eddie Dunmore ('The Chapman'), Keith Roberts of Wigan, Dave Scott and Michael Yates.

A main channel for the revivalist movement in its role of protest literature was the Campaign for Nuclear Disarmament, and the Aldermaston marches gave a natural setting for new political ballads. Some other aspects of the contemporary scene recorded in balladry included taxation, food prices, anti-smoking, greedy landlords, Mass X-ray campaigns, the Street Offences Bill, Billy Graham, beatniks, sputniks, and of course the Viet-Nam war. It is unfortunate that many so-called peace songs have exuded partisan aggression and hatred.

Pioneer writers of modern broadsides of social criticism included Ewan MacColl, Peggy Seeger, John Hasted, Eric Winter, Fred Dallas, Dr Alex Comfort, and science-fiction writer John Brunner.

Sydney Carter has been responsible for some beautiful folk-style carols, as well as amusing topical songs. The late Leslie Haworth was a great balladist, whose *Ascent of Everest* captured much of the feeling of ancient minstrelsy.

There are now several gramophone record companies devoted to authentic folk music recordings. Even poetry has been given a new stimulus by the broadside revival, underlined by the vogue for Brechtian verse declaimed to a jazz background. Christopher Logue's vigorous *Song of the Dead Soldier* was issued as a broadside, and many other modern poets circulate their pieces on cheaply priced sheets.

With nearly a thousand folk clubs in Britain, and a network of clubs in Europe, America, Israel and elsewhere, the folk circuit has attempted to create an alternative culture to the modern world of exploitation. This sincere movement has involved scholars and working people, old and young, in a genuine search to re-create tradition and rediscover meaning in life.

Is all this a true renaissance of the traditional impulse in the old folk music and street literature, or is it a romantic form from which the essence has already receded? It is too early to say, for there are many other influences in modern society.

Pop music is more firmly entrenched, and has become a symbol of nonconformity and anti-culture. It began innocently enough and with a certain talent, but the prizes were too glittering for top performers and investors. With millions of pounds involved and the prospect of instant fame, every gimmick and saleable outrage was mobilised; the world of folk music rhythms, melodies and themes was ransacked for the ingredients of the new psychedelic sound, amplified all over the world. Year by year the pop festivals grow as large as the Nuremberg rallies in prewar Germany. Aggressive flyposters of pop groups with sensationalist names and violent themes appear on street hoardings as a new kind of graffiti in lavish colour printing, side by side with the manifestos of the New Left.

Many of the old folk songs that made our flesh tingle with sad stories of true love, suffering, or injustice became false—beautiful lies drawing their power from an ancient pity but distorting it into contemporary protest themes of expediency and bitterness.

In Northern Ireland, folk songs were recruited by the IRA. Thousands of penny song cards eulogising the legendary lives of dead IRA gunmen were sold in the Belfast pubs, reinforcing a new mythology of hatred. In the 1971 troubles the militants in Londonderry barricaded themselves behind physical and mental barriers in the Bogside and Creggan estates, and men, women and children joined together in a daily campaign of killing and maiming civilians and British soldiers, a compulsive hostility that became a psychopathic way of life. Rival fanatics from the Protestant areas committed atrocities against Catholic sympathisers. In the IRA pubs the folk groups sang haunting old folk songs side by side with hostile ballads with lines like:

> On Rossville Street Sunday the blood ran like wine
> Of those who were marching for freedom that day.

On the street walls, crude slogans and posters announced: 'Give us guns not stones', and 'All soldiers are bastards'.

A future historian, with only the confused remains of our printed and recorded ephemera, might find it difficult to analyse the tangled story of our momentous times, and document the transformations of past forms.

Something of the mythic impulse in ballads and Gothic chapbooks passed into science-fiction magazines, where the old heavens and hells became the setting of spaceship sagas. A cheaply printed literature industry developed in the mass-produced pornographies of condoned sexual fantasy. Throughout the cities of Europe and America there are chains of sleazy shops peddling sex and horror comics to poor people and their children, and the rich rewards have bred protection rackets. At a middle-class level are the sexy paperbacks at every news-stand, a popular literature that has replaced chapbook romances. A vague hunger for something beyond materialism generated freak cults, pop religions, and a bourgeois preoccupation with witchcraft and the occult.

In the high-pressure profit and loss of an expanding consumer society that would have staggered the oldtime pedlars, much of the wonder and awe of existence dissolved into mundane preoccupations. The mass media of newspapers and television record the optimism of success and the ideals of comfortable affluence, but they also reflect the mounting unrest of widespread power struggles, exploitation, ruthless big business, reckless strikes, political confrontations, power coups and wars. They do not elucidate the mass emotional sickness of preoccupation with money, power, ego, self-indulgence, sensationalism, and irrational hatreds in a materialistic society poised uneasily on a vast arsenal of atomic weapons. Why did centuries of topical preoccupation culminate so briefly in the prosperity and technological triumphs of affluence, only to collapse suddenly in universal confusions?

Meanwhile, we study past ages to deepen our understanding of history and the connections between literature and life, to find clues to interpret a baffling and intimidating present. Books have given us one sort of history, but the rise and fall of street literature is also the story of mankind, roughly printed, but with a simplicity and passion lacking in more intellectual literature. History comes to life in the thousands of ephemeral sheets which show us the hopes, fears, opinions and events (both great and small) that preoccupied ordinary people now long dead, what they believed, what they loved or hated, their tragedies, and what made them laugh.

And so we are coming to the last verses of this long broadside story, and the complex struggle between tradition and topicality in the world of cheap printing. This could never be a conventional history, for the sheets themselves only form a framework for philosophy. Like the patterer and the pinner-up in nineteenth century London, I stand before you with a bundle of old papers. As always, your balladmonger has Strange, Terrible, and Wonderful News, and a Warning Against Sin:

'Ladies and Gentlemen—Welcome to my picture gallery! The

theme is the story of man (and woman) in all the most varied aspects from the sublime to the ridiculous, told by the genius of the most talented authors of the day (for the small price of one penny) and illustrated by the brilliant technique of the leading artists and engravers (all for the small price of one penny). The whole of life is here, from the noblest aspirations of mankind to the copy of verses written by the unfortunate criminal the night *after* he was executed, with a warning to young men and women to avoid bad company and sinful vanity—all for the incredibly small and sufficient charge of one penny!'

So the cheapjack shows us life—the facts, follies and sins of the day, fluttering on penny and halfpenny sheets like puppets on a string, the non-books of their time, the literature of poor people before the age of cheap newspapers, books or television.

It is a long way from the heroic images and rituals of ancient myth to the vanishing folklore and paper souvenirs of the twentieth century. A little penny chapbook kept alive the story of Cinderella, a retelling of an ancient Hindu myth. A Scottish folk ballad hints at a myth of creation, first told in sacred scriptures thousands of years earlier. A nursery song echoes a primitive religious rite. Sometimes the trashy catchpennies of the streets preserve the deepest metaphysical speculations of mankind in a secret language of archetype.

In an age far removed from traditional roots, tradition has worn paper thin, and all that is left of the fantastic mythology of Lord Vishnu as Vahara the great boar, who shook out the mighty Himalayan mountain range in his battle with a demon, is the comic ballad of 'Sir Eglamore' (lanky down dillo!), or 'Old Bangham' with his wooden knife. Only the bones of a thousand men remind us of a cosmic event, and it may be that tradition will not be re-stated in living language until after an equally titanic upheaval.

In a world in which the super-powers plan their final takeover bids in a proxy war at every pressure point of the globe, against a background of universal confusion, neo-hedonism, and mass psychopathology, the new broadside sound is neurotic violence. In many countries the myths have already come off the pages of literature as living letters of confrontation in the streets, where the masses are the chorus of a theatre of cruelty where there is no purging by pity and terror, because there is only terror. And in spite of a shrill protest movement and hostile cries for peace, the fault is not simply in our rulers and teachers, but in ourselves. We have made every way out a new trap.

The great conflicts of religion and politics are magnified distortions of the split within each man's inner life, and externalise the individual conflicts of love and hate, desire and fear, creation and destruction. We do not see how the lie starts in ourselves, nor how it spreads outwards. The irrational forces of modern society are not an incomprehensible evil—rather they are brought into being and intensified by the subtle commitments of millions of ordinary people every day, unaware of the common ground of the emotions, the secret psyche of the mass. Because of this, all our literature has special responsibilities.

Yet if the proud libraries of the world are burnt down, as they were in ancient times, the great secrets of life remain open secrets, since the mere shape of printed words and the noise of their sounds means little without some personal initiation. The old magic of tradition is still here, against all the bureaucrats, the vanity of property and prestige, pop idolatry, the struggles for power and the destruction of meaning, but it is not simply in a revived folklore, a drug, a slogan on a banner, the book of the month, or a broadside bought for a penny. The key is in our own integrity, and the ordinary man or woman in the street may yet discover that he is a king's son or she a princess, just as in the old, old folk tales. The essential truths of life are still revealed to a pure heart and a humble understanding. All else is vanity and will pass away, and even death may be a high adventure.

You may protest that I exceed my license as a broadside patterer in all this sober moralising, but I claim the privilege of the ballad-monger in sermonising against the sins of the times. And history supports my warnings if you think back only as far as the horrors of Hitler's Germany. Yet who listens to an old man with an ancient history?

Years ago, I saw an old man selling broadside ballads in Dublin city, Ireland. He has moved on. There was only one old man in Puerto Rico with sheets of décimas, and the crudely printed handbills had verses on the assassination of President Kennedy.

Today there is still a ballad-seller in the market-place of Northeast Brazil. He is selling the epic poem of *Carlos Magno e os Doze Pares de França*—the eight hundred year old legend of Charlemagne and the Twelve Peers of France, still in chapbook tradition. Hanging on strings in a battered suitcase are other chapbook pamphlets—the *literatura de cordel*—'literature on a string'. Some of these chapbooks relate apocalyptic visions of the end of the world, the resurrection of the dead, and the last judgement:

> A Communist country will begin the Third World War
> Will drop fire from the clouds and burn the
>   mountains and the plains
> Will invade many nations, sweeping away the
>   populations from every corner of the earth . . .
>
> A burning wind blows across the north east
>   and a rain of boiling water falls everywhere.
> No one escapes alive, the poor, the rich, the
>   innocent must die in the scalding rain.

Centuries ago it was rumoured that the emperor Charlemagne did not really die, but was only sleeping until the hour of his people's need. Is it a modern world that sleeps, caught up in a vain dream of materialism and power games?

Business is bad, and few people bother to listen to the ballad-seller or buy his chapbooks. Now the great Charlemagne hangs on a string in a market-place, for the last time. . . .

Look closely, then, at my broadside picture gallery, of tragedy and comedy, tears and laughter, wisdom and folly, before we too are pinned to the wall of history by relentless time.

7: Examples and Notes

These examples illustrate something of the variety of street literature, in form and subject-matter. There are many examples of broadside ballads and chapbooks, since they were well-established forms, but there are also specimens of transitional forms of the popular newspaper—news ballads, prose broadsides, and the literary news-sheet. Other types of popular street ephemera represented include street notices, pamphlets, lottery advertisements, almanacs, and cheap literature for children.

The examples have been grouped under convenient categories, as will be seen from the section of NOTES that follows, where there are comments on individual items and details of actual size of originals.

In addition to the need to give some impression of the rich variety of street literature, I have also felt it helpful to include items that reflect themes and ideas touched upon in the text of the book, so that these facsimiles will, in a sense, help to tell their own story. I believe that street literature has been closer to life than the world of books. Ordinary people, without intellectual pretensions or special social position, spelt out the letters of street notices, sang the ballads, or treasured the chapbooks and pamphlets as a poor man's library. If we can study the function of so much that is trivial, novel, catchpenny, and ephemeral, as well as romantic, inspiring, significant and timeless, we may come nearer to understanding the age-old riddle of the importance and place of every single created being in the great scheme of things. That is the task of literature.

The LOVER's Magazine,

B E I N G

A Choice Collection of S O N G S;

Containing,

1. There was a Lady fine and gay.
2. Whenever green Myrtles afford a green fhade.
3. It is I believe.
4. Whilft our Anchor it is weighing.
5. The Lafs who would know how to manage a Man.
6. All you that will have a wife.
7. The Lafs of Patty's Mill.
8. Upon a Summer's Evening clear.
9. How hard is the fate of all women kind.
10. As I went forth one May morning.
11. Wou'd you tafte the Noon-Tide Air.
12. O'er half the fky the blufhing dawn.
13. Away to the Field, fee the Morning looks gay.
14. God blefs great GEORGE the Third.
15. Bufy, curious, thirfty Fly.
16. What is Life we fo prefer?
17. As by Bedlam I was walking.
18. Says Plato, why fhould man be vain?
19. Since ev'ry charm on earth combine.
20. The Bird that hears her Neftling cry.

Printed and Sold in Aldermary Church-Yard,
Bow-Lane, LONDON.

Great, and wonderful News to all Chriftendom in particular, and the whole World in General.

B E I N G A

Strange and Wonderful Relation

OF THE

Apearance of an Angel

TO A

M I N I S T E R

As he was going Abroad to Preach,

WHO TOLD

His moft SECRET THOUGHTS, and likewife the TEXT he was to PREACH from.

A L S O,

Of his telling the MINISTER many wonderful THINGS tnat will fhortly come to pafs.

L I K E W I S E

The Minifter's Name, the Place where he lived, the Year, Month, Day, and Hour of the Angel's Appearance to him; with a true and faithful Account of the Words the Angel fpoke to the Minifter.

A L S O

An Account of the great Prodigies and Signs that will be feen in the Month of January next in many Parts of England.

Seven
OF THE MOST
POPULAR SONGS.

THE BRIDAL RING.
WHAT ARE YOU GOING TO STAND.
THE LASSIES OF SCOTLAND.
THE MACGREGOR'S GATHERING
FAREWELL TO THE MOUNTAIN
THE BANKS OF THE BLUE MOZELLE.
'TWAS MERRY IN THE HALL.

GLASGOW:
PRINTED FOR THE BOOKSELLERS.
45

M A R Y,
THE
MAID OF THE INN;
AN INTERESTING NARRATIVE;

DETAILING THE

Singular way she discovered her Lover to be a

ROBBER AND MURDERER;

HIS CONVICTION AND EXECUTION;

WITH

Her forlorn and deftitute Wanderings, and unhappy Death.

ALNWICK:
PRINTED AND SOLD BY W. DAVISON,
BONDGATE STREET,
Where may be had, a large Affortment of Hiftories, Songs, Pictures, Children's Books, &c.

THE FAMOUS
HISTORY
OF
FRIAR BACON,
With the Lives and Deaths of
BUNGEY and VENDERMAST.

PART the FIRT.

Printed in the Year, 1796.

THE
HISTORY
OR
Jack & the Giants.

Part the First.

COVENTRY;
Printed and Sold by J. Turner.

1790

THE
PILGRIM'S PROGRESS,
FROM THIS WORLD TO THAT WHICH IS TO COME,

GLASGOW;
PUBLISHED BY ORR AND SONS, BRUNSWICK ST.

43

THE COLRAIN LASS,
to which are added
The Lamentation of Pat. Maguire for
Violating Mary Keys.
and
The HIGHLAND LASS.

OMAGH:
Painted for the Flying Stationers,
1847

ENTERTAINING LESSONS FOR CHILDREN.

Frontispiece.

Train up a child in the way he should go, and when he is
old he will not depart from it.

THE

CHILD'S EASY
PRIMER:

BEING THE

BEST INTRODUCTION TO

READING AND SPELLING.

Embellished with Cuts.

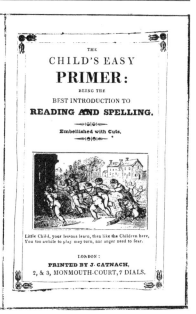

Little Child, your lessons learn, then like the Children here,
You too awhile to play may turn, nor anger need to fear.

LONDON :

PRINTED BY J. CATNACH,
2, & 3, MONMOUTH-COURT, 7 DIALS.

C. N. WRIGHT'S

NEW & IMPROVED BATTLEDORE.

af ef of af il em on
if uf el il an in

ab eb ob ac ic uc
ub ec oc ed ad od
id

A B C D E F G H
I J K L M N O P Q
R S T U V W X Y Z

a b c d e f g h i j k l
m n o p q r s t u v
w x y z ffi ffl fi ff fl

D L R H X Z A V N
U T I Q G O C W S
Y K M E B P F J

w s f l b n z u g m p h i
e v j o r c q k a x d t y

COCK.

GOAT.

CROW.

STAG.

LEOPARD.

BEAVER.

NURSERY POEMS,

FROM THE

ANCIENT AND MODERN POETS.

BANBURY:
PRINTED BY J. G. RUSHER.

FRONTISPIECE.

The fields provide me food, and show
The goodness of the Lord:
But fruits of life and glory grow
In thy most holy word.

AN ELEGY

ON THE

Death and Burial

OF

COCK ROBIN.

Ornamented with Cuts.

YORK:
Printed by J. Kendrew, 23, Colliergate.

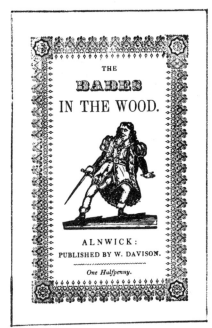

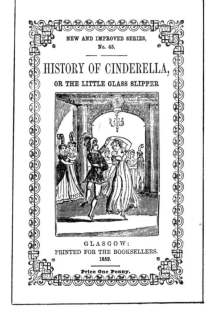

SIX PRIZES
OF
£20,000
IN THE
State Lottery,
WHICH BEGINS DRAWING
THIS MONTH,
TUESDAY, June 28th.

SCHEME.

6	of £20,000 ....are..	£120,000
2	---- 10,000 ----------	20,000
2	---- 5,000 ----------	10,000
3	---- 2,000 ----------	6,000
5	---- 1,000 ----------	5,000
7	---- 500 ----------	3,500
20	---- 100 ----------	2,000
30	-------- 50 ----------	1,500
1,000	-------- 22 ----------	22,000
4,000	-------- 15 ----------	60,000

25,000 Tickets. £250,000
NO FIXED PRIZE.

THIS IS THE
ONLY LOTTERY
THAT EVER CONTAINED
SIX PRIZES of £20,000!

Tickets and Shares are selling by

SWIFT
& CO.

Poultry & Charing-Cross.

Evans & Ruffy, Printers, 29, Budge Row, Wallbrook.

FORTUNE FAVORS THE FAIR.

YE British Fair, whom Nature has supplied
With charms resistless; you, her darling pride,
When Fortune smiles, receive redoubled grace;
Her gifts add lustre to each beauteous face:
She lays her freewill off'ring at your feet,
In Lott'ry treasures, for a new year's treat.
Tens, Twenties, Thirty Thousands, sure to rise
Above your wishes ;—many a noble Prize
May be obtain'd !—The Goddess now is kind ;
Embrace her offers while she's in the mind.

Next Day's Drawing,
Thursday, January 22, 1807.

Evans & Ruffy, Printers, 29, Budge-row, Wallbrook.

Can you give this ex-Service Man a Job or help him by buying this Bill,
PRICE 2d.

The Battle of Neuve Chappelle

The charge was over and the battle won,
Some girl lost a sweetheart, some mother a son;
Sadly did we hear of a comrade who fell
For the honour of Britain at Neuve Chappelle.

Honour had been won in that glorious fight:
The lads who died for the cause and the right;
There's a price to be paid, and the Germans know well,
For the cold blooded murder at Neuve Chappelle.

We fell in for roll call after that fight,
And some of them made a piteous sight;
Some never answered, and we knew well
They had fallen, like heroes, at Neuve Chappelle.

Some homes will be lonely, some mother's heart sad,
Some lass will be crying for the soldier lad
Who died in that battle: for his country he fell,
Defending his home at Neuve Chappelle.

JULIET.—*Romeo and Juliet*
Ask for WARREN's BLACKING, made at
30, STRAND—all others are inferior.

————"Oh, gentle Romeo,
If thou dost love, pronounce it faithfully !"
When love unites too faithful hearts,
But Death the band can sever,
And woman's troth, and honour's vow,
Truth consecrates for ever.
For honour will in every case,
The public praise command :
Thus for his Blacking Fame has crown'd
R. WARREN, 30, STRAND,

Vox Stellarum:

Or, a Loyal

ALMANACK

FOR THE

Year of Human Redemption,

₥753.

Being the Firſt after Bissextile or Leap-Year.
In which is contained all Things fitting for
ſuch a Work ; as,

A Table of Terms and their Returns ;
the Fulls, Changes, and Quarters of the Moon ;
the Riſing, Southing, and Setting of the Seven
Stars, and other Fix'd Stars of Note ; the Moon's
Age, and A Tide Table fitted to the ſame ; the
Riſing and Setting of the Sun ; the Riſing, Southing and Setting of the Moon ; Mutual Aſpects,
Monthly Obſervations, and many other Things
uſeful and pleaſant.

Unto which are added,

Aſtrological Obſervations on the Four Quarters
of the Year ; an Hieroglyphick alluding to
theſe preſent Times. A remarkable Chronology ;
the Eclipſes, and other Matters both curious and
profitable.

By FRANCIS MOORE, Phyſician.

LONDON: Printed by J. Bettenham, for the
Company of Stationers.

THE
SPEECH
OF THE
Prince of Orange,
TO SOME

Principle Gentlemen of *Somerfetfhire* and *Dorfetfhire*, on their coming to Joyn his Highnefs at *Exeter* the 15th of *Nov.* 1688.

THo' we know not all your Perfons, yet we have a Catalogue of your Names, and remember the Character of your Worth and Intereft in your Country. You fee we are come according to your Invitation and our Promife. Our Duty to God obliges us to Protect the Proteftant Religion, and our Love to Mankind, your Liberties and Properties. We expected you that dwelt fo near the place of our Landing, would have join'd us fooner, not that it is now too late, nor rhat we want you Military Affiftance fo much as your Countenance, and Prefence, to Juftifie our Declar'd Pretentions; rather than accomplifh our good and gracious Defigns. Tho' we have brought both a good Fleet, and a good Army, to render thefe Kingdoms happy, by Refcuing all Proteftants from Popery, Slavery, and Arbitrary Power; by Reftoring them to their Rights and Properties Eftablifhed by Law, and by Promoting of Peace and Trade, which is the Soul of Government, and the very Life-Blood of a Nation; yet we rely more on the Goodnefs of God and the Juftice of our Caufe, than on any Humane Force and Power whatever. Yet fince God is pleafed we fhall make ufe of Humane means, and not expect Miracles, for our prefervation and Happinefs: Let us not neglect making ufe of this Gracious Opportunity, but with Prudence and Courage, put in Execution our fo honourable purpofes. Therefore Gentlemen, Friends and Fellow-Proteftants, we bid you and all your Followers moft heartily Wellcome to our Court and Camp. Let the whole World now Judge, if out pretentions are not Juft, Generous, Sincere, and above Price; fince we might have, even a Bridge of Gold, to Return back; But it is our Principle and Refolution rather to dye in a Good Caufe, than live in a Bad one, well knowing that Vertue and True Honour is its own Reward, and the Happinefs of Mankind our Great and Only Defign.

FINIS.

EXETER, Printed by *J.B.* 1688.

DIARRHŒA
&c.

**All Persons suffering from DIARRHŒA
and other like BOWEL COMPLAINTS,
in the PARISHES of**

WAPPING
AND
SHADWELL,

**MAY, ON APPLICATION, OBTAIN ALL
NECESSARY**

MEDICINES

At the Dispensary at

WAPPING WORKHOUSE;
AND
Medical Attendance
AT ALL TIMES,

NIGHT and DAY,

**Will be given at the homes of all who
may require it.**

JULY 31, 1866.   **Limehouse Board of Works.**

Oppertunity Lost, Or

The Scotch Lover Defeated.

Here *Willy* followes *Peggy* ftill
But ne'r attains to have his will
His flownefs caus'd the hafty Maid
To call a Miller to her ayd :
Who nimbler then her Lover feaz'd
And ftraight her hafty paffion eas'd.

To a pleafant Northern tune.

With Allowance.

There was a Lafin our Town
   Sing *Willy Scotſon,*
He lov'd a Lafs bonny and brown
   Was pretty *Peggy Benſon.*

Each morn as he gang'd to the field
   Sing *Willy Scotſon,*
He tou'd fome piece of kindnefs yeild
   To pretty *Peggy Benſon.*

Her Beauty far his heart had ftir'd
   Sing *Willy Scotſon,*
Yet cou'd not tell what he defir'd
   Of pretty *Peggy Benſon.*

He follow'd her through thick and thin
   Sing *Willy Scotſon,*
But gain not yet becaufe his weell
   To pretty *Peggy Benſon.*

But once upon a Summer day
   Sing *Willy Scotſon,*
He gang'd abroad a making hay
   with pretty *Peggy Benſon.*

Be blith and bonny was that day
   Sing *Willy Scotſon,*
Caufe it might wanton in the hay
   with pretty *Peggy Benſon.*

Quo he, did Lafs the liggethe down
   Sing *Willy Scotſon,*
An 'thout delay impelling thy green gown,
   my pretty *Peggy Benſon.*

He haftly ranne off the rauge
   Sing *Willy Scotſon,*
Then liggs and woont and fayt me too
   Quo pretty *Peggy Benſon.*

Quo the Lad, life tell thee what
   Sing *Willy Scotſon,*
He aw gang hame, and fetch my Clark
   for pretty *Peggy Benſon.*

He turnt home, and came agen
   Sing *Willy Scotſon,*
But he found a Miller on her term
   By fthat *Peggy Benſon.*

He thinks this Clark had been ith fire
   Sing *Willy Scotſon,*
Sen he banifht his wearie befire
   And pretty *Peggy Benſon.*

She bade him come another day
   Sing *Willy Scotſon,*
She left himfelf and the cloup
   O naughty *Peggy Benſon.*

Printed for P. Brooksby in weft-finithfield.

A TRAGICAL BALLAD
OF THE UNFORTUNATE LOVE'S

LORD THOMAS
AND
FAIR ELEANOR

LORD Thomas he was a bold forrefter,
And a chaser of the King's Deer,
Fair Eleanor was a fine woman,
And Lord Thomas he loved her dear.

Come riddle my riddle dear mother, he said,
And riddle us both in one.
Whether I shall marry with fair Eleanor,
And let the Brown Girl alone.

The brown Girl she has got money,
Fair Eleanor she has got none,
Therefore I charge thee on my blessing,
Bring me the crown Girl home.

And as it betel on a holiday,
As many more do beside,
Lord Thomas he went to fair Eleanor,
That should have been his bride.

But when he came to fair Eleanor's bower,
He knocked at the ring,
Then who was fo ready as fair Eleanor,
To let Lord Thomas in.

What news, what news, Lord Thomas she faid
What news, haft thou brought unto me,
I am come to bid thee to my wedding,
And that is fad news for thee.

O God forbid I Lord Thomas she faid,
That fuch a thing ever fhould be done,
I thought to have been the bride myfelf,
And thou to have been the bridegroom.

Come riddle thy riddle, dear mother she faid,
And riddle it all in one,
Whether I fhall go to Lord Thomas's wedding
Or whether I fhall let it alone.

There's many that are our friends daughter,
And many that are our foes,
Therefore I charge thee on my blessing,
To Lord Thomas's wedding don't go.

There's many that are our friends, mother,
It's thoufand were our foes,
Betide me life, betide me death,
To Lord Thomas, don't go.

She cloathed herfelf in gallant attire,
And her merry men all was dreft.

And as fhe rode through every place,
They took her to be fome Queen.

When fhe came to Lord Thomas's gate,
She knocked at the ring,
And who was fo ready as Lord Thomas,
O let fair Eleanor in.

He took her by the lilly white hand,
And led her through the hall,
And he fat her in the nobleft chair,
Amongft the Lady's all.

As this your bride fair Eleanor faid,
Methink fhe looks wond'rous brown,
Thou might'ft have had as fair a woman,
As ever trod upon the ground.

Defpife her not, Lord Thomas he faid.
Defpife her not unto me,
For better I love thy little finger,
Then all her whole body

This Brown Girl had a little penknife,
Which was Both keen and fharp,
And betwixt the fhort ribs and the long,
She prick'd fair Eleanor to the heart.

O Chrift now fave me, Lord Thomas he faid,
Methinks thou look wond'rous van,
Thou ufed'ft to look as good a colour,
As ever the fun fhin'd on.

O art thou blind Lord Thomas fhe faid,
Or can ft thou not very well fee,
O doft thou not fee my own heart's blood,
Runs trickling down my knee.

O dig my grave Lord Thomas reply'd,
Dig it both wide and deep,
And lay fair Eleanor by my fide,
And the Brown Girl at my feet.

Lore Thomas he had a fword by his fide,
As he walk'd about the hall
He cut his brides head from off her fhoulders,
And flung it againft the wall.

He fet his fword upon the ground,
And the point againft his heart,
There never was three lovers fure,
That fooner did depart.

Printed and sold by J. Pitts, 6, Great St. An
drew-street, seven-Dials.

The UNHAPPY MEMORABLE SONG of the

HUNTING OF

Chevy Chace.

Howard & Evans, Printers, No. 42, Long-
lane, Wel.Smithfield, London.

1856.

THE

Juſt Judgment of GOD ſhew'd upon Dr. John Fauſtus.

To the Tune of, *Fortune my Foe*, &c.

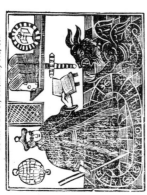

ALL Chriſtian Men give Ear a while to me,
How I am plung'd in Pain, but cannot ſee:
I liv'd a Life, the like did none before,
Forſaking Chriſt, and I am damn'd therefore.

At *Wertemburgh*, a Town in *Germany*,
There was I born and bred of good Degree,
Of honeſt Stock, which afterwards I ſham'd,
Accurſt therefore, for *Fauſtus* was I nam'd.

In learning high my Uncle brought up me,
And made me Doctor of Divinity:
And when he dy'd he left me all his Wealth,
Which curſed Gold did hinder my Soul's Health.

Then did I ſhun the Holy Bible Book,
Nor on God's Word would never after look;
But ſtudied the accurſed Conjuration,
Which was the Cauſe of my utter Damnation.

The Devil in Frye's Woods appeared to me,
And ſtraight to my Requeſt he did agree,
That I might have all Things at my Defire,
I gave him Soul and Body for his Hire.

Twice did I make my tender Fleſh to bleed,
Twice with my Blood I wrote the Devil's Deed,
Twice wretchedly I Soul and Body fold,
To live in Pleaſure, and do what Things I would.

For four and twenty Years this Bond was made,
And then at length my Soul for it was paid;
Time ran away, and yet I never thought,
How dear my Soul our Saviour Chriſt had bought.

Would I at firſt been made a Beaſt by Kind,
Then had not I ſo vainly ſet my Mind;
Or would not when Reaſon began to bloom,
Some darkſome Den had been my deadly Tomb.

Wo to the Day of my Nativity!
Wo to the Time that once did foſter me!
And wo unto the Hand that fealed the Bill!
Wo to myſelf the Cauſe of all my Ill!

The Time I paſſ'd away with much Delight,
'Mongſt Princes, Peers, and many a worthy Knight,
I wrought ſuch Wonders by my Magick Skill,
That all the World may talk of *Fauſtus* ſtill.

The Devil carried me up in the Skie,
Where I did ſee how all the World did lie:
I went about the World in eight Days' Space,
And then return'd into my native Place.

What Pleaſure I did wiſh to pleaſe my Mind,
He did perform, as Bond and Seal did bind:
The Secrets of the Stars and Planets told,
Of Earth and Sea, with Wonders manifold.

When four and twenty Years was almoſt run,
I thought on Things that then was paſt and done;
How that the Devil will ſoon claim his Right,
And carry me to everlaſting Night.

Then all too late I curſt my wicked Deed,
The Dread thereof docs make my Heart to bleed:
All Days and Hours I mourned wond'rous ſore,
Repenting then of all Things done before.

I then did wiſh both Sun and Moon to ſtay,
All Times and Seaſons never to decay:
Then had my Time ne'er come to dated End,
Nor Soul and Body down to Hell defcend.

At laſt when I had but one Hour to come,
I turn'd the Glaſs for my laſt Hour to run:
And call'd in learned Men to comfort me,
But Faith was gone, and none could ſuccour me.

By Twelve o'Clock my Glaſs was almoſt out,
My grieved Confcience then began to doubt:
I pray'd the Studious to ſtay in Chamber by,
But as they ſtaid they heard a doleful cry.

Then preſently they came into the Hall,
Whereas my Brains were caſt againſt the Wall:
Both Arms and Legs in Pieces they did fee,
My Bowels gone, there was an End of me.

You Conjurors and damned Witches all,
Example take by my unhappy Fall!
Give not your Souls and Bodies unto Hell,
See that the ſmalleſt Hair you do not fell.

But hope in Chriſt his Kingdom you may gain,
Where you ſhall never fear ſuch mortal Pain;
Forſike the Devil and all his crafty Ways,
Embrace true Faith that never more decays.

F I N I S.

The WANDERING JEW;

Or, The Shoemaker of JERUSALEM.

Who lived when Our Saviour JESUS CHRIST was Crucified, and by him appointed to Wander till his Coming Again.

WHEN as in fair Jerusalem,
And Our Saviour Christ did live;
His own dear life did give.
The wicked Jews with scoffs and scorns,
Did daily him molest;
That never till he left his life,
Our Saviour could have rest.
Repent therefore, Old England,
Repent while you have space,
And do not like the wicked Jews,
Despise God's profferd Grace.
When they had crown'd his head with thorns,
In sorrowful sort they led him forth

Upon a street, the which a wretch
Did charitably control
And said, Away thou King of Jews,
You shall not rest you here;
Pass on your execution place
You lose now draweth near.
And thereupon he thrust him thence,
At which our Saviour said,
I sure will rest, but thou shalt walk
And have no Journey stay'd
With that this cursed Shoemaker,
For offering Christ this Wrong,
Left Wife and Children, house and all,
And went from thence along.
So when he had the precious blood
Of Jesus Christ thus shed,
And to the cross his body nail'd,
Away with speed he fled,
Without returning back again.
Unt his dwelling place,
And Wandereth up and down the World,
A renegade most base.
No resting could he find at all,
Nor eate nor heart's content,
Ne house, nor home, nor dwelling place,
But wandering forth he went
From Town to Town in foreign lands,
With grieved conscience still,
repenting for the heinous guilt
Of his forepassed ill.
Thus after some ages past,
With Wandering up and down,
He once again desired to see
Jerusalem's fair Town.
But finding it was quite destroy'd,
He Wandered full of Woe,
Our Saviour's Words which he had spoke
To verify and shew.
I'll refusal be, but thou shalt walk,
So doth the Wandering JEW,
From place to place, but cannot stay,
For seeing countries new.
Declaring still the power of him,
Where'er he comes or goes,
And all things done in the East,
Since Christ's death he doth shew.
The world he still doth compass round,
Who hearing of the name of Christ,
Their idol Gods do change.
To whom he hath told wondrous things,

Of time, how past and gone,
And to the princes of the World
Declar'd his cause of Moan.
Desiring still to be dissolv'd,
And yield his mortal Breath;
But as the Lord had thus decreed,
He must not yet see Death.
For neither looks he young or old,
But as he did those times,
When Christ did suffer on the Cross
For mortal sinners crimes
He passed many foreign lands,
Arabia, Egypt, Africa,
Greece, Syria, and Greet Thrace,
And quite thro' Hungara,
Where Paul and Peter preach'd Christ,
Those blest Apostles dear,
Where he hath told our Saviours words,
In the countries far and near,
And lately in Bohemia,
With many a German town;
And now in Flanders as 'tis thought,
He wandereth up and down.
Where learned Men with him confer,
Of those his lingering days,
And wonder much to hear him tell
His journies and his ways,
If people give this Jew an alms,
The most that he will take,
Is not above a great a day,
With which for Jesus sake,
Doth kindly give unto the poor,
And therefore make no spare;
Affirming still that Jesus Christ
Of him hath daily care;
He was not seen to laugh or smile,
But Weep and make great moan.
Lamenting still his Miseries,
And Days far spent and gone.
If he hears any one blaspheme,
Or takes God's name in vain,
He tells them that they crucify
Their Saviour Christ again.
If thou hadst seen grim Death said be,
As these my eyes have done.
Ten thousand thousand times would ye,
His torments thinks upon.
And suffer for his sake all pains,
All torments and all woes :
These are his Words, and this his life
Where'er he comes or goes.

JOCKEY's Escape from bonny *Dundee.*

To it's own proper Tune.

W⁷Here got thou the Haver-meal Bannock?
Blind Bubby, can't thou not see?
I got them out of a *Scotch* Man's Wallat,
As he lay Easing under a Tree.
Come fill up my Cap, come fill up my Can,
Come Saddle my Horse, and call up my Man,
Come open the Gates, and let me go free,
And show me the Way to bonny Dundee.

For I have neither rob'd nor stolen,
Nor have I done any Injury,
But I have got a fair Maid with Bairn,
The Minister's Daughter, of bonny Dundee.
Come fill up my Cap, come fill up my Can,
Come Saddle my Horse, and call up my Man,
Come open the Gates, and let me go free,
And I'se gang na mare to bonny Dundee.

Altho' I've gotten her Maiden-head,
Good tooth I've given her mine in Lieu,
For when at her Daddies I'se gang to Bed,
I'se kiss her without any more ado.

I'se cuddle her close, and give her a Kiss,
Pray tell me now who 'tis the Harm in this?
Then open the Gates and let me go free, -
And I'se gang no more to bonny Dundee.

All *Scotland* ne'er had such a Lass,
So bonny and blyth, as *Jenny* my Dear,
I give her a Gown of Green on the Grass,
But now I no longer muit tarry here.
Then Saddle my Nag that's bonny and gay,
For now, it is Time to go hence away;
Then open the Gates and let me go free,
She's ken me no more in bonny Dundee.

In Liberty still I recon to Reign,
For why I have done no honest Man Wrong,
The Parson may take his Daughter again,
For I'll be a Mammy before it's too long.
And have a young Lad or Lass of my Bread,
For I have done her a general Deed,
Then open the Gate, and let me go free,
For I'se gang no more to bonny Dundee.

Since *Jenny* the fair was willing and kind,
And came to my Arms with right good Will;
A Token of Love I've left her behind,
Thus have I required my Kindness still.
The *Jenny* the fair I often had kiss'd,
Another may reap the Harvest I sow'd,
Then open the Gates, and let me go free,
And I'll never come more to bonny Dundee.

Her Dadd would have me to make her my Bride,
But to have and to hold, I could never endure,
From bonny Dundee this Day I will ride,
It being a Place not safe and secure.
Then *Jenny* farewell, my Joy and my Dear,
With Sword in my Hand the Pallage I'se clear,
Then open the Gates and let me go free,
For I'se gang no more to bonny Dundee.

My Father he is a mukle good Laird,
My Mother a Lady bonny and gay,
Then while I have Strength to h..ndle a Sword,
The Parson's Request I'll never obey.
Then *San'ty,* my Man, be thou of my Mind,
In bonny Dundee we's ne'er be confin'd,
The Gates we will force to set our selves free,
And never come more to bonny Dundee.

Then *Sandy* reply'd, I'll never refuse,
To fight for a Laird so valiant and bold,
While I have a Drop of Blood for to loose,
E're any fickle Lown shall keep me in Hold.
With Sword in my Hand, I'll valiantly stand,
And fight by your side to kill or be kill'd,
For forcing the Gates, and let our selves free,
And to bid adieu to bonny Dundee.

With Sword ready drawn they rode to the Gate,
Where being deny'd an Entrance through,
The Master and Man they fought at that rate,
That some ran away, and others they flew.
Thus *Jockey* the *Laird* and *Sandy* the *Man,*
They valiantly fought as Highlanders can,
In Sight of the *Lown's* they set themselves free,
And so bid adieu to bonny Dundee.

F I N I S

THE FAITHLESS CAPTAIN,
Or Betrayed Virgin.

ALL ye maidens fair I pray while draw near,
It will make your heart bleed when farther I proceed
A victim the truth it has befel,
In London, let me tell,
Blest with a store of wit and beauty bright,
Unto a lady fair she a servant dwelt,
A down right lady in each modest delight,
She had a son we hear who a captain were,
A ship the Burford call'd he did command,
And but was bound, was to India bound,
And he must forsake the English land.
His mother's waiting maid had his heart betray'd,
Of great kindness unto her did treat,
Tho' she was poor, yet he did her adore,
But at length he did her heart's delight
With some rich things he did bestow,
The joyful day we hear appointed were,
For the marriage as you shall understand,
Him they many a share for the maidens fair,
Hard it is for maids to trust mankind,
The right before they married were to be
Ere they the maiden her did doom.
Saying, my heart's delight go with me to-night,
About some business that I must have abode,
Unto a tavern we took the maid straightway,
Her poor innocent maid did think so ill,
There the morning fair it did then appear,
Blest with a store of virtue and delight,
And ever her gentle senses did betray
Finding that her cheeks the charming streams did pour,
My heart's opened in your ... I am tell.

Now my virgin bloom you've cropt too soon,
All joy and pleasure now I bid farewell,
Within do you know the knot was to be ty'd,
For ever undone, now my honour's gone,
I am undone I shall not be deny'd,
To your charming person I have enjoyed,
If I forsake my dear, heaven be aware,
My life ... the sad time ... is today,
The ship that I command, when I leave the land,
May it never more return again.
And my silent tomb I in thy youthful bloom—
Be in the deep and raging main
But first I'll go to sea, wed I married be,
To look after honour and renown
Now my virgin's honour it is gone,
With many vows and oaths from her arose
And on board the ship he soon did steer

The beauteous damsel bright went that same night
And ... unto his cabin the sorrow ...
Her lovely locks of hair white as the silver were,
She cut off that morning bright her knew,
Combed like a sailor bright she went that night
To steer at the rendezvous did go,
Being sail and slim and straight every limb
She was so to your charms, heaven knows best,
The crew at her did gaze, the lieutenant says
Young man have you ever been at sea
No, kind sir reply'd he but desire me
I soon shall become a sailor bold
For I have a mind to go where the showers do blow
She was entered straight to be a second mate
And so bound in little did go
But when the ... her charms did betray,
The captain his true love did not know,
Once upon a day he too love did go?

Mate, thy person doth so much appear,
Just like a love of mine, I think many a time,
When I look on you, I look upon my dear,
She was my mother's maid I her heart betray'd,
Now I have left her thus to grieve about,
I will that she soon may married be,
To some other man, were my mind ...
This was a piercing dart to her tender heart,
With a deep sigh she from him turn'd away,
Enough to ... she said on the purl'd ...
Who crush'd my honour did betray,
Now comes the tragical part enough to pierce a heart
Quick she the blood did pour around,
This cut her bosom almost in twain,
The ship's crew we hear did love her most dear,
Began to look quite thick about the waist,
Forty ... from her eyes came on so fair,
She trembling to the captain then did come,
He said, I plainly see, madam, who you be,
At his feet she then fell immediately,
And said, do not lie so me severe
For my distress my dearest dear,
You have been you know my real sweet-throw,
But since it is so, soon pay to me show,
Favour a poor ill toward one ... here
Soon as the maiden he did say,
So poor of this matter you let know,
Soon as she can get sight of steel.
Prettily he thought her for love he knew
So said, my dearest dear be not so severe,
Call to mind the oaths you made to me,
The night before we married were to be
Do not from me part, in this wild desert,
Freely I'll comply this moment to die,
So let me now love by, you be slain
Earnestly upon her as she reply'd,
He unto her did say and made their grave,
I cannot cruel be to such constancy,
But to your charms, heaven knows best
We are far from home now the billow roar
... danger do me fear
Then had me tell what has befel
And will be married upon the sea,
... maid the news
But as we hear they married were
Life in sporting light did appear

Yet fortune at we find, to them proves unkind
Those unhappy lovers to divide,
As night came were by his loving fair,
The winds blew high and dreadful storms air
all hands aloft they run, all dangers for to shun,
While the swelling bosom of the sea,
Tore them mountains high they for help did cry
To the Lord in their extremity
At last the dreadful rock they received a shock
Expecting every moment for to die
The women on the deck she came among the rest
In the hurry ever board o'er fell
The ... ploy'd dear to save their lives
No one could see her but she was her grave
A tragical story to her I ... to tell,
The powers did decree she arrived should not be
For this happiness they thanked kind heaven
The captain cry'd where is my lovely bride
Having searched no one could see
For oh unlucky day she was cast away
At that the swelling billows beat more bitterly
No rest he could take but sat on the beach,
Earnestly of heaven he did implore,
That her corpse he might see floating on the sea
To gaze upon her he did pray
When two days were past he found her at last
Her body floating upon the main
O Neptune kind said he then to favour me
With a ... upon her again
Now I see her dear I'll go to my dear
Like a Leander here, I'll go my dear
Ever more before her arms to sleep
it was on the ... the she slumber'd in the deep
A silent tomb in the silent deep
Her love in realities I will share her fate
And upon the same watery billow she
Mr promise I perform this unhappy morn
I, So instantly he leaped into the sea,
Many of them were there
When too true it was his fatal hour
For the swelling wave did become his grave
I this ... of honour and renown
With a cold ... he went down
Oh young virgins do not make game
Keep your vows and oaths as you propose
Then happy blessings will attend the same.

J. Pitts, Printer, Wholesale Toy and Marble Ware-house, 6, Great St. Andrew street, 7 dials

DEATH and the LADY;
Or the Great Messenger of Mortality.

DEATH.

FAIR lady, lay your costly robes aside,
No longer may you glory in your pride;
Take leave of all your carnal vain delights,
I am come to summon you away this night !!!

LADY.

What bold attempt is this ? pray let me know,
From whence you come, or whither I must go?
Must I, who am a lady, stoop and bow,
To such a pale-fac'd visage,—who art thou ?—

DEATH.

Do not you know me ?—well, I tell you then,
It's I that conquer all the sons of men !
No pitch of honour from my dart is free,
My name is DEATH ! have you not heard of me ?—

LADY.

Yes I have heard of you time after time,
But being in the glory of my prime,
I did not think you would have call'd so soon,
Why must my morning sun go down at noon ?—

DEATH.

Talk not of noon, you may as well be mute,
This is not time at all for to dispute;
Your riches, jewels, gold, and garments brave,

Houses and lands must all new masters have,
Tho' thy vain heart to riches was inclin'd,
Yet thou must die and leave them all behind.

LADY.

My heart is cold, I tremble at the news,
Here's bags of gold, if thou wilt me excuse,
And seize on them, and finish thou the strife,
Of those that are a weary of their life :—
Are there not many bound in prison strong,
In bitter grief of soul have languish'd long,
And fain would find a grave, a place of rest,
From all their grief in which they are opprest ?
Besides, there's many with their hoary head,
And palsy joints, by which their joys are fled ;
Release thou them, whose sorrows are so great,
And spare my life to have a longer date ?

DEATH.

Tho' they by age are full of grief and pain,
Yet their appointed time they must remain ;
I come to none before my warrant's seal'd,
And when it is they must submit and yield;
I take no bribe, believe me this is true,
Prepare yourself to go, I come for you !

LADY.

Death, be not so severe, let me obtain,
A little longer time to live and reign ?
Fain would I stay, if thou my life will spare,
I have a daughter beautiful and fair,
I'd live to see her wed whom I adore,
Grant me but this, and I will ask no more ?—

DEATH.

This is a slender, frivolous excuse,
I have you fast, and will not let you loose,
Leave her to providence, for you must go
Along with me, whether you will or no.
I, death command kings for to leave their crowns,
And at my feet they lay their sceptre down !

If unto kings this favour I don't give,
But cut them off, can you expect to live,
Beyond the limits of your time and space ?—
No; I must send you to another place.

LADY.

You learned doctors now express your skill,
And let not death of me obtain his will ;
Prepare your cordials, let me comfort find,
My gold shall fly like chaff before the wind !

DEATH.

Forbear to call, their skill will never do,
They are but mortals here as well as you ;
I give the fatal wound, my dart is sure,
And far beyond the doctor's skill to cure !
How freely can you let your riches fly,
To purchase life, rather than yield to die !—
But while you flourish'd here in all your store,
You would not give one penny to the poor,
Tho' in God's name, their suit to you did make,
You would not spare one penny for his sake !
The Lord beheld wherein you did amiss,
And calls you hence to give account for this !!

LADY.

Oh ! heavy news ! must I no longer stay ?
How shall I stand at the great judgement day ?
Then from her eyes the chrystal tears did flow,
She said none knows what I do undergo :
Upon a bed of sorrow here I lie,
My carnal life makes me afraid to die !
My sins, alas ! are many, gross, and foul,
O righteous Lord, have mercy on my soul !
And tho' I do deserve thy righteous frown,
Yet pardon, Lord, and pour a blessing down :—
Then with a dying sigh her heart did break,
And did the pleasures of this world forsake ! !

Thus do we see the high and mighty fall,
For cruel death shews no respect at all ;
To any one of high or low degree,
Great men submit to death as well as we :
Tho' they are gay their lives are but a span,
A lump of clay, so vile a creature's man !
Then happy those whom Christ has made his care,
Die in the Lord, and then they blessed are.

[Printed by J. Turner, High Street, Coventry.

The Bloody Gardener's
CRUELTY,

SHEWING HOW THE

MOTHER

OF A

Young Nobleman

BRIBED THE

GARDENER

TO COMMIT

MURDER

ON A

Young Shepherdess.

BECAUSE

HER SON

HAD FELL IN LOVE

WITH HER

And she wished them not to be

MARRIED.

THE GARDENER

Found out, and afterwards

Hung in Chains.

Come all you constant lovers, & to me lend an ear
And mind this sad relation which I do give here,
'Tis of a maiden fair,
A shepherd's daughter dear,
But love did prove her utter overthrow.

She was of beauteous mould, fair and clear to behold,
And by a noble Lord she courted were,
But was too young we find,
As yet fond love to mind,
Yet little Cupid did her heart ensnare.

His parents they were all of high degree,
They said she is no match at all for thee,
If you'll a blessing have,
Grant us but what we crave,
And wed with none but whom we shall agree.

Dear son we have for you a chosen bride,
With store of gold and beautiful beside,
Of a temper kind and free,
She is the girl for thee,
But not a shepherd's daughter of mean degree.

And if by us you'll not be ruled or led,
You from our presence shall be banished,
No more we will you own,
To be our only son,
Then let our will be done to end the strife.

Madam, said he, if a begging I should go,
I should be contented so to do,
If that I could but have,
The girl that I do crave,
No curs'd gold shall part my love and me.

Was she as poor as Job, and I of royal robe,
And lord of all the globe, she should be mine,
His mother said in scorn,
Thou art most nobly born,
And with a beggar's brat shall never join.

He hearing his mother to say so;
His eyes them with tears like fountains flow,
Saying a promise I have made,
And her beauty betray'd,
Therefore no other for my bride I chuse.

A cruel snare then for her life she laid,
And then for to act this thing, O then she did,
With her gard'ner she agreed,
To do the bloody deed,
And butcher her forthwith and dig her grave.

To the gardener she gave four score pounds
To murder her and lay her under ground,
All in a grave so deep,
In everlasting sleep,
Hoping her fair body would not be found.

She wrote a letter and sent it with speed,
Saying, my dearest, with haste now proceed,
Meet me this night I pray,
I've something to say,
Poor girl she little thought upon the deed.

The youthful shepherdess of this nothing knew,
But went to seek her true love as she us'd to do,
She search'd the garden round,
But no true love she found,
At length the bloody gardener did appear.

What business have you here, madam, I pray?
Are you come here to rob the garden gay?
Cries she, no thief I am,
To meet my love I'm come,
Which did this night appoint to meet me here.

He spoke no more but straight a knife he took,
And pierc'd her heart before one word he spoke,
Then on the ground she fell,
Crying sweet love farewell,
O welcome Death, thy fatal stroke.

Was this done now my dear by your design,
Or by your cruel parents most unkind,
My life is thus betray'd,
Farewell vain world she said,
I hope in heaven I a place shall find.

But when he saw her life was really gone,
Immediately he laid her in the ground,
With flowers fine and gay,
Her corpse did overlay,
Intending that her body should not be found.

Now all the time this Lord he little knew,
But went to meet his love as he used t.
He search'd the vallies round,
But no true love he found,
The little lambs were wandering to and fro.

Lamenting greatly for his shepherdess,
Then he did lay him down upon the grass
The heavens he did implore,
To see his love once more,
O then ye Gods above I'm sure,

O whither shall I seek that angel bright,
Who is alone my pleasure and delight,

Pray if alive she be,
Let me my true love see,
Or el e my soul will quickly take its flight.

Whereas the woods and groves began to mourn,
The small birds they did sing a mournful tune,
Crying your love is gone,
And left you quite alone,
Then on a mossy bank he laid him down.

He had no sooner clos'd his eyes to sleep,
But a milk white dove came to his breast,
Her fluttering wing did beat,
Which wak'd him out of sleep;
And then the dove took wing and he was blest.

To his mother's garden he did repair,
For to bemoan the loss of his dear,
Here once more the dove he see,
Sitting on a myrtle tree.
With drooping wings she did disconsolate appear.

O dove, disconsolate, why do you come?
Have you lost your love as I have done,
Then you dodge me here,
No comfort can I bear,
Then thus the dove replied, and then flew down.

Saying it was your mother ordered it so,
That from her milk-white breast her blood did flow
To the grave he did repair,
But found no true love there.
Homeward then to his mother he did go.

I fear you have kill'd my joy and only dear,
He said, mother most cruel and severe,
For a dove a dove I do declare,
Did all in blood appear,
And said if she is dead her fate I'll share.

His mother hearing what the son did say,
She turn'd as pale as death and swoon'd away,
Then into destraction ran,
And told him what she had done,
And where the virgin's body it then lay.

He said no more but straight took a knife,
And said, now farewell to the comforts of life,
Then into the garden he flew,
And pierc'd his body through,
And said it was curs'd gold that caus'd all this strife

These two lovers is one tomb were laid,
And many a briny tear for them was shed,
And the gard'ner as we hear,
Was apprehended then,
And hung in chains for being so severe.

Printed by T. Bloomer, 53; Edgbaston Street.

REASON;

OR, THE

Unwilling MAID

AND

Amorous SQUIRE.

A new Song

YOUNG Virgins attend, believe me your
friend,
And do not refuse to hear Reafon ;
Ten guineas was offer'd me, twety was prof-
fered me,
If I would but hearken to Reafon.
Fol lol de lol, &c.

My fpark he came in, with a fmile and a grin,
And argu'd, but 'twas not the Seafon
For me to comply, fo I did deny,
But I wifh I'd comply'd with his Reafon.

He gave me a bufs, and he pull'd out his purfe,
And told me he'd marry in feafon ;
If I would comply, and not him deny,
But liften a while to his Reafon.

I could hardly deny, yet afraid to comply,
For fear of fomething elfe in feafon,
Should make me look big, likewife hop the twig,
For liftening too much to his Reafon.

But I vow and declare I never will fear
'Of any thing's coming in feafon ;
Come well, or come ill, for twenty guineas ftill,
I always will hearken to Reafon.
Fol lol de lol, &c.

THE

Beaver's Prize.

By a Lad of Yarmouth, fourteen Years of Age,
who was on board the PRIZE during the
Engagement off Flamborough Head.

YE brave Britifh youth if to fame you would rife,
Your fortunes come try in the bold Beaver's Prize
With five fcore brave feamen and fourteen carriage guns
Soon as we appear fee the enemy runs.
CHORUS.
Of us they turn tail, afraid for to fight,
Whilft Britons purfue them,
Far as we can view them,
And the cowardly dogs are preferv'd by their flight.

Off Flamborough Head as our courfe we did fteer,
A fignal was made for an enemy near,
We perceived them to be two French privateers,
And for an engagement we ftrait did prepare.
With courage refolv'd to fight both as one,
We being all fteady,
For fighting, Boys, ready,
But they run away ere we fcarce had begun.

They had twenty guns each, and men thirteen fcore,
And with them a Brig they had ta'en juft before,
Which we foon did retake, and on board did find,
Six French Men the cowardly dogs left behind,

Such Britons courageous our annals have prais'd,
Of heroes contending,
Their country defending,
From fame's noble lords let it not be aras'd.

In a day or two after we chas'd them again,
They being far off, it proved in vain ;
For as foon as they faw us away they did run,
Not giving us time to fire one Gun.
But we hope ere 'tis long to meet them once more,
together uniting,
And ready for fighting,
We will not give them leave to run as before.

Come fill up your glaffes, our Captain's the toaft,
Sure one more courageous England never could boaft,
With heroic ardor he dares the proud foe,
Impatient to meet them does chearfully go.
Example for us, who his orders fullfil,
We ne'er think of flying,
But of conqueft or dying,
When the foe we purfue with a hearty good will.

Next to him our Lieutenant of courage fo bold,
Whofe heart pants for glory as mifers for gold ;
And then to our bold Britifh feamen a glafs,
Their valour unnotic'd fure never can pafs.

But let us in praife of their bravery fing,
Who never refufes,
With idle excufes,
To venture their lives for their country and king.

William far Away.

A New SONG.

[Sold at No. 4e, *Long Lane.*]

I'VE loft my dear William, and well I
    may defpair,
For his prefence would footh me from each
    anxious care,
My fighs fhall fill the lazy fails, and fwift
    him back convey,
Ah! what can *I* do now, fweet William's
    far away.

The lads of our village all hail'd me their
    queen,
My beauty proclaim'd me the toaft of the
    green
But grief has ftole the opening rofe which
    in my cheeks did play,
Too fatally, alas! I love, my William far
    away.

Ah! fortune, unrelenting, you fwell the
    mifer's ftore,
And ftill your fmile refufing to thofe who
    love adore,
Adieu delufive dreams of hope, I'll feek my
    native clay,
Bleed, bleed my poor bofom, for William's
    far away.

THE

BEGGAR.

Printed for and sold by J. Pitts, No. 14, Great
Saint Andrew Street, Seven Dials.

OF all the trades in London,
    A beggar is the best,
For when he is tired,
    He can sit him down and rest.

CHORUS.

With his whim, wham way a low, way a low
    His Jack staff stay a low,
Lillies be the baby O,
    Lo! bonny was the bloom,

He's a bag for his wheat,
    Another for his rye,
And a little bottle by his side,
    To drink when he is dry.

He's a bag for his oatmeal,
    And another for his salt,
And a little pair of crutches,
    To see how he can halt.

And if you go to Pimlico,
    The lasses you will see,
With every lad a glass in hand,
    And a lass upon his knee.

If any man refuses,
    To lend us half a crown,
When we are in need,
    Why d—n him knock him down.

MANTZ, FINSBURY.

The Belfast
Mountains

Pitts Printer andToy Warehouse, 6, Great
st Andrewstreet 7 dials

'TWAS on the Belfast Mountains,
  I heard a maid complain,
Making a lamentation
  Down by a purling stream,
She said I am confined,
  All in the bands of love,
All by a false pretender,
  That does inconstant prove

O Johnny my dear jewel,
  Don't treat me with disdain,
Nor leave me here behind me,
  In sorrow to complain,
His arms he clasp'd around me,
  Like violets round the vine
his bonny Irish laddie,
  Has stole this heart of mine.

Had I but all the diamonds,
  That on the rocks do grow,
I'd give it to my Irish laddie,
  If he to me his love would shew,
Wringing her hands and crying
  O Johnny dear farewell,
To yon Belfast Mountains.
  My sorrows I will tell,

'Tis not Belfast Mountains,
  Can give to me relief,
Nor is it in their power,
  To ease me of my grief,
Had they but a tongue to prattle
  Or tell me a loving tale,
To my bonny Irish laddie,
  My mind I would reveal

Cold Winter is
PAST.

Pitts printer. wholesale Toy and Marble ware
house, 5, Great st Andrew street 7 dials,

COLD Winter is past,
  Pleasant summer come at last,
And small birds on every green tree,
  The hearts of those are glad,
  While mine is very sad,
For my truelove is absent from me.
I should not think it strange,
The wide world to range
If I could but find my delight,
  But here in Cupid's chains,
  I am forced to remain,
And in sorrow to spend the whole night,
I'll comb back my hair,
And my livery I'll wear,
I'll dress myself in velvet so green
  All things I'll undertake.
  For my truelove's sake,
While he rides in the borough of Kildare
I'll put on a suit of black,
With a fringe about my neck
And gold rings on my fingers I'll wear
  Straightway I will repair,
  To the borough of Kildare,
And there I'll get a fight of my dear.
With patience I did wait,
While he rode for the plate,
Expecting young Johnson to see,
  But fortune proved unkind,
  To that darling of mine,
And he's sent to the Loughens for me,
My love is like the sun,
That in the firmament does run,
Which always prove constant and true
  But yours is like the moon.
  Which wanders up and down
And every month it is new,
Farewell my joy and heart,
Since you and I must part,
You are the finest Lad that e'er I see,
  I never do design,
  To alter my mind,
Altho' you are below my degree.

THE

MAIDEN'S
BANTAM COCK.

There was a farmer's daughter, she lived in Hertfordshire,
She was wild and rakish, but she was young and fair;
Geese and ducks she'd plenty, and hens a tidy stock, [cock.
But what she stood in want of most was a brisk and lively

CHORUS.

Of all the pretty birds that fly, the best in all the stock,
To keep a maid in exercise, is a brisk and crowing cock.

Says she "I can't wake in a morn, I don't know what to do,
I have no clock to tell the hour, nor yet a cock to crow;
I mean to go to market, I'll sell my shawl and smock,
But I will have some money to buy a crowing cock!

"Father's timepiece will not go, and mother does declare,
The weights run down the pendulum, and has been many
    a year:
I feel so queer, I can't tell how, and stupid as a block—
I shall go mad, and silly too, if I can't get a crowing cock!"

Away she went to market and a handsome cock did buy,
With comb so red, and wings so black, to please a maiden's
    eye,
And as she trotted home again the men around did flock,
And prais'd the size and beauty of this maiden's pretty cock.

Young William met her by the wood, and caught her in
    his arms,   [alarms;
And swore that he would shield her, and keep her from
Then he kissed her cherry lips—she started with a shock!—
"Through teazing me and squeezing me you've spoil'd my
    pretty cock!"

She gazed upon her pretty cock, and stroked it with her
    hand,   [couldn't stand!—
Its feathers ruffled, its head hung down, poor thing, it
"Oh! William, what shall I do, 'twas the best in all the
    stock?   [my poor cock!"
With your rough pranks and wicked tricks you have ruin'd

"Oh, never fear!" young William said, "nor put yourself
    in pain,
If you nourish it and coax it well, it's sure to mend again."
Then up it rose and shook its wings, it beat both dial and
    clock,   [cock.
And waked this maiden every morn, 'twas such a crowing

650.

Vilikins
And His Dinah

Oh! 'tis of a rich merchant, in London did dwell,
He had but one daughter, an uncommon nice young gal,
Her name it was Dinah—scarce sixteen years old,
She had a large fortune in silver and gold.
    Singing—Too-ral-loo, &c.

As Dinah vas valking, in the garden vun day,
    Spoken—The front garden
Her papa came to her, and thus to her did say:—
Go and dress yourself, Dinah, in gor-ge-ous array,
    Spoken—Take your hair out of paper.
And I'll get you a husband, both vally-ant and gay!
    Singing—Too-ral loo, &c.

    Spoken—This is what the infant progeny said to the
    author of her being.

Oh, papa! oh, papa! I've not made up my mind,
To marry just yet, I do not feel inclin'd:
And all my large fortue I'll gladly give o'er,
If you'll let me stay single a year or two more.
    Singing—Too-ral-loo, &c.

    This is what the indignant parient replied,—I repeat the
    father.

Go, boldest daughter, the parient replied,
If you don't consent to be this here young man's bride,
I'll give your large fortune to the nearest o'kin,
And you shan't have the benefit of one single pin,
    Singing—Too-ral-loo, &c.

    Chorus of indignant parients,—very bass,—Too-ral loo.

    Spoken—Now comes the epiflabber-gas trimum of the
    lover.

As Vilikin's was a valking the garden around,
    Spoken—The aforesaid front garden.
He espied his dear Dinah, lying dead upon the ground,
A cup of cold pison it lied by her side,
And a Billy Dux, stating 'twas by poison she died!
    Taken inwardly, Singing—Too-ral-loo, &c.

    Spoken—This is what the lovier did.

Then he kiss'd her cold corps, a thousand times o'er,
He call'd her is dear Dinah—although she was no more!
He swallow'd the pison, like a lover so brave—
And Vilikin's and his Dinah, lies buried in one grave!
    Both on 'em, Singing—Too-ral-loo, &c.

    MORAL.

Now all you young vimmens, take a varning and nor
Never by no means disobey your guv'ne ;   [on.
And all you young feilers, mind who you clapt your eyes
Think of Vilikin's and his Dinah, and the cup of cold pison.
    Else you'll be singing—Too-ral-loo, &c.

Chanting Benny,

OR THE

BATCH OF BALLADS.

When quite a babe my parents said,
  As how I'd got a woice, sir.
They would not give me not no trade,
  So singing I took for choice, sir.
All other chanter's I outshine,
  In fact I'm localist sir,
And since I've been out in the line,
  I'm a regular vocalist, sir.

CHORUS

  So listen to me while I cry,
    Songs three yards a penny,
  Then if you feel inclin'd to buy,
    Encourage chanting Benny.

Come give me this, and give me that,
  I'm ask'd by many a don, sir.
As if they thought each stupid flat,
  Could sing them all at once, sir,
My songs have had a tidy run,
  I've plenty in my fist, sir,
And if you like to pick out one,
  I'll jist run through my list, sir.

Here you see my daughter Fan,
  She wore a wreath of roses,
Here you see my son Tom,
  The sun what lights the roses.
Green grows the rushes O,
  On the banks of Allan water,
Sich a getting up stairs,
  With brave Lord Ullin's daughter.

Poor Bessy was a Sailor's bride,
  Sitting on a rail, sir,
Is there a heart that never lov'd,
  The rose of Allandale, sir,
The maid of Judah, out of place
  With plenty to be savat,
I say my rum'un who are you,
  What a dreadful shocking bad hat.

Here's Molly Dodd and I fell out,
  Going to the Nore, sir,
Here's Barney Bralleghan too,
  At Judy Callagghan's door, sir,

Come let us dance and sing,
  Mr. and Mrs. Wrangle,
My dearest Jane, my pretty Jane,
  Has your mother sold her mangle?

Here's Dolly the dancing dairy maid,
  In the harbour taking tea sir,
And here you see the nice young gal,
  Under the walnut tree sir,
Adam was a gentleman,
  Him what was the first man,
And here you find lost Rosabel,
  With the little hairy dustman.

Here you see the handsome man,
  With the pretty little dear sir,
Its all very fine Mr. Ferguson,
  But you really can't sleep here sir,
I want money, never mind,
  Miss Nichols with a thorn sir,
Here's the rose shall cease to blow,
  The merry mountain horn sir.

Not a drum was heard at Paddy's grave
  While the village bells was ringing,
'Twas in the merry month of Ma,
  While I was out a singing,
Why did I love, ax my eye,
  Any green in me do you spy out,
Flare up, sweet lass of Richmond hill,
  There you go with your eye out.

The ladies' man at the garden gate,
  With Giles Scrogging's ghost man,
Salley in our alley, we met,
  With Walker the twopenny postman,
Here's on a washing day,
  We'll die for love and whiskey,
The man wot sweeps the crossings,
  In the bay of Biscay.

No. **38.**

I CANOT MIND MY WHEEL.

Uncle Tom's Cabin.

J. O. Bebbington, Printer, 31, Oldham Road, Manchester, sold by H. Andrews, and J. Beaumont, Leeds.

Air—Jim-along Josey.
There's Uncle Tom's Cabin written by Mrs. Stowe,
Of which the contents you must know ;
If not, I shan't be doing wrong,
To give you some idea in the shape of a song.

Air—Yankee Doodle.
The first I mention'd was a slave, whose face was rather yellow,
Georgy Harris was his name, a noble hearted fellow ;
He had a wife and chubby child, and dearly he did cry sir,
When he came home from work at night, he shouted for Eliza.
But then there was a trading man, he used to traffic daily,
Who drank & smok'd & flew the lash, they call'd him Mr. Haley
Poor uncle Tom too had a wife, and Chloe was her name,
He lov'd her dearly as his life, and she lov'd him the same.
Mr. Shelly used them well, but being short of cash sirs,
Poor uncle Tom was forc'd to sell, or else he'd make a smash sir,
Poor Tom he fell upon his knees, and like a ghost turn'd pale'y,
And as they drag'd him from his home he sang this song to Italy,

Air—Bridal Waltz.
Why did my massa sell me, why did my massa sell me,
Why did my massa sell me, and bear me from my home.

Air—Susannah don t you cry.
Aunt Chloe then began to cry, and turn'd just like a sloe,
And tho' the tears came in Tom's eyes, he could not blubber loud
He strok'd his woolly head to her's, and roll'd his goggle eyes,
He smack'd his sausage lips to hers, saying Chloe don t you cry.
Oh aunt Chloe stop it if you can,
Keep up your spirits, be a brick,
And stand it like a man.

Air—Lucy Long.
When Eliza heard the news, she nearly did run wild.
No sooner then she started, she went off with the child,
She travelled oe'r the ice sirs, up to her neck in snow,
And when she got safe landed, she sung like any crow,
Oh I have saved my picaniny, and now I'm everjoyed,
They may go to Putney on a pig, now I have saved my child.

Air—Boatman's Dance.
Topsy here and Topsy there and Topsy wanted everywhere,
I never had a mother I never had a father,
Never was born so 'spects I grow'd.

Air—Lucy Neal.
The story says I've suffer'd much,
And hardships that they've passed
But like all tales that I've been told,
They meet again at last'
Alive or dead I cannot say,
But our rulers they should roam
Within our courts and alleys,
To see our slaves at home,
And sing that good old strain that Britons rule the waves,
Twould-be-a-blessing to this land to boast we had no slaves.
CHORUS—RULE BRITANNIA.

398

THE POPE HE LEADS A HAPPY LIFE.

The Pope he leads a happy life,
He knows no care of marriage strife,
He drinks the best of Rhenish wine,'
I would the Pope's gay lot were mine ;
But yet all happy's not his life,
He loves no maid, nor wedded wife :
Nor child hath he to cheer his hope—
I would not wish to be a Pope.

The Sultan better pleases me.
He leads a life of jollity,
Has wives as many as he will—
I would the Sultan's throne then fill.
But yet he's not a happy man,
He must obey the Alcoran,
And dares not taste a drop of wine—
I would not that his fate were mine.

So here I take my lowly stand,
I'll drink my own my native land—
I'll kiss my maiden's lips divine,
And drink the best of Rhenish wine ;
And when my maiden kisses me,
I'll fancy I the Sultan be !
And when my cherry glass I tope,
I'll fancy that I am the Pope.

I CANNOT MIND MY WHEEL.

I cannot mind my wheal, Mother,
I cannot mind my wheel ;
You know not what my heart must know,
You feel not what I feel,—
My thread is idly cast, Mother,
My thought is o'er the sea ;
My hopes are fading fast, Mother,
Yet feel you not for me.
I cannot mind my wheel, &c.

I had a dreadful dream, Mother,
'Twas of a ship at sea ;
I saw a form amidst the storm,
I heard him call on me.
I heard him call on me, Mother,
As plain as I now speak,
I thought my brain would burst, Mother,
I thought my heart would break.

For me he perils his life, Mother,
The weary ocean wide,
And yet a word, one word from you,
Had kept him by my side.
My wheel had gaily sped, Mother,
My thoughts at home smil'd free ;
But now my smiles have fled, Mother,
My heart is o'er the sea.

I SHALL BE MARRIED

ON MONDAY MORNING.

As I was walking one morning in spring,
I heard a fair maiden most charmingly sing,
All under her Cow, as she sat a-milking,
Saying, I shall be married, next Monday morning.

You fairest of all creatures, my eyes e'er beheld,
Oh ! where do you live love, or where do you dwell,
I dwell at the top of yon bonny brown hill,
I shall be fifteen years old next Monday morning.

Fifteen years old love, is too young to marry,
The other five years love, I'd have you to tarry,
And perhaps in the mean time love you might be sorry
So put back your wedding, next Monday morning.

You talk like a man without reason or skill,
Five years I've been waiting against my will,
Now, I am resolved my mind to fulfil,
I wish that to-morrow was Monday morning.

On Saturday night it is all my care,
To powder my locks and curl my hair,
And my two pretty maidens to wait on me there,
To dance at my wedding next Monday morning.

My husband will buy me a guinea gold ring,
And at night he'll give me a far better thing,
With two precious jewels he'll be me adorning,
When I am his bride, on Monday morning.

My two pretty maids shall put me to bed,
Then I'll bid adieu to my maidenhead,
And over my true love my legs I will fling,
Good morrow fair maidens, on Tuesday morning.

He leads a happy life.

The Pope he leads a happy life,
He knows no cares of marriage strife,
He drinks the best of Rhenish wine—
I would the Pope's gay lot were mine.
But yet all happy s not his life,
He loves no maid, nor wedded wife ;
Nor child hath he to cheer his hope—
I would not wish to be the Pope.

The Sultan better-pleases me,
He lives a life of jollity,
Has wives as many as he will—
I would the Sultan's throne then fill.
But, yet he's not a happy man;
He must obey the Alcoran,
And dares not taste a drop of wine—
I would not that his fate were mine.

So here I take my lowly stand,
I'll drink my own, my native land—
I'll kiss my maiden's lip divine,
And drink the best of Rhenish wine,
And when my maiden kisses me,
I'll fancy I the Sultan be,
And when my cherry glass I tope,
I'll fancy that I am the Pope.

WILLIAMSON, PRINTER, NEWCASTLE.

[27]

The Banks of
INVERARY.

J. Catnach, Printer, 2, Monmouth-Court, 7 Dials.
Battledores, Primers, &c. Sold very Cheap.
Sold by W. Marshall, Bristol ; Also, by T.
Batchelar, 14, Hackney Road Crescent.

EARLY one summer's morning, along as I
　did pass.
On the banks of Inverary I met a bonny lass,
Her hair hung o'er her shoulders broad, her
　eyes like stars did shine,
On the banks of Inverary I wish'd she had been
　mine.

I did embrace this fair maid, as long as e'er I
　could,
Her hair hung o'er her shoulders broad, just
　like threads of gold,
Her hair hung o'er her shoulders broad, her
　eyes like drops of dew,
On the banks of Inverary I'm glad to meet
　with you.

I pray young man give over embracing of me so.
For after kissing then comes sorrow, after that
　comes woe ;
If my poor heart should be ensnar'd, and I be-
　guil'd by thee,
On the banks of Inverary I am glad you for to
　see.

Some people say, I know you not, but I know
　you, said she,
On the banks of Inverary to flatter maids like
　me.
For once I us'd to flatter maids, but now it must
　not be,
On the banks of Inverary I have ound my wife
　said he.

I put my horn unto my mouth, and blew both
　loud and shrill,
Six of my servant men came out, to wait their
　master's will,
Now, will you not consent, this night, my
　charming maid, said he,
On the banks of Inverary my wedded wife to be?

'll set my love on horseback, on horseback very
　high,　　　　　　　　　　　　　　　　 [delay ;
We'll go unto some parson, without any more
then will sing all sorts of love, until the day I
　die,　　　　　　　　　　　　　　　　 spied.
On the banks of Invarary where first my love I

THE
Constant Lovers.

Printed by J. CATNACH, 2, Monmouth-Court, Dials.

A SAILOR courted a farmer's daughter,
　　That liv'd convenient on the Isle of Man
But mark good people what followed after,
A long time courting against his parents will.
A long time courting, and still discoursing,
All things concerning the ocean wide,
He said my darling, at our next meeting,
If you will consent I'll make you my bride.

Why as for sailors I don't admire,
Because they sail in so many parts,
The more we love them, the more they slight us,
Leave us behind with broken hearts.
Don't you say so, my dearest jewel,
I ne'er intend to serve you so,
I have once more to cross the ocean,
You know my darling I must go.

This news was carried unto his mother,
Before he set his feet on board,
That he was courting a farmer's daughter,
Whose friends and parents doth afford,
One penny portion going to the ocean,
Like one distracted his mother ran, [make her,
If you don't forsake her, and your bride never
I will disown you to be my son.

My mother, he said, you are in a passion,
I'm very sorry you've spoke too late,
Don't you remember your first beginning,
My father married you a servant maid :
Don't you despise her, I mean to rise her,
As my own father with you has done,
So I will take her, and my bride I will make her,
You may disown me to be your son.

But when his love did hear the story,
Away to the ocean she did run,
Saying in you. passion you need not mind it,
For I have had money and you have had none,
Money or not money, you are my lot,
You have my heart and affections still,
So I will take her, and my bride I will make her,
Let my scolding mother say what she will.

So the constant lovers got married, and had an
excellant fat duck for dinner.

SALE

OF

A WIFE.

Come all you lads and lasses gay, and banish care and strife,—In the market-place, a mason did by auction sell his wife;—Thirteen shillings and a penny for the lady, was the sum,—And to see the curious spree some thousands soon did run;—In the market-place, I do declare, its true upon my life,—A mason did, the other day, by auction sell his wife.—This man and wife, good lack-a-day! did often disagree;—For she often pawned her husband's clothes to go upon the spree. So he led her to the market, with a halter, I am told, And there she was, so help my bob, by public auction sold. When the auctioneer began the sale, a jolly farmer cried, Here's five and fourpence half-penny for the mason's lushy bride; A tanner cried out seven and six, and then a butcher said, I'll give you ten and seven pence, beside a bullock's head. She's going, cried the auctioneer, she's going upon my life; Tinkers, cobblers, sailors, will you buy a charming wife? Such fighting, scratching, tearing too, before no one did see, Such roaring, bawling, swearing, O! blow me, it was a spree. At length a rum old cobbler did give a dreadful bawl, Here's thirteen and a penny with my lap-stone and my awl. Thirteen and a penny, when down the hammer dropt, With whiskers, apron, bustle, shawl, stays, petticoat, and——A lushy mason's lady was this blooming damsel gay, She did unto the hammer come upon a market-day; Bakers, butchers, masons, did bid for her, we hear; While a lot of rum old women pitched into the auctioneer. Young men and maids did hallo, while married folks did sneer; They frightened the old cobbler and knocked down the auctioneer. The cobbler took the lady up just like a Scotchman's pack, And the funny mason's lady rode upon the cobbler's back. Some laughed till they bursted, while others were perplexed, But the cobbler bristled up his wife with two big balls of wax. The cobbler sat her on his knee, and joyfully did bawl, While the lady knocked about the seat the lapstone and awl. Then the mason he did sell his wife, as you shall understand, And thirteen and a penny was popt into his hand; He whistled and capered, for to banish care and strife; He went into a gin-shop, singing, I have sold my wife! So the divorced mason he may go, to banish care and strife, Unto the market-place again and buy another wife. Now the cobbler and the lady are both in a stall, While the cobbler works the bristle, why the lady works the awl. And they upon the lapstone do so merry play together, Singing, heel and toe, gee up gee woe, big balls of wax and leather. And day and night, in sweet delight, they banish care and strife; The merry little cobbler and his thirteen-shilling wife.

Song 221.

UNCLE NED'S

Description of the Bloomers.

"Do you know Mrs. Pinchmug, I have just been to the corner for a drop of the comfort of life, and there I saw a Bloomer serving behind the bar; she looked quite charming, and I think I shall have a Bloomer dress made for myself."

"Ah, my dear Mrs. Jollymutton, directly I get rid of this cold, I shall be a Bloomer too; I wouldn't be out of the fashion for the world."

COME all you pretty maidens of every degree
   That dwells on Britannia's charming ground,
You must be blithe and gay, throw your petticoats away,
Your dandy caps, your bonnets and your gown.
      CHORUS.
Away with the petticoats and skirt,
  And the gown too that draggles in the dirt,
High and low degree mean bloomers for to be
And be dressed in the breeches, hat and shirt.

You British ladies gay something starts new every day
  I think Mrs. Bloomer has proved kind,
The ladies for to please, with the buttons on their knees—
In the trousers you'll look so very fine.

Your dandy shift and stays you must quickly throw away
  Your shawl and flounc'd petticoat
So charming you will look in a pair of Blucher boots
And a stunning handsome Bloomer velvet coat.

One old Duchess I declare who lives in Bloomer square
To her housekeeper said we shall be parrots
So handsome and so fine with the breeches tied behind
And a spicy three-cocked hat and a stunning carrot.

Ladies must look out for jobs, be carpenters and snobs,
Tailors and sailors—it's true,
If their husbands them offend they'll give them the ropes end,
And make them whistle yankey-doodle-doo.

They'll think it very hard when they go into the yards,
  And into a fever they will get,
Their braces to let down will cause them for to frown,
  And I'm fearful their trousers they will wet,
Dandy trousers I declare and braces they must wear,
  They must toddle down to Moses for a suit.
And every pretty maid, instead of Adelaid's,
  Must try and buy a pair of Wellington boots.

To make them look quite prim, their shirts they must tuck in,
  They'll be gay and fresh as any mutton.
They will think it quite a bore, for their fingers will be sore,
  In practicing their trousers to unbutton.

You must be Bloomers all, throw away the gown and shawl,
  The shirt, stays, and petticoat too;
So funny you will look, in a pair of big top-boots
Singing Bloomers gay and cock-a-doodle-doo

The Queen rose in a fright, as she lay in bed one night,
  And threw away her bustle, gown, and skirt,
Then she danced in high glee, such a Bloomer I will be,
  And slipped on Prince Albert's hat and shirt,
So my ditty for to end, all the women must be men,
  And wear a coat instead of dandy shawls,
Be ready day and night if they are wanted for to fight,
  And polish off old Nosey's cannon balls.

Ryle & Co., Monmouth Court, Bloomsbury

BABY FARMING.

MOTHERS BEWARE.

Oh, mothers, fond mothers, your attention
    I pray.
And listen awhile to a pitiful lay,
It's a out baby farming, a scandalous trade,
And shocking disclosures have lately been
    made,
Near Brixton, in Surrey, this system so base,
Has at last been discoverd, a social disgrace.

CHORUS.

Then mothers, fond mothers, of your children
    take care,
And against baby farming I pray you beware.

What is baby farming, some mothers may say
'Tis a practice that takes a poor infant away
From the care of it's mother by a stranger
    instead,
The poor little creature is foster'd and bred.
It encourages vice, and one i won't name,
'Tis a means to get rid of the off-pring of shame

Sometimes a young woman has been led
    astray,
Sends the child of her guilt to be out of the
    way.
She pays a few pounds, 'tis a bargain and then
She gives it up never to see it again,
While the indolent wife in luxvry fed,
Pays a stranger to suckle her offspring instead

In a Terrace, at Brixton, two sisters did dwell
How they tempted poor mothers their
    offspring to leave,
To their tender care, but alas to deceive.
They starved them to death, for of late has
    been found,
The bodies of infants in the fields there
    around.

Poor children half-naked, their state we
    deplore,
Too weak for to stand, they laid on the floor
Unwashed and neglected by night and by
    day,
Till their dear little souls from life pass away
And what cared the nurse for the dead ones,
    not she.
The death of a child, why a saving would be

Will the hen drive the chicken from under
    under her wing.
And leave it to perisn, the poor little thing,
Or will dumb brutes desert their offspring,
    ah ! no,
What proofs of affection animals show.
Yet mothers alas their children will slay,
Or else pay another to put it away.

THE
IVY GREEN.

Aʜ! a dainty plant is the ivy green,
　That creepeth o'er ruins old ;
Of right choice food are his meals, I ween,
　In his cell so lonely and cold.
The wall must be crumbled, the stone decay'd,
　To please his dainty whim ;
And the mouldering dust that years have made,
　Is a merry meal for him.
　　　Creeping where no life is seen,
　　　A rare old plant is the ivy green.

Fast he stealeth on, though he wears no wing
　And a staunch old head hath he,
How closely he twineth—how tightly he clings,
　To his friend, the huge oak tree !
And slily he traileth along the ground,
　And his leaves he gently waves,
As he joyously hugs, and crawleth around
　The rich mould of dead men's graves.
　　　Creeping where grim death hath been
　　　A rare old plant is the ivy green.

Whole ages have fled and works decayed,
　And nation's have scatter'd been ;
But the stout old ivy shall never fade,
　From its hale and hearty green.
The brave old plant in its lonely days,
　Shall fatten on the past ;
For the stateliest building man can raise,
　Is the ivy's food at last.

[1]

WOODMAN
Spare that Tree.
───

Woodman spare that tree,
　Touch not a single bough—
In youth it shelter'd me,
　And I'll protect it now.
'Twas my forefather's hand,
　That placed it near this cot ;
There, woodman, let it stand,
　Thy axe shall harm it not.

That old familiar tree,
　Whose glory and renown
Are spread o'er land and sea,
　Say, would'st thou hack it down ?
Woodman, forbear thy stroke,
　Cut not its earthbound ties—
Oh, spare that aged oak,
　Now tow'ring in the skies.

Oft, when a careless child,
　Beneath its shade I heard
The wood notes sweet and wild,
　Of many a forest bird.
My mother kiss'd me here,
　My father press'd my hand,
I ask thee, with a tear,
　Oh, let that old oak stand.

My heart-strings round thee cling,
　Close as thy bark, old friend,
Here shall the wild bird sing,
　And still thy branches bend.
Old tree, the storm still brave,
　And, woodman, leave the spot,
While I've a hand to save,
　Thy axe shall harm it not.

WALKER, PRINTER, DURHAM.

GOD:

A POEM, BY DERZHAVIN,

A RUSSIAN GENTLEMAN,—BORN 1763.

[DERZHAVIN, after serving sometime in the Army, was made successively a Councillor of State, Ambassador of the Senate, President of the College of Commerce, Public Cashier, and, in 1802, Minister of Justice. He has since retired, on his full allowance, to pass the evening of his days in the enjoyment of the fruits of his long and active labours. The Poem on God, by this Author, has been translated into Japanese, by order of the Emperor, and is hung up, embroidered with Gold, in the Temple of Jeddo. It has been translated into the Chinese and Tartar languages, written on a piece of rich silk, and suspended in the Imperial Palace of Pekin.]

O Thou eternal One! whose presence bright,
All space doth occupy, all motion guide;
Unchanged through time's all-devastating flight;
Thou only God! there is no God beside!
Being above all beings! Mighty One!
Whom none can comprehend and none explore;
Who fill'st existence with Thyself alone,
Embracing all—supporting—ruling o'er;
Being whom we call God—and know no more!

In its sublime research, philosophy
May measure out the ocean-deep—may count
The sands of the sun's rays—but God! for Thee
There is no weight nor measure: none can mount
Up to Thy mysteries; reason's brightest spark,
Though kindled by Thy light, in vain would try
To trace Thy counsels, infinite and dark:
And thought is lost ere thought can soar so high,
Even like past moments in eternity.

Thou from primeval nothingness didst call
First chaos, then existence:—Lord, on Thee
Eternity had its foundation;—all
Spring forth from Thee:—of light, joy, harmony,
Sole origin:—all life—all beauty Thine.
Thy word created all, and doth create;
Thy splendour fills all space with rays Divine.
Thou art, and wert, and shall be, glorious! great!
Light-giving, life-sustaining Potentate.

Thy chains the unmeasured universe surround:
Upheld by Thee, by Thee inspired with breath!
Thou, the beginning with the end hast bound,
And beautifully mingled life and death!
As sparks mount upwards from the fiery blaze,
So suns are born, so worlds spring forth from Thee;
And as the spangles in the sunny rays
Shine round the silver snow, the pageantry
Of heaven's bright army glitters in Thy praise.

A million torches lighted by Thy hand
Wander unwearied through the blue abyss:
They own Thy power, accomplish Thy command,
All gay with life, all eloquent with bliss.
What shall we call them? Piles of crystal light—
A glorious company of golden streams—
Lamps of celestial ether, burning bright—
Suns lighting systems with their joyous beams?
But Thou to these, art as the moon to night.

Yes! as a drop of water in the sea,
All this magnificence in Thee is lost:—
What are ten thousand worlds compared to Thee?
And what am I then? Heaven's unnumbered host,

Though multiplied by myriads, and array'd
In all the glory of sublimest thought,
Is but an atom in the balance weigh'd
Against Thy greatness—is a cypher brought
Against infinity: What am I then?—Nought!

Nought! but the effluence of Thy light Divine
Pervading worlds hath reach'd my bosom too;
Yes! in my spirit doth Thy Spirit shine,
As shines the sun-beam in a drop of dew.
Nought! but I live, and on hope's pinions fly
Eager towards Thy presence; for in Thee
I live, and breathe, and dwell; aspiring high,
Even to the throne of Thy Divinity.
I am, O God! and surely Thou must be!

Thou art! directing, guiding all—Thou art!
Direct my understanding then to Thee;
Control my spirit, guide my wandering heart:
Though but an atom 'midst immensity,
Still I am something, fashioned by Thy hand!
I hold a middle rank, 'twixt heaven and earth,
On the last verge of mortal being stand,
Close to the realms where angels have their birth,
Just on the boundaries of the spirit land!

The chain of being is complete in me;
In me is matter's last gradation lost,
And into next step is spirit—Deity!
I can command the lightning, and am dust!
A monarch, and a slave! a worm, a god!
Whence came I here, and how? so marvellously
Constructed and conceived! unknown? this clod
Lives surely through some higher energy;
For from itself alone it could not be!

Creator, yes! Thy wisdom and Thy word
Created Me, Thou source of life and good!
Thou Spirit of my spirit, and my Lord!
Thy light, Thy love, in their bright plenitude
Fill'd me with an immortal soul, to spring
Over the abyss of death, and bade it wear
The garments of eternal day, and wing
Its heavenly flight beyond this little sphere,
Even to its source—to Thee—its Author there.

O thought ineffable! O visions blest!
Though worthless our conceptions all of Thee,
Yet shall Thy shadowed image fill our breast,
And wait its homage to Thy Deity.
God! thus alone my lowly thoughts can soar,
Thus seek Thy presence—Being wise and good!
'Midst Thy vast works, admire, obey, adore;
And when the tongue is eloquent no more,
The soul shall speak in tears of gratitude.

Wonderful Adventures of Mr. O'Flynn in
Search of Old Mother Clifton!

Understanding that old Mother Clifton's house was blown 336 miles above the moon, I went in search of her. I was searching nine days, running as hard as I could with my two shin bones in my pocket, and my head under my arm, by order of Old Joe Buck, the pensioner, who lost his middle eye at the battle of Waterloo, chewing half-boiled stirabout. I then got upon a buck flea's back, which carried me over large hills of skilligolee and bog-holes of buttermilk, till I met Jarvis the coachman, driving two dead horses under an empty post-chaise loaded with eighteen milliners, two tambour workers, two loads of apples, a roasted mill stone, and half-a-dozen grenadier cock magpies, belonging to the French flying artillery, drinking tea till they were black in the face. I asked Mr. Jarvis if he had any account of the old woman of Rad-cliffe highway, who was drowned in a shower of feathers last night, about a fortnight ago, and he told me he had no account of her whatever, but if I went to John Ironsides, I'd get some intelligence : and where John Ironsides lived he told me was two miles beyond all parts in the parish, up and down a street where a mad dog bit a hatchet next week, and pigs wrestle for treacle. I thanked him for his information, and bid him good night. I then began to run as fast as I could sit down by the side of a ditch, with my two shin bones and my head in my pocket, till I met with a gentleman with the Custom-house of Dublin on his back, the Manchester Exchange in his pocket, and Lord Nelson's pillar in London stuck in his hand for a walking-stick. The Lord help you, poor man, said I, I am sorry for you, and the devil skewer you, why had you not better luck. I asked him what was the matter, and he told me he was bad with the gravel in the eye, the daddy wrumble in the guts, and the worm cholic in his toe. I then put him into a coach and drove him into a druggist's shop, and ordered him two pennyworth of pigeons' milk, three ounces of the blood of a grasshopper, a pint of self-basting, the head and pluck of a buck flea, the ribs of a roasted chew of tobacco, and the lights and liver of a cobbler's lap-stone, boiled seperately altogether in a leathern iron pot,

Immediately after taking the mixture, he was delivered of a pair of blacksmith's bellows and a small tombstone a ton weight.

Then proceeding on to Johnny Goola's house, said I to him, John, did you get any account of Mother Clifton's house, that was blown 336 miles above the moon by a gale of wind from a sow gelder's horn. I got no account, says Johnny, only I wrote a letter to her to-morrow night, when I was snoring fast asleep, with my eyes open, knowing her father to be a smith, and farrier to a pack of wild geese, and her mother nurse to a nest of young monkies that was held in the said parish of Up-and-down, were pigs wrestle for stirabout. But John told me I should not go till I had dined with them, we then sat down, and what should be brought up but a dish of stewed paving stones, mixed with the oil and ribs of a chew of tobacco, and two quarts of the blood of a lamplighter's snuff box. The next wonder she showed me, she brought me into a fine garden and placed me by a cabbage stalk which only covered 52 acres of ground, and where I saw ten regiments of artillery firing a royal salute of 21 guns. The next great wonder she shewed me, was a big man standing upon a small table of heath, dressed in a scarlet black cloak, who made a very great sermon, but a north buck-flea bit him in the pole of the neck and made him roar murder. The next wonder I saw a small boy only a thousand years old, thrashing tobacco into peas ; one of the peas started through a wall eighteen feet thick, and killed a dead boy on the other side. Then there was the London Privateer and the Channel Royal Mail Coach in a desperate engagement, firing boiled oyster shells, stewed lapstones and roasted wigs one at the other ; one of the lapstones struck Mother Clifton over the right eye, and delivered her of the Old Woman of Radcliffe Highway, who was sister to Mother Clifton, who had nine rows of bees'-wax teeth, and a three-cocked hat made of the right side of a crab's nostril. I then took the old hag, and made a short leap from Liverpool to Nass in the north of Ireland, where I saw a French frigate coming with Nelson's monument at the top of her mainmast. So now to bring my story to an end, this Old Woman and me step-ping out of the vessel into the port-hole, I made my escape, but the Old Woman was always tipsy with drinking Chand-ler's tobacco, so she sunk to the bottom, and if you go there you will find her making straw hats of deal boards.

[HARKNESS, PRINTER, PRESTON.]   518.

FAIRBURN (SENIOR'S) PORTRAIT

OF THE

PIG-FACED LADY,

OF

Manchester-Square.

DRAWN FROM THE INFORMATION OF A FEMALE WHO ATTENDED ON HER.

SECOND EDITION, WITH ADDITIONS.

DESCRIPTION.

THIS most extraordinary Female is about Twenty Years of Age, she was born in Ireland, and is of high family and fortune; on her life and issue by marriage a very large property depends.

Her body and limbs are of the most perfect and beautiful shape, but her head and face resembles that of a *Pig*. She eats her victuals out of a *Silver Trough*, in the same manner as *Pigs* do; and, when spoken to by any of her relatives or her companion, she can only answer by a *Grunt*.

The *female* who attends on her and sleeps with her is paid at the rate of One Thousand Pounds per Annum for her attendance; but, although the salary is so great, her late companion has quitted her situation, having been terribly frightened by her.

The following Advertisement, from a young Female to attend on her and be her companion, appeared in the *Times* of Thursday, February 9, 1815:

" A young gentlewoman having heard of an advertisement for a person to undertake the care of a lady who is heavily afflicted in the face, whose friends have offered a handsome income yearly, and a premium for residing with her seven years, would do all in her power to render her life most comfortable; an undeniable character can be obtained from a respectable circle of friends: an answer to this advertisement is requested, as the advertiser will keep herself disengaged. Address, post paid, to X. Y. at Mr. Ford's, Baker, 12, Judd-street, Brunswick-square."

Also the following Advertisement, from a young gentleman of respectability, declaring his sentiments respecting a final settlement (matrimony) with this most Wonderful Female, and stating his intentions to be sincere, honourable, and firmly resolved, appeared in the Morning Herald, of Thursday, February 16, 1815: " Secrecy.—A single gentleman, aged thirty-one, of a respectable family, and in whom the utmost confidence may be reposed, is desirous of explaining his mind to the friends of a person who has a misfortune in her face, but is prevented for want of an introduction. Being perfectly aware of the principal particulars, and understanding that a final settlement would be preferred to a temporary one, presumes he would be found to answer the full extent of their wishes. His intentions are sincere, honourable, and firmly resolved. References of great respectability can be given. Address to M. D. at Mr. Spencer's, 22, Great Ormond-street, Queen-square."

Another advertisement, from a *Fortune-Hunter*, was sent to the *Times* for insertion, offering to *marry her*, however deformed, but which was refused insertion, (although accompanied with a One Pound Note!!) for reasons best known to the editor of that paper.

This prodigy of nature is the general topic of conversation in the metropolis. In almost every company you join the *pig-faced Lady* is introduced,—and her existence is firmly believed in by thousands, particularly by those who reside at the west end of the town.

Published by JOHN FAIRBURN, 2, Broadway, Ladgate-Hill.

(Price One Shilling, coloured.)

THE

Royal Fortune Teller!

Being a Warning to Old and Young, Rich and Poor, Married and Single; but particularly to all Young
Men and Women, who by perusing this Publication, may well be suited with good Husbands and Wives.

THE DUMB ALPHABET.

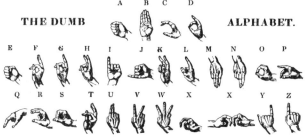

ALL you who wish your fortunes for to know
Unto astrologers you need not go;
Your destinies I can explain at large,
One single penny is my highest charge.
'Tis not by moles or marks that I foreknow,
Nor by the wrinkles in your palms I go;
I cut no cards, nor twirl the coffee cup,
Nor ask the stars, nor raise the devil up.

I shew the way your fortunes to explain:
All other methods are but false and vain,
By which designing men make you their tools—
Taught by knaves, and but believ'd by fools.
And none but silly girls and foolish fellows,
Will spend their money now on fortune-tellers
Some foolish ask, and wish they should be told
Should I die young? or live till I be old?

Do you oft tipsy go to bed at night?
And are you apt to quarrel oft and fight?
Do you in the morn oft lie long in your bed?
And among vicious company often are you led
Were you to live long you would live to no good
To lead such a life, 'twere a pity you should,
Do you ask the question shall I ever get rich?
I can give a shrewd guess, tho' I am not a witch

Why should you not if industrious you are,
And always content with a moderate share!
Must you have no less than a horse or a gig?
Some think themselves rich with a cow and pig
If you had now all you've by idleness lost,
And all your tobacco and liquor have cost;
If this were laid up in a corner so sly,
No doubt but a cow and a pig it would buy.

But if no more care of your money you take,
But spend it at play, the fair, or the wake,
No influence of stars, no gipsy, or witch,
Nor yet all the wise-men can e'er make you rich
There's flashy folks, I know it to my sorrow,
Ofttimes put off with call again to-morrow;
Although they dress themselves so very fine,
Some of their pockets are as low as mine,
Some wear a veil, and on their breast a locket,
They have not got one shilling in their pocket
And some of these fine folks it is well known,
Have oft been seen to put their clothes in pawn
Those make the best of wives, for I have tried,
Who to pay their debts is their chiefest pride,
To find such faults there would be less occasion
If women dressed according to their station,
But the fortune all young girls want to know,
Is this— Shall I ever get married or no?

Some that are in haste, and want to know when,
Cry; what can the matter be now with the men
Now I can tell you when brought to the test,
It may be your temper is none of the best.
To tell you the truth, if one may be so bold,
The men are afraid you should turn out a scold
They can't get time I heard them say,
Either to read the word of God or pray
But many a time in every day that passes,
They can view themselves in looking glasses,
Tho' laying long in bed made numbers ill,
Yet many follow that bad practice still,
And when they get into that idle way,
They are behind hand with their work all day
Young women must dress decent I grant,
But pride is as low as a beggar in want,
For they get white stockings, fine shawl and pelisse
They want a new gown to be all of a piece;
The times are far worse our grandmothers say
Since women are fond of dressing so gay.
With knitting or spinning you seldom now meet
But milliners shops are in every street.

In every place some say you may find
A certain idle class of women kind,
Who rest not till their neighbour's faults are known
To all the town---but they forget their own
Wherever they good entertainment find,
They often visit, and seem very kind.
But if a person be both sick and poor,
These gossips they will always shut the door;
And she that can afford a glass of gin,
Is sure to have th m after lying in;
One comes and asks how she the night did pass
The bottle's ready, she must have a glass,
O! what a pretty babe, another cries,
It's daddy's picture, see its nose and eyes.
Now all you women that gossiping have gon
If this cap fits you, you may put it on;
Unto the wise I think I've said enough,
I pray excuse my language being rough
You drunken husbands who your wives abuse
Then plead drunkenness for their excuse,
Take care lest you be brought to know
That drunkenness is no excuse in law;
The times are hard with drunkards, oft they fail
When without money, the landlord is unkind,
To ask for trust, they have been there before,
And have not yet paid off their last old score.

J. Catnach, Printer, 2, Monmouth-court, 7 Dials

THE EVERGREEN.

CAROLS
For Christmas Holidays.

God rest you

God rest you merry gentlemen
Let nothing you dismay,
Remember, Christ, our Saviour,
Was born on Christmas day.
To save poor souls from Satan's power,
Which a long time had gone astray.
And 'tis tidings of comfort and joy.

From God, that is our Father,
The blessed Angels came,
Unto some certain shepherds.
With tidings of the same:
That there was born in Bethlehem,
The SON of GOD by name.
And 'tis tidings, &c.

" Go fear not," said God's Angels,
" Let nothing you affright,
For there is born in Bethlehem,
Of a pure Virgin bright;
ONE able to advance you,
And beat down Satan quite."
And 'tis tidings, &c.

The shepherds at these tidings,
Rejoiced much in mind,
And left their flocks a feeding,
In tempest, storms, and wind
And straight they went to Bethlehem,
The Son of God to find.
And 'tis tidings, &c.

Now when they came to Bethlehem,
Where our sweet Saviour lay ;
They found him in a manger,
Where oxen fed on hay,
The blessed Virgin kneeling down,
Unto the Lord did pray.
And 'tis tidings, &c.

With sudden joy and gladness.
The Shepherds they were filled,
To see the babe of Israel,
Before his mother mild
Said they, " upon this blessed day,
The Scriptures are fulfill'd."
And its tidings, &c.

Now to the Lord sing praises,
All you within this place ;
And like true loving Christians,
Each other then embrace
For the merry time of Christmas,
Is drawing on apace.
And its tidings, &c.

God bless the rulers of this house
With great prosperity,
And many a merry Christmas,
May in y live again in see,
Amongst their friends and kindred.
That live both far and near.
And God send us all a happy New Year.

St. Stephen's Day.

IN friendly love and unity,
For good St. Stephen's sake.
Let us all this bless-ed day
To Heaven our prayers make;
That we with him the cross of Christ,
May freely undertake.
And Heaven will bless us evermore.

Now, while we all here banqueting,
Of charitie having store,
Let us not forgetful be,
To cherish up the poor.
And give what is convenient,
To the needy at the door
And Heaven will bless you evermore

For God hath made you stewards here,
Upon the earth to dwell,
He that gathereth for himself,
And will not use it well,
'Gainst the kindness of his Maker,
Does wickedly rebel.
And Heaven, &c.

May every blessing from on high,
Attend each family dear,
Long life, health, and prosperity,
To enjoy good Christmas cheer.
Now kind y for your pretty song,
Good butler draw mine beer.
And Heaven, &c.

St. John's Day.

THE moon shines bright, the stars give light
A little bef re 'tis day;
And hark ; the bellman of the night,
Awakes us all to pray.
Awake ! awake ! good people all
Awake ! and do shall sing
How Christ the Lord, holi day was born,
To be our Saviour dear.

Ari e, arise, and let us sing,
Glad songs to hail the day,
The day that Christ our Heavenly King,
Did in a manger lay.

To save poor sinners such as we,
From everlasting pain :
Christ died upon the cursed tree,
And rose from death again.

The life of man is but a span,
He came forth like a flower.
For presently he is cut down,
And withered in an hour.
Princes and kings, with those that sing,
These ditties through the streets,
Though fortune does them here divide,
In death at last shall meet.

Holy Innocents.

NOW cruel Herod with wrath and anger
fill'd,
Did order that all infants should be kill'd,
Thinking to murder our dear Saviour then
O cruel, cruel, savage hearted man.

Hail ! ye first flowers of martyrdom,
Whom, heedless of your tender age,
Christ's persecutor, blind with rage,
Destroy'd—as
does the storm young roses in their bloom.

The Joys.

THE first good joy our Mary had,
It was the joy of one ;
To see her own Son Jesus
To suck at her breast bone.
Both Father, Son, and Holy Ghost,
To all eternity.

The next good joy that Mary had,
It was the joy of two ;
To see her own Son Jesus,
To make the man to read.
Both Father, Son, and Holy Ghost,
To all eternity.

The next good joy that Mary had,
It was the joy of three ;
To make the blind to see.
Did make the blind to see.
To make the blind to see—God-man,
And blessed may be ;
Both Father, Son, and Holy Ghost,
To all eternity.

The next good joy our Mary had,
It was the joy of four ;
To see her own Son Jesus,
To read the Scriptures o'er.
To read the Scriptures o'er—God-man,
And blessed may be be,
Both Father, Son, and Holy Ghost,
To all eternity.

The next good joy that Mary had,
It was the joy of five ;
To see her own Son Jesus,
To raise the dead to life,
To raise the dead to life—God-man,
And blessed may he be ;
Both Father, Son, and Joly Ghost,
To all eternity.

The next good joy our Mary had.
It was the joy of six,
To see her own Son Jesus,
To wear the Crucifix.
To wear the Crucifix—God-man,
And blessed may he be
Both Father, Son, and Holy Ghost,
To all eternity.

The next good joy that Mary had,
It was the joy of seven,
To see her own Son Jesus,
To wear the Crown of Heaven.
To wear the Crown of Heaven—God man,
And blessed may he be ;
Both Father, Son, and Holy Ghost,
To all eternity.

AS I sat on a sunny bank,
A sunny bank, a sunny bank,
As I sat on a sunny bank,
On Christmas-day in the morning.

I spy'd three ships come sailing by,
Come sailing by, come sailing by ;
I spy'd three ships come sailing by,
On Christmas-day in the morning.

And who should be with these three ships,
With these three ships, these three ships
And who should be with these three ships,
But Joseph and his fair lady.

O he did whistle, she did sing,
And all the bells on earth did ring,
For joy that our saviour he was born,
On Christmas-day in the morning.

W. S. FORTEY, Printer & Publisher, Monmouth Court, London, W.C.

The Ladies Concert.

Love was once a Little Boy

[The left broadside consists of numerous closely printed ballad columns, largely illegible, including the following song headings:]

KING AND COUNTRYMAN

MARCH TO THE BATTLE FIELD

THE WOLF

SONG TO LOVE a ROUNDELAY

THE MOUNTAIN MAID, a favourite Song, by Sung, Mr. Sinclair.

JAMIE OF DUNDEE

THE QUEER LITTLE MAN

THE MINUTE GUN AT SEA

LOVING LABOUR LOST, Sung by Madame Vestris.

YOUNG LOVE

HEARY AND LUTE

WILLIAM AT EVE

FROM

BUT A BROOM, Sung by Madame Vestris.

LOVELY WOMAN

Stiggli-Schränzer
Nohwux

D'Goliath-Risewal-Stinkballade

Mit sauvyl Lärm und Gachyss und Bum
macht s'Volk me wider aimool dumm,
he jo, em Stink-Goliath sy Baiechli.
In jedem Käsblatt list me's brait
wie lang är zyg, wss är verdrait
und fangt so s'Schyzer Riechli.

Zerscht gir's am Zoll zwor no-n-e Hält
und d'Zellner bschaue jede Falt
vo däm ganz baundere Wääli,
doch dä stinkt so, s'wird alle huul,
dend är schmeckt nit nur uus em Muul,
s'macht drum au kain e-n-Aeli.

Denn kunnt in d'Quärrantäque s'Vih,
zerscht waiss zwor niemerts gnau wohi,
jä, alles glopft gärn d'Finke,
denn, wie scho gsait, dä Risewal
dä hett e „Parfum", s'isch e Quai,
so haarig duet är stinke!

Doch ändlig isch's-drno so wyt,
dr Goliath kunnt, s'isch, hegächni Zyt,
doch s'Volk giebach gar nit käse.
Denn wär zer Muschtermäss jetz goht
dä schnupperet in dr Luuft — stoht
gly still, denn s'duet z'arg jäse....

So stoht dä Langholzkare dert
und hett s'fyn Basler Näsli gstert,
au d'Ohre rebilliere,
dyan r'duudlet dert vo frisch bis spoot
e Grammophon aint d'Leffel root,
dä sott g'Lyt animiere...?

Doch oha läts, es git kai Stem,
me giggelet am Dählähau-
und scho duet me sich ummräe,
's isch nit wie als im Jamer gitt,
denn bruucht's kai baunderen Appäll,
Billjeh för s'Monstre-Drumele...

... das zieht bi-n-uns, d e n n kenne-d'Lyt,
denn häan dä greeschte Gachährzyt,
doch vör dä Risenchuure,
mir häan's scho gsait, macht niemerts Halt,
is, d'Buebe giele dur e Spalt,
doch sunscht haut me's helt dsare....

Doch mir sin schynts nur Afang gsi,
uff Tournée goht jetz s'Risewih,
ringsum im Schwyzerländli
und, glaubsch es kuum, doch s'isch eso:
in zwai Stedt din d'Lyt scho und froh,
s'Volk druggs vor de Zältwändli.

Und luegt und stuunt und zieht Vesgych
und merkt, dä Wal isch gar nit schych,
dä ka-n-is s'Wasser biete,
dä sotte mir im Wappe ha,
denn wiset me wäa mir biete, Ma,
so frooge si und briete....

He jo, die Stadt isch Ziri gsi,
dert stuunt e jedes ab däm Vih
und sait, wenn as mit Mure:
„Da hännd mir's ja, säb Goliath,
s'isch't dänn scho wtickli cheibeglast,
hätt na die grösseri Schnuure!"

Die anderi Stadt aber isch Bärn!
Und waisch worum r'en deft so gäm
häan au samt Rise-Muuli! —
Das kunnt in Bärn vom Bundeshuus,
is, looset jetz, denn s'isch e Gruus,
d'Goliathli, hesch au gnuuke,
mir häan is alles gaet notiert,
das hett ze-n-unserem Wage gfiehrs,
drum tien mir di hio tunke!

Und hänn drmit gwis s'Richtig braicht,
hett di au hie kai Hund s'g's... schlißt!

Wottsch unsere Goliath gnu bschaue, denn hausch's ief
Fasnachts-Zyschtig in d'Ladärne- und Wäguh-Usställt
in dr Basler-Halle vo dr Muschtermäss.
S'isch offe vom Morge-n-am Nyni bis z'Nachs am Nün.

Numb. 1659

The London Gazette.

Publiſhed by Authority.

From Monday October 10. to Thurſday October 13. 1681.

Vienna, Octob. 5.

THe Emperor has ordered 6000 Men, that are quartered about *Oedenburg*, to march towards the *Upper Hungary* for that the Rebels increaſe very much in ſtrength and are now able to act in two Bodies; with the one they beſiege *Calo* and batter it with 18 pieces of Cannon. The Dyet at *Oedenburg* is to end the 18th Inſtant.

Liege, Octob. 11. The Deputies which our Magiſtrates had ſent to *Cologne*, to endeavour to compoſe the differences between his Electoral Highneſs and this City, returned hither ſeveral days agoe, and have made report of what they had done. Since an Expreſs ſent by the Imperial Commiſſioner arrived here, and brought a Letter written by the Popes Nuncio, and the ſaid Imperial Commiſſioner, to our Magiſtrates, wherein they give them an Account, That being very deſirous to prevent the ill conſequences which theſe miſunderſtandings between their Prince and them may at laſt have, they were, notwithſtanding the ill ſucceſs they had hitherto had, reſolved to continue their Endeavours, in order to an Accommodation, and that for that purpoſe, they had been in Conference with the Electors Miniſters, and had with them agreed on four Preliminary Articles; which in caſe this City did conſent to, they doubted not ſo to order Matters, as that all other points in difference ſhould be adjuſted to mutual ſatisfaction: Whereupon our Magiſtrates have had ſeveral Meetings to conſider of the ſaid Articles; which are, That this City ſhall acknowledge his Electoral Highneſs as their Sovereign Prince, and ſhall pray his Pardon for what they have offended him in. That all Hoſtilities ſhall ceaſe. That all Priſoners ſhall be releaſed; and that all that's paſt ſhall be forgotten. And it's ſaid that they will agree to them, and have accordingly reſolved to return the Expreſs with an Anſwer to the Imperial Commiſſioners Letter.

Francfort, Octob. 12. On Wedneſday laſt the Count *de Roſenberg*, the firſt of the Imperial Plenipotentiaries for the Conferences that are to be held here, arrived at *Hanaw*, and we expect his Excellency in this City in few days; as likewiſe the French Ambaſſadors, and the other Miniſters that are to aſſiſt at the ſaid Conferences. Our Letters from *Ratisbonne* tell us, That the States Aſſembled there, have ſince the taking of *Strasbourg*, wholly applyed themſelves for the ſetling the Points that yet remain undetermined, concerning the Raiſing and the Maintaining the Army, they ſome time ſince reſolved to keep on foot for the defence of the Empire; and that the Duke of *Holſten Ploen*, and Count *Waldeck* were propoſed to be Generals of the ſaid Army.

Hamburg, Octob. 14. The King of *Denmark* is returned to *Copenhagen*. And from *Berlin* we have an Account, that both the Imperial and French Miniſters had had ſeveral Audiences of the Elector of *Brandenburg*, upon the preſent conjuncture of Affairs;

The Firſt preſſing his Electoral Highneſs to take ſuch meaſures as are neceſſary for the preſervation of the Peace of the Empire; and the Latter, endeavouring to ſatisfie his Electoral Highneſs, that the King his Maſter has not any intentions to diſturb it. We are told that the Duke of *Zell* is about forming a Body of 10000 Men, which he will have in a readineſs to march, as there ſhall be occaſion, for the defence of the Empire.

Ghent, Octob. 15. One *Louis Picar*, formerly a Captain of Dragoons in *Holland*, who is accuſed of having committed ſeveral Murthers, and other heynous crimes in the Province of *Utrecht*, having at the deſire of the States-General been ſeized in this City, (whither he was fled,) by order of the Prince of *Parma*, and committed priſoner to the *Caſtle*; and his Highneſs having Commanded, that he ſhould be put into the hands of the *Fiſcael* of *Utrecht*, purſuant to the Directions he had received from *Spain*, the ſame was executed yeſterday; but the ſaid *Picar* had not been long in the cuſtody of the *Fiſcael*, who was carrying him away in a Coach, when he was reſcued by a number of Armed Men, and made his eſcape.

Bruſſels, Octob. 15. We have an account from *Lille*, and ſeveral other places, of the Motions of the French Troops; which does not a little allarm us, and the Countrey-People, who know what it is to have their company, and are therefore affrighted at every report of their March, beginning already in ſome places to remove their Cattle, &c. though we hope they have no reaſon for it. There are Letters from *Strasbourg* which ſay, that the King would be at *Sebleſtadt* the 18th Inſtant, where it was believed he would ſtay a day or two, and that he was not expected at *Strasbourg* till the 18th or 20th Inſtant.

Hague, Octob. 17. The States-General, as we are told, have ordered the Fleet *Van Amerongen* to return forthwith to *Berlin*, thinking it neceſſary to have a Miniſter at that Court in this Conjuncture; We have an account from *Amersoort*, that the Princeſs of *Orange* paſſed through that place yeſterday on her return from *Aix la Chappelle*. The States of *Holland* and *Weſt-Friesland* have publiſhed a Placaet, by which they Declare, that all ſuch Proteſtants as ſhall ſeek Protection and Shelter in this Province, ſhall for twelve years be exempted from all extraordinary Taxes, which ſhall be raiſed.

Newmarket, Sept. 10. The following Addreſs have been preſented to His Majeſty.

To the Kings moſt Excellent Majeſty.

The humble Addreſs of the Single Men, and Apprentices of the City and County of *Norwich*.

Moſt Gracious and Dread Soveraign,

WE Your Majeſties truly Loyal and Obedient Subjects, the Single Men, and Apprentices

Rumb. 34

The TATLER.

By *Ifaac Bickerftaff* Efq;

Quicquid agunt Homines noftri Farrago Libelli.

From *Saturday June 25.* to *Tuesday June 28.* 1709.

White's Chocolate-houfe, June 25.

HAving taken upon me to cure all the Diftempers which proceed from Affections of the Mind, I have labour'd, fince I firft kept this publick Stage, to do all the Good I could poffibly, and have perfected many Cures at my own Lodgings; carefully avoiding the common Method of Mountebanks, to do their moft eminent Operations in Sight of the People; but muft be fo juft to my Patients as to declare, they have teftified under their Hands their Senfe of my poor Abilities, and the Good I have done 'em, which I publifh for the Benefit of the World, and not out of any Thoughts of private Advantage. I have cured fine Mrs. *Spy* of a great Imperfection in her Eyes, which made her eternally rolling 'em from one Coxcomb to another in publick Places, in fo languifhing a Manner, that it at once leffen'd her own Power, and her Beholders Vanity. Twenty Drops of my Ink, plac'd in certain Letters on which fhe attentively look'd for half an Hour, have reftored her to the true Ufe of her Sight; which is, to guide, and not miflead us. Ever fince fhe took this Liquor, which I call, *Bickerftaff's Circumfpection-Water*, fhe looks right forward, and can bear being look'd at half a Day without returning one Glance. This Water has a peculiar Virtue in it, which makes it the only true Cofmetick or Beauty-Wafh in the World: The Nature of it is fuch, that if you go to a Glafs, with Defign to admire your Face, it immediately changes it into downright Deformity. If you confult it only to look with a better Countenance upon your Friends, it immediately gives an Alacrity to the Vifage, and new Grace to the whole Perfon. There is indeed a great deal owing to the Conftitution of the Perfon to whom it is apply'd: It is vain to give it when the Patient is in the Rage of the Diftemper; a Bride in her firft Month, a Lady foon after her Husband's being Knighted, or any Perfon of either Sex who has lately obtain'd any new good Fortune or Preferment, muft be prepar'd fome Time before they take it. It has an Effect upon others, as well as the Patient, when it is taken in due Form. Lady *Petulant* has by the Ufe of it cured her Husband of Jealoufy, and Lady *Gad* her whole Neighbourhood of Detraction. The Fame of thefe Things, added to my being an old Fellow, makes me extreamly acceptable to the Fair Sex. You would hardly believe me, when I tell you there is not a Man in Town fo much their Delight as my felf. They make no more of vifiting me, than going to Madam *d'Epingle's*. There were two of them, namely, *Damia* and *Clidamira*, (I affure you Women of Diftinction) who came to fee me this Morning in their Way to Prayers, and being in a very diverting Humour, as Innocence always makes People chearful, they would needs have me, according to the Diftinction of pretty and *very* pretty Fellows, inform them, if I thought either of them deferving the *very* pretty among thofe of their own Sex; and if I did, which was the more deferving of the Two. To put 'em to the Tryal, Look ye, faid I, I muft not rafhly give my Judgment in Matters of this Importance; pray let me fee you dance: I play upon the Kit. They immediately fell back to the lower End of the Room. You may be fure they curt'fy'd low enough to me: But they began. Never were Two in the World fo equally match'd, and both Scholars to my Name-fake *Ifaac*. Never was Man in fo dangerous a Condition as my felf, when they began to expand their Charms. Oh! Ladies, Ladies, cry'd I, not half that Air, you'll fire the Houfe. Both fmil'd; for by the by, there's no carrying a Metaphor too far, when a Lady's Charms are fpoke of. Some body, I think, has call'd a fine Woman dancing, a Brandifh'd Torch of Beauty. Thefe Rivals mov'd with fuch an agreeable Freedom, that you would believe their Gefture was the neceffary Effects of the Mufick, and not the Product of Skill and Practice. Now *Clidamira* came on with a Crowd of Graces, and demanded my Judgment with fo fweet an Air— But fhe had no fooner carried it, but *Damia* made her utterly forgot by a gentle finking, and a Rigadoon Step. The Conteft held a full half Hour; and I proteft, I faw no mannerr of Difference in their Perfections, till they came up together, and expected my Sentence. Look ye Ladies, faid I, I fee no Difference in the leaft in your Performance; but you *Clidamira* feem to be fo well fatisfied that I fhall determine for you, that I muft give it to *Damia*, who ftands with fo much Diffidence and Fear, after fhowing an equal Merit to what fhe pretends to. Therefore, *Clidamira*, you are a pretty; but *Damia*, you are a *very* pretty Lady. For, faid I, Beauty lofes its Force, if not accompanied with Modefty. She that has an humble Opinion of her felf, will have every body's Applaufe, becaufe fhe does not expect it; while the vain Creature lofes Approbation, through too great a Senfe of deferving it.

From my own Apartment, June 27.

Being of a very fpare and hectic Conftitution, I am forc'd to make frequent Journies of a Mile or two for frefh Air; and indeed by this laft, which was no further than the Village of *Chelfea*, I am farther convinc'd of the Neceffity of travelling to know the World. For as it is ufual with young Voyagers, affoon as they land upon a Shore, to begin their Accounts of the Nature of the People, their Soil, their Government, their Inclinations, and their Paffions, fo really I fancied I could give you an immediate Defcription of this Village, from the five Fields where the Robbers lie in wait, to the Coffee-houfe where the *Literati* fit in Council. A great Anceftor of ours by the Mother's Side, Mr. Juftice *Overdo*, (whofe Hiftory is written by *Ben. Johnfon*) met with more Enormities by walking *incog.* than he was capable of correcting; and found great Mortifications in obferving alfo Perfons of Eminence, whom he before knew nothing

of.

COPY OF VERSES ON THE LATE
DREADFUL FIRE
In James Street, Lisson Grove.

PRAY give ear you feeling Christians,
  For a moment pray attend,
List, oh, listen with attention,
  To those lines which here are penned,
Concerning of a dreadful fire,
  As I will unfold to you ;
The which occurred on Saturday Morn.,
  In Great James St., Lisson Grove.

————CHORUS————

The dreadful sight it was bewildering,
  Awful and sad you may suppose,
A Father and his lovely children,
  Burned to death in Lisson Grove.

At 1 o'clock on Saturday morning,
  Oh ! how dreadful to relate,
They also did without warning,
  Meet with their unhappy fate,
They soundly in their beds was sleeping,
  And no power could them save,
Now their friends for them are weeping
  While they sleep in Lisson Grove.

In health and youth they did retire,
  To their beds on Saturday night,
E're occurred the dreadful fire,
  Which did the neighbourhood affright·
The nurse who did attend the children,
  That night her precious life lost there
And also the tender Father,
  And his three little children dear.

Oh, what may occur to-morrow,
  None of us on earth can tell,
There may be much·pain and sorrow,
  In the home wherein we dwell ;
God above is all sufficient,
  For to keep us from alarms,
He is willing to protect us,
  Guide & guard us from all harm.

That fatal night when they retired,
  And their tender eyelids closed,
The house e're morning would be fired,
  While they did sleep in sweet repose ;
They for a moment had no morning,
  They did not dream of sad alarms,
They did not think before the warning,
  They would sleep in deaths' cold arms

Oh ! God receive their souls in glory,
  There to dwell for ever more ;
This distressing dreadful story,
  Causes many to deplore.
Six poor souls from hence was hurried,
  Their earthly days was at an end,
Their bodies in the earth lie buried,
  And their spirits up to Heaven ascend

London :—Printed and Published by H. SUCH,
123, Union Street, Borough.
Where all the new Songs may be
had as soon as Published

LONG LIFE TO

CAPTAIN WEBB !

THE CHAMPION OF THE SEAS·

A New Song written on the wonderful task completed by Captain Webb, who Swam from Dover to Calais on the 24th of AUG. being above twenty hours in the water.

Air—Oyster Shell Bonnets.

About Captain Boynton a lot has been said,
But we're jolly well proud of our bold Captain Webb,
He wants no Cork Dresses to soothe his alarms,
He can swim like a duck, with his good legs & arms.

CHORUS.

Captain Boynton's defeated you'll see at a glance,
By Captain Webb swimming from England to France

Captain Boynton came over to take us all in,
His dresses to sell and the dollars to win,
But the Yankee's are done cork jackets and all,
Captain Webb done the journey with no dress at all.

Captain Boynton we know could'nt sink in the sea,
Paddling along he's as safe as could be,
But poor Webb had nothing but good English pluck,
He must be wet footed for he swims like a duck.

'Ere the dawn of the day he left Dover pier,
He jump'd in the water without any fear,
The fishes were startled to see his legs go,
They bob'd up their tails and they bob'd down below.

As bold Captain Webb thro' the channel did fly,
He stuck his big toe in a mackarel eye,
And in their own language the poor fishes said,
Here's a fish with two legs, knocking about over head

But he went on his way thro' the glistening tide,
Till a jelly fish gave him a nip in the side,

It was like a big flea and behaved very rough,
Perhaps he thought the bold Captain was tarnation tough.

About twenty hours he stuck to his task,
And then by success was rewarded at last,
The astonished Frenchmen were anxious to learn,
If the Captain had got any steam in his starn.

The Captain was cheer'd as he landed on shore,
Altho' he was tired he was not done o'er,
He shook hands with friends and the truth must be said,
Had something to drink and toddled to'bed.

Now altho' Captain Boyton is a wonderful man
Let him take off his dress and do this if he can,
We've a little girl in London Miss Beckwith I mean,
Could wack all the Yankee's that ever was seen.

So let us give honor were honor is due,
Success to the Captain so fearless and true,
We hope that his bold eyes, will never grow dim,
Till every man in this Country can swim.

London :—H. P. SUCH, Machine Printer & Publisher,

177, Union-street, Borough, S.E.

bec 1875

LORD PALMERSTON
He is a Clever Man,
And they won't get over him

Britannia sons, you'll hear some fun,
  If you will lend an ear,
It's about our staunch old Veteran—
  I mean our old Premier;
He's not a flat, caught in a trap,
  And that the world will see,
Let them do their best, and do their worst
  They won't get over he.

He's a rum cove, fol de riddle I do,
  Our Premier so free;
Lord Palmerston is a funny old chap,
  And they won't get over he.

It seems some chap has set a trap,
  And caused a deal of strife,
And he wants to say the gay old man,
  Oh! dear, has kissed his wife;
He's going to sue for a divorce,
  But it is on slippery ground,
And he's going to lay the damages
  At thirty thousand pounds

Lord Palmerston is a funny chap,
  The Queen does him adore,
Because he does his duty,
  And his age is fourscore;
They won't get over Palmerston,
  Neither by this or that,
Jack Temple never was afraid
  Of any man or trap.

His Lordship said, I have a wife,
  An honour to a man,
And once upon a time she was
  A tender bit of lamb;
But now she's getting old and tough,
  Still we banish care and strife,

I neither want the jealous fool,
  Neither do I want his wife.

Lord-Palmerston won't frighten'd be,
  He knows what he's about,
Though he has one foot in the grave,
  And the other not far out;
He can enjoy his bit of lamb,
  That's wholesome, sweet, and sound,
And they won't bounce Jack Temple
  Out of thirty thousand pounds.

He will not give a penny,
  The result of all he'll see;
As he said last night to his lady bright,
  They shan't get over me;
Whatever may be the consequence,
  He'll brave it like a man,
And while he lives he will enjoy,
  His sweet old bit of lamb.

All men throughout the nation will
  Protect our old Premier,
And he always shall be guarded
  By Britannia's Volunteers.
And suppose he kissed the covey's wife,
  But proof cannot be found,
It ought to be a stunning kiss
  For thirty thousand pounds!

Here's jolly good luck to Palmerston,
  And although near fourscore,
We hope that he may live in health,
  For twenty years or more;
We could not find a better,
  If we hunted through the land,
Then here's success to Palmerston,
  He's a regular good old man.

Disley, Printer, 57, High Street, St. Giles.

Purchased of a Ballad-singer in Eccleston Square, Pimlico, 9 December, 1863.

WE'LL NOT FORGET
Poor ROGER now.

Britons all, come pay attention,
  And list awhile to my sad song,
And when you've heard some facts I'll mention,
  You'll say they've proved that right is wrong.
That the claimant is the right man,
  To many people it is quite clear,
But the jury found him guilty,
  His sentence is fourteen years.

Tho' in prison they have cast him,
  To speak one word they'd not allow.
Our friendship for him still is lasting,
  We'll not forget poor Roger now.

As the case it was proceeding,
  From the day it did begin,
It was clear to all by reading,
  They never meant that he should win
If he dared to ask a question,
  Like a dog he was put down,
While the other side indulged in—
  Jokes more fitting for a clown.

The witnesses against poor Roger,
  I think it is a shocking thing,
Dragged up from the back slums of Wapping,
  To take their words it was a sin,
While among the friends of Roger,
  Were soldiers who in battle, cool,
Had nobly fought for England's glories,
  They were put down as rogues or fools.

A deal of sympathy and humbug,
  Was got up for Cousin Kate,
You may abuse the lower classes,
  But mind you do not touch the great,
That they are angels dropped from heaven.
  Divorce court trials will prove to you,
But then of course we must excuse them,
  Because they've nothing else to do.

If there's any mothers standing round me,
  I ask you truely, every one,
If you think that you could ever—
  Once forget a long lost son,
And so his mother recognised him,
  Which filled the family with dismay,
But suddenly she died, poor lady,
  Or a different tale they would tell to day.

Then jolly good luck to brave Kenealy,
  Their threats he did not care a jot,
Thought he had five to one against him,
  His voice was heard above the lot,
They may call the Claimant an impostor,
  A lump of fat—the counsel bawl,
But it is the universal feeling,
  That he is the right man after all

Disley, Printer, London.

Outrage & Murder

On a Little Child at PURFLEET.

A Little girl named **Alice Boughen**, was supposed to have been dreadfully **outraged** and murdered by a School-master, on **Wednesday**: she left her home at **2** o'clock, to go to school. At half-past 3 she left the room to go into the back, and **was** not seen alive afterward.

TUNE:— Just before the Battle Mother.

You parents dear that love your children,
Just listen to this dreadfull deed,
A little girl she has been murdered,
It will cause each mother's heart to bleed;
Poor child she was outraged by a soldier,
Then brutaly murdered as we're told,
At Purfleet poor Alice Boughen,
She was jurs 5 Years and ten months old.

CHORUS :—

Poor little child her death was dreadful,
How sad her fate to die so young,
Outraged and murdered by a soldier,
At Purfleet thio deed was done.

Poor Alice dear sweet little angel,
Was carried by this monster bold,
Into a field for his vile purpose,
Then she was murdered as we'er told ;
To hide her quite this cursed monster,
He concealed his victim in some hay,
Near the Magazine her frozen body,
Was found a mass of lifeless clay,

Then he sent home her little brother,
With his sisters hat and jacket to,

The father he was broken hearted,
At first he scarce knew what to do;
No doubt dear Alice cried for mercy,
He heeded not her pityous cry,
On this little dear he had no pity,
Poor child a dreadful death to die.

Oh, what must be the parents feelings,
Now their dear daughter is no more,
When she was found the site was dreadful,
Poor child lay weltring in her gore,
May her soul rest with its maker,
Were angles dwell both night and day,
At her tender age she had no notion,
That fiend would take her life away.

Richard Coote, was a school master,
Of the Royal Artillery as we hear,
His little victim suffered dreadful,
Her nose was torn away we hear;
The murderer then to stop her screaming.
He prest his hand on her sweet face,
With her little strength she struggled with him,
On his clothes her inocent blood was traced.

MURDER AT CAMBRIDGE.

Robert Brown, stands charged with the murder of Emma Rolfe, by cutting her throat with a razor, on a Common near Cambridge, on Thursday night, Aug. 28th, 1876. The Prisoner has confessed the crime to Police Constable Wheel.

The victim was an "UNFORTUNATE GIRL,"

Tune:—Driven from Home.

In the quiet town of Cambridge a deed has been done,
That I'm sure has surprised and startled each one ;
An unfortunate woman but just in her prime,
Alas ! is the victim of this cruel crime.
Well known in Cambridge, from virtue betrayed,
In the path of dishonour too early she strayed ;
But whatever she's been we can all understand,
Her life was as sweet as the best in the land.

CHORUS.

Poor Emma Rolfe had no time to repent,
On Midsummer common to eternity sent ;
Robert Brown was her murderer, in prison he's cast.
From virtue she strayed to be murdered at last.

God only knows what a hard life she led,
The sale of her honor was the price of her bread ;
Exposed to the scoffs and the jeers of the world,
Her short life was passed, in deep misery hurled.
In cheap gaudy clothes obliged to dress gay,
Poor women like her their days pass away ;
They must wear a smile tho' the heart is sick and sore
Till they go to their graves and are heard of no more

She met with her murderer on Thursday night,
They both went together soon after twilight ;
They went to the common for a purpose we know,
They quarrelled and then he gave her a death blow ;
He then cut her throat with a razor so keen,
The poor woman's blood on the pathway did stream,
Her sad wretched life, alas ! it was o'er,
Ere the morning had dawn'd, Emma Rolfe was no
       more.

A policeman was brought and the murderer confess'd,
For the crime he committed he now has no rest,
He would give all the world to recall that sad hour,
But what has been done is beyond earthly power.
She was murdered that night, with her sins on her
       head,
We hope they're forgiven now she's laying dead ;
Tho' lost to the world, despised and forlorn,
Someone will miss the poor girl now she's gone.

Robert Brown will be tried for this unmanly crime,
And if he's found guilty must suffer in time ;
We pity his brother and relations as well,
Who are grieving for him as he lies in his cell :
His poor victim lies in her cold narrow be,
Never no more to her ruin be led ;
Young girls beware you are not led astray,
For plenty will quickly decoy you away.

Don't be too hard on this poor woman's fate,
She might have reformed, but now it's too late
Perhaps she had no one to snatch her away,
To save her from ruin or going astray :
When the first step is taken 'tis hard to return,
Many a poor girl this and lesson must learn,
And many a kind mother has had a dear child,
By some wealthy young flatterer to ruin beguiled.

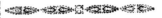

London:—H. P. SUCH, Machine Printer & Publisher
177, Union-street, Borough, S.E.

Murder of M. Marten,
BY W. CORDER.

Printed by J. CATNACH, 2, Monmouth-court, 7 Dials.
Sold by Bennett, Brighton.

COME all you thoughtless young men a warning take by
me,
And think on my unhappy fate to be hanged upon a tree,
My name is William Cerder to you I do declare,
Icourted Maria Marten most beautiful and fair.
promised I would marry her upon a certain day,
ostead of that I was resolved to take her life away ;
went into her father's house the 18th day of May,
O come my dear Maria we'll fix the wedding day.
you will meet me at the red barn as sure as I have life,
will take you to Ipswich town and there make you my wife
straight went home and fetched my gun, my pickaxe and
my spade,
I went into the red barn and there I dug her grave.
With heart so light she thought no harm to meet him she
did go,
He murdered her all in the barn and laid he body low ;
The horrid deed that he had done, she lay bleeding in her
gore,
Her bleeding mangled body he threw under the red barn
floor.
Now all things being silent she could not take no rest,
She appeared in her mother's house, who suckled her at her
breast ;
For many a long month or more her mindbeing sorely op-
pressed,
Neither night nor day she could not take no rest.
Her mother's mind being so disturb'd she dream'd three
nights o' er,
Her daughter she lay murdered under the red barn floor ;
She' sent her father to the barn wh cn un the ground he thrust
And there he found hi daughter m ingling with the dust.
My trial is hard I cou not stand, most woeful was the sigh
When her jaw bone was brought to prove, which pierc'd my
heart quite ;
Mie aged mother stan n g by, likewi his loving wife,
And with her grief h er hair she tore, sehe scarcely could
keep life.
Adieu, adieu my loving friends my gla ss is almost run,
On Monday next wil be my last, when I am to be hange'u ;
All you young men that do pass by with pity look on me,
rot the murder of Maria Martin I was hang'd upon a tre

Wilt thou
SAY
Farewell Love.

Catnach, Printer, 2, Monmouth
Court, 7, Dials.

Wilt thou say farewell, love,
And from Rosa, part ?
Rosa's tears will tell, love,
  The anguish of her heart : —
  I'll still be thine,
  If thou'lt be mine,
I'll love thee though we sever,
  Oh, say, can I
  E'er cease to sigh,
  Or cease to love ?
  No never.

Will thou think on me, love
When thou art far away,
I think on thee, love,
And never never stray.
I'll still be thine, &c.

Let not other's wiles, love
Thy ardent heart betray ;
emember Rosa's smiles, love,
  When Rosa's far away.
  I'll still be thine,
  thou'lt qe mine,
  e thee though we sever.
  Oh say, can I
  E'er cease to sigh,
  Or cease to love !
  No never.

THE
CONDEMNATION
OF
Oliver Plunket

Titular Primate *and Arch Bp. of* Dublin *in* Ireland.

And likewise of
Edw. Fitz Harris,

For HIGH-TREASON, *at the* KING·S-
Bench *in* Westminster-Hall, *June* 15. 1681.

THE Court being set, *Oliver Plunket* was brought to the Bar, and Mr. Attorney General moved in behalf of the King, for Judgment against the Prisoner, whereupon he was Ordered to hold up his Hand, and demanded what he had to say, why Judgment of Death should not be pronounced against wim, for the High-Treason, upon which he was lately Arraigned and found Guilty, in that Court.

Whereupon Mr. *Plunket* insisted upon his want of Evidence, whom he expected should have appeared on his behalf at his Tryal; likewise the improbability of the Evidence against him, since the place where they Deposed an Army was to be Landed, was not capable of receiving them, and, that it was not possible for him to raise so much Money in *Ireland* as should maintain them: He also insisted upon the Jury, alledging That the Laws of *England* are so favorable to take a Jury out of the place where the Fact was Committed, that they may the better Judge of Time,s Places, and other Circumstances; He acknowledged he was a Priest and a Bishop in that Kingdom, which he said was not Treason there, and that while there was connivance, till the Proclamation did forbid him, he did Exercise his Function there; concluding with many Protestations of his Loyalty.

The Court having with patience heard what he could say, proceeded to Sentence; and he was told he had been Convicted of the greatest and most horrid of all Crimes, even Treason of the highest nature, Treason against God, his King and Country: against God, in endeavouring to bring in a false Religion, and the most pernicious of all others whatsoever; for whereas True Religion teaches men their duty to God and man, this on the contrary, teaches men (for advancing the Church) to commit all manner of Villanies and Treasons: and, as it was against God, so certainly he had committed a very high Crime against his Lawful Prince, since the design was to be carried on by taking away his Life, to whom he owed all manner of Allegiance and Obedience; and, though he alledged, That it was not Treason to be a Bishop or a Prelate in *Ireland*, yet the Court told him, That, f the Pope to set up Bishops and Prelates in his Majesties own Kingdom, against his Majesties Authority, though it were not formal Treason, yet it seemed to be of a Treasonable nature, since it set up another Power against his natural Prince: and, then the Design was likewise to have brought Blood and Destruction upon the poor People of *Ireland*, which had been fully proved against him.

And as to what he alledged of being Tryed in the same place where the Fact was Committed, he was told, That the Law whereby he was Tryed, was not made with a design to ensnare him, but that there were many Presidents and Examples, that divers have been Arraigned and Condemned in *England*, for Treason Committed in *Ireland*.   He

An Account of the Execution of Brigadier *Rookwood*, Major *Lowic* and Mr. *Cranburn*, at *Tyburn*, *April* 29th. 1696.

Jacobites

WHEN the Prisoners came first up into the Cart, Mr. *Lowick* and Mr. *Rookwood* (being *Roman Catholicks*) Kneeled down together, and Mr. *Lowick* Read some Prayers, for above half an hour, out of a small *English* Book of Devotion (Writ by an Abbot). And Mr. *Cranburn*, Kneeling down by himself, Prayed to this effect:

' O Lord Jesus forgive me all my Sins, and forgive all
' my Persecutors ; grant me true Repentance now I
' suffer for thy Cause ; let me have thy assistance and
' support now I suffer for thy Cause. Give stedfastness
' to thy Followers, and repentance to all their Persecu-
' tors. Carry me to those happy Mansions prepared for
' all those that suffer for thee : and all I beg for Christ
' Jesus sake : *Our Father which art in Heaven,* &c.
' Almighty and most Gracious God, support, I pray
' thee, thy unworthy Servant in this last and great busi-
' ness of laying down my Life ; let me not dishonour
' the Cause and Truth that I suffer for : It is not my
' mistrust of the Righteousness of my Cause, but the
' common Sins and Errors of my Life, which makes me
' afraid to appear before the Righteous Bar. But cleanse
' me from my Sins, and then I shall meet Death with
' confidence : I know when the sting of Death is taken
' out, there is an aversion in our Nature ; but let the in-
' fluence of thy Grace overcome it in my Spirit ; possess
' my mind more and more with a sense of the Righte-
' ousness of the Cause I suffer for : And whatever Terror
' would otherwise strike into me, let it arm my Spirit
' with confidence, that I die for thee and thy Cause, and
' that I shall be received into thy Rest. *Lord, into thy*
' *hands I command my Soul.*

Mr. *Sheriff.* Mr. *Cranburn* take what time you will, we will stay for you.

Then the Hangman tied the Rope about Mr. *Cranburn.*

Mr. *Sheriff.* If you will retire again, Mr. *Cranburn*, we will wait for you.

Then *Cranburn* Kneeled down and Prayed again. And after a little time they all rose up, and kissed each other.

Mr. *Sheriff.* Take your own time Mr. *Lowick.*

Mr. *Lowick.* I thank you, Sir.

Then *Cranburn* had the Rope put about his Neck.

Executioner. Have you got a Cap, Sir ?

Mr. *Cranburn.* Yes I have: And the Executioner took it out of his Pocket, and a Paper with it.

Executioner. What is in this Paper ?

Mr. *Cranburn.* Nothing.

Executioner. Do you deliver no Paper to the Sheriff ?

Mr. *Cranburn.* No, my Papers have been taken from me. There is a Paper in my Bosom, which I would have you take out ; open my Breast, and you will see it ; which the Executioner did, and took it out, and ask'd him if he should give it to the Sheriff.

Mr. *Cranburn.* No, There is nothing in it but a Memo-randum of what I would say ; my Papers were taken from me.

Mr. *Sheriff.* Who took them from you ?

Mr. *Cranburn.* Tokefield.

Mr. *Sheriff.* You made it with your own hand, Did you not ?

Mr. *Cranburn.* Yes, Sir.

Mr. *Sheriff.* We cannot Read this (it being Writ with a Pencil) make your self as easy as you can. Will you speak the Words your self ?

Mr. *Cranburn.* Yes, Sir.

Mr *Sheriff.* Read it audibly and leisurely, for you f there is one writes, for we would do you no wrong and we will command silence.

Mr. *Cranburn.* Gentlemen, I am in a few moments appear before the Great and Righteous Judge of a Men, to whom I am to give an account of all my Act ons ; I confess I have been a great and wicked Sinner but I hope to find Pardon by the Merits and Intercession of our Lord and Saviour Jesus Christ. I would advise all of you to be diligent and conscientious in your Dut to God ; and whoever is so, it will make him a goo Christian ; and I am sure, he that is a good Christian can never be a Rebel to his Lawful King. As to the Assassination of the Prince of *Orange*, I had notice of t on *Saturday*, between the hours of Nine and Ten, F bruary the 22d. Mr. *Charnock* after I had carried the Names of the Persons to him, ——

Mr. *Sheriff.* Who had you the Names from ?

Mr. *Cranburn.* From Captain *Porter* , and after I car ried the Names to Mr. *Charnock* , he made an addition of Six of his own, and sent me back to Mr. *Porter* to ac quaint him that it was necessary to come to him, and they Two to go to the Knight together.

Mr. *Sheriff.* What Knight was it ?

Mr. *Cranburn.* That I cannot tell.

Mr. *Sheriff.* Go on.

Mr. *Cranburn.* The 22d I had Knowledge of this De sign between Ten and Eleven ; between Eleven and Twelve the time was over. And when I came from Mr. *Porter* to Mr. *Charnock*, he told me the Knight had alter'd his measures, and he desired Mr. *Porter* would take care of himself, and he would not have him make too much haste out, for fear of surprizing any of the Gen tlemen that were with him. What was Sworn against me by Mr. *Porter*, Mr. *Pendergrass*, and Mr. *La Rue*, was true : 1. That I sent a Sword to Mr. *Pendergrass* ; and 2d. I was at the *Sun-Tavern* ; and 3d. I did carry the Note. But I did not know what it was for. I wish they may have Repentance for the same. As I am to do Justice to all men, for I am more especially to my Sove reign King *James* ; I believe he had no Knowledge of the Design ; and I doubt not but God will restore him o his Ancient and Rightful Kingdoms : And as I am in Duty bound to pray for him (then he Kneeled down)
' I humbly beseech God to Bless, Prosper, and Keep
' him, and give him patience under all his Sufferings,
' and a happy issue out of all his Afflictions, and to
' grant that no Plot against him may prosper : Be a strong
' Tower against the face of his Enemies ; as for those
' that would not have him to Reign over them, let them
' be cloathed with Shame ; but upon himself let his
' Crown flourish. Bless our Gracious Queen *Mary, Ca-*
' *therine* the Queen *Dowager*, and his Royal Highness the
' Prince of *Wales* : Prosper them with all Happiness ,
' enrich them with thy heavenly Grace, and bring them
' to thine everlasting Kingdom ; through Jesus Christ our
' Lord. (Then he stood up.)

Mr. *Sheriff.* Mr. *Cranburn*, take your own time.

Mr. *Cranburn.* I do believe that very few persons knew of this Design, but those that were the principal Promo-ters of it ; and I beseech God no more Blood may be spilt. I beseech Almighty God to open the eyes of this Nation, that this Nation may not become a Prey to a Foreign Power.

Mr. *Sheriff*

The LAST DYING WORDS and CONFESSION of

Benjamin Wike, alias John Smith,

Who was Tried, Caſt, & Condemned *for Highway Robbery, near* Knutsford,
in Cheſhire, and was executed on Saturday, *the* 20th *of* Auguſt, 1785.

I BEN WIKE was born at *Barnſley*, in the county of *York*, of poor but honeſt parents, who brought me up, and gave me good education; the buſineſs I followed was a collier for ſome time, but giving myſelf to drinking and gambling, occaſioned me to ſell all I had. I then took to travelling as a pedlar, ſelling gingerbread, toys, and other articles in the town and neighbourhood of Barnſley; which occupation reduced me to ſuch diſtreſs, I was not able to ſupport myſelf, therefore I was reſolved to take another courſe of life, and accordingly I did, where I bought a piſtol and other things fit for my deſign: I was then reſolved that night to begin my wickedneſs, and accordingly out I went with a heart like ſteel, betwixt the hours of ten and eleven I met a man coming from ſome country farm, and of him I made my prey; I not only robbed him of his money and watch, but likewiſe took his ſhoe and knee-buckles, and then made my eſcape into another country, where I met a drover, and robbed him of his money, amounting to two pounds ſix ſhillings and ſixpence; whereupon the drover told me, if I would let him have his money, he would tell me how to get ten times as much; however, I would not part with his money, ſtill I was certain of the other, where he told me was drinking in a public houſe, where there were ſome gentlemen much in liquor, and they had to come home that road, for he knew them very well, and they only lived in the next village; ſo I reſolved to lay wait for them, and accordingly I met two of them very much in liquor, and bid them ſtand, and robbed them of 37 guineas in gold, 17 ſhillings in ſilver, and two ten pound notes.—— Having made theſe bold attempts I was pretty fluſh in the pocket, and determined to have a horſe, but thought it better to ſteal than buy one, ſo I did ſo, and ſet out on the road between Leeds and Wakefield, where I committed ſeveral great robberies; for then I feared no-body, having plenty of money, and the appearance of a Lord.

Then I uſed great Inns, expecting to hear ſomething, which I did ſhortly; I ſoon learnt that there had been ſeveral gentlemen to a fair in the country in their carriages, and I laid wait for ſome of them; about the hour of eleven I came up with a carriage that had a gentleman and his lady in it; I rode boldly up to the driver, bidding him ſtop, which he refuſed to do, but firing a piſtol ſoon put them all to the rout, and the lady cried out bitterly, but I ſoon ſtopped their noiſe by giving a whiſtle and firing a piſtol, as this made them think I was calling more of my gang. So the gentleman deſired me not to hurt him, or his lady, and he would give me his purſe; but I deſired it in a moment, or both him and his lady's brains ſhould be blown out, ſo he delivered his purſe, containing 52 guineas in gold, and four ſhillings in ſilver; but not ſatisfied with that I told them that death was their doom if they not give me more, whereupon the lady gave me a purſe, containing 29 guineas in gold, and two half crown pieces. I then demanded their watches and rings, which they gave me, but the lady cried bitterly, hoping I would not take her diamond ring, as ſhe valued that more than her life, but I told her ſhe die firſt, ſo I bid them good night, and away I rode, fearing nobody I had not gone 3 miles before I met a gentleman, being from the ſame feaſt, ſo I bid him ſtand, thinking a ſtore was no ſtore, and robbed him of his watch and 42 guineas, wiſhing him a very good night. Away I then ſet out in haſte of ſome of the reſt that preſently met with 9 or 10

of them together, bidding them good night, and told them ſome of their companions had gone before them. I ſtill rode on making the beſt of my way home, where I continued till next day at noon, then refreſhed myſelf in expectation of going out that night, ſo I went to a tavern and called for a bottle of wine, and joined myſelf in that company which was the likelieſt to ſerve my purpoſe, ſo we drank merrily round till the hour of twelve, when ſome of them ſaid, they would ſet off home, and accordingly they did, except one who was left drowſy laying his head on the table, I puſhed him, telling him his companions were all gone; then up he gets, bidding me good night; now that was all I wanted, ſo I ordered them to get me a horſe ready, telling the landlord one of them had flung me out of my watch.

Another gentleman hearing my loſs ſaid, friend, I'll have a horſe, and go with you, if you pleaſe. I told him I was much obliged to him, and would make him amends ſome way: Which I did ſhortly; for we had not gone a mile before I deſired him to ſtop. The gentleman ſaid, Sir, you are joking. Not I, by G—d, ſaid he, ſo out goes your brains in one moment, if you do not deliver your watch and money. So with much ado, he gave me all he had, which was about 33 guineas, with his watch, buckles, and ring. I then bid him good night, and rode after the other, and came up with him in the ſpace of half an hour. He was much in liquor, and could hardly rule his horſe. Whereupon I ſaid, What is the matter, friend? Friend, ſaid he, are you a friend of mine? Yes, replied I, and as you are in liquor, I will take care of you and ſee you ſafe home.—— Pray, how far have you to go? Two miles replied the gentleman. Two miles, ſays I, then there is no better place to ſettle our affairs, ſo ſtand and deliver; but the gentleman refuſed, ſo I knocked him off his horſe, and told him, he was a dead man if he did not give me his money: But, without making much ado, I rifled his pockets, took 9 guineas 2 ſhillings and his pocket book, wherein I found 4 fifty pound notes, 2 ten pounds, and 2 twenty pound notes, leaving him in the road to take that night's recreation, and away I went to mine quietly.

Next day paſſed my time in counting my booty, and found it very proper to my mind; but I was not long after I underſtood there had been ſome farmers ſelling cattle in a market, and I was reſolved to meet one of them coming home, which I did, and robbed him of 400 pounds in ready caſh, and two hundred in notes. But an alarm was ſoon made, and I was taken and committed to Nottingham goal for ſtealing a Bag of Cotton, and tried at the Aſſizes; but, by good friends, ſent me tranſported for three years to the river Thames, where I ſerved my time; and coming to my own part again, having no money, but what little my clothes fetched, I was fully bent on taking up my old courſe of life, and carried it on for the ſpace of three years. Then making a bold attempt to rob two men, I was taken, ſent to the high goal of Cheſter, tried, caſt, and condemned.

On Saturday morning the unhappy culprit received the Holy Sacrament from the hands of the Rev. Chaplain; and about eleven o'clock was put into a cart, in order to be conveyed to the place of execution; attended by the under ſheriff and proper officers. By twelve o'clock the proceſſion arrived at the fatal tree, when, after the uſual time ſpent in Prayer, he was launched into a boundleſs eternity, amidſt a great concourſe of people, whom he had previouſly exhorted to take warning by his untimely end.

EXECUTION

OF

FIVE PIRATES

At Newgate, on Monday, Feb. 22nd, for Murder on board the Flowery Land.

H. DISLEY, Printer, 57, High Street, St. Giles, London. — W.C.

Oh ! what numbers did flock to see,
Five murderers die on the gallows tree,
For those cruel deeds which they have done,
Their fatal glass is now quite run ;
When they were sent to the shades below,
No tears of pity for them did flow,
No mercy did they expect to have,
Only to fill a murderer's grave.

    Those five men on the drop did stand,
    For their deeds on board the Flowery Land.

Children and mothers they have caus'd to weep,
For those who were slain and sunk in the deep ;
We hope they are number'd with the blest,
And with God above their souls at rest ;
Their sufferings were great, no tongue can tell,
Welt'ring in blood, on the deck they fell.
On their knees, for mercy they did crave,
But were murder'd and sunk beneath the waves

They've took from wives their husbands dear,
And griev'd their hearts the sad news to hear,
But in the hour of their distress,
God protect them and the fatherless !
For what those murderers did on board the
    Flowery Land,
At the throne of God they will have to stand,
On the scaffold their lives did forfeit pay,
Oh, what will they feel on the Judgment day

In the mighty deep, where the billows roar,
Their victims sleep for evermore,
Tho' they parted them from those they love,
We hope their friends will meet them in Hea-
    ven above,
Where their sufferings will be all o'er
On another bless'd and peaceful shore,
Where they will feel no grief or pain,
But for ever dwell ne'er to part again.

In the murderers' last hour, the solemn bell,
Warn'd them to bid this world farewell,
To resign their breath they did on the gallows
    stand,
Life for life's required by God and man ;
The murderers on the fatal morn,
On the gallows did die, expos'd to scorn,
For them there was no sympathy,
When they were launched in eternity.

We hope that this will a warning be,
To all, either by land or sea,
From the paths of virtue never to stray,
And never take precious life away ;
Or like those mutineers, your fate may be,
Have to end your days on the fatal tree,
No one for them could pity have,
When they were sent to the murderer's grave.

The English Murderer at Work

26/7/1917.—WM. PARTRIDGE, T.C.—Slow-murdered in Lewes Jail.

25/9/1917.—THOMAS ASHE.—Brutally murdered in Mountjoy Jail.

29/11/1917.—JOE NORTON.—Slow-murdered in Lewes Jail.

29/5/1918.—FRANK CULLEN.—Slow-murdered in Lewes Jail.

9/12/1918.—RICHARD COLEMAN.—Slow-murdered in Usk Jail.

6/1/1919.—**PIERCE McCANN—Slow-murdered in Gloucester Jail.**

21/1/1919.—SEAN ETCHINGHAM, T.D.] Dropped in shattered
12/2/1919.—MRS. THOMAS CLARKE] health from the Murderer's grip.

Within the past few months also COUNT PLUNKETT and many others have been released for "health reasons" after a slow, deliberate reduction of their vitality.

To-day there are still in the hands of the Murderer hundreds of men and women.

IN BELFAST JAIL the prisoners have been in handcuffs DAY AND NIGHT from 21st January, 1919, to the middle of February, and they are still in solitary confinement there. Since 21st January, 1919, they have not been permitted to attend Mass.

IN MOUNTJOY JAIL, the prisoners have been in handcuffs from 13th January, 1919, up to the middle of February, except on Sundays, and some are still in solitary confinement.

IN CORK the prisoners are in handcuffs since the 17th January, 1919.

IN MARYBORO', LIMERICK, DERRY the Murderer is at work, too.

FROM ENGLAND comes, to tell us what our loved ones have been suffering there,

THE
DEAD BODY
OF
PIERCE McCANN.

WHAT ARE YOU GOING TO DO?

GRAND PROTESTANT ASSOCIATION OF LOYAL ORANGEMEN.

This Protestant Association was formed at Exeter, on the landing of William the Third, Prince of Orange, in 1688, and under his auspices. The first code of laws to govern it was drawn by the Rev. Dr. Burnet, afterwards created Bishop Burnet, its principles and objects were then, what they are now, viz.,—for the protection of life, property, and the protestant religion; in fact, a defensive society against the inroads of popery.—It is a *politico-religio* society; its politics being, "The husbandman that laboureth shall be first partaker of the fruits;" or in other words, "A fair days wages for a fair day's work," and religiously it means, "Honour all men, love the brotherhood, fear God, honour the king." It is an eminently loyal body, and perfectly legal, as admitted by Lord Palmerston, the ex-premier; and Lord Derby, the present premier. It has been more maligned and traduced than any other society or association in the known world; but it has out-lived and surmounted all difficulties and opposition, and is more prosperous at the present moment than it ever was, having its ramifications in almost all parts of the globe—next to the Masonic body. It was resuscitated or re-organized at the Battle of the Diamond, in September, 1795;—and it assisted in putting the Irish rebellion down, in 1798—the Canadian rebellion, under the leadership of Sir Allan McNab, in 1837,—and had an arm put into its hands by the Whig Government, to assist in crushing the rebellion of Smith O'Brien, in 1848. These are shortly its principles, objects, and actions; and it invites all loyal, patriotic protestants, who value their civil and religious liberties, the purity of their wives and daughters from the disgusting, obscene, filthy popish confessional, and the protection of their own firesides from the encroachments of popery, to band themselves together in connexion with this loyal band of brotherhood; and preserve intact, the present liberties we now enjoy—so dearly purchased for us by the martyred blood of our forefathers—and hand them down to unborn generations!

It provides for the sickness of its members; and relief when in search of employment; their decent interment, and also that of their wives; thereby, combining benevolence with principle.

The motto on the Orange Lodge Laws:—"The members are called Orangemen in honour of William the Third, Prince of Orange, and King of England, whose name they assume, and whose memory they cherish in grateful consideration of the deliverance from popery and tyranny, effected under Providence, by that wise and resolute man."

In conclusion, this society condemns all ill-feeling towards any man; it is slow to take offence, and offering none; but is firmly attached, and determined to support, maintain, and defend the sovereign,—the protestant religion and the liberties of the empire.

By order of the North Eastern Province of the Grand Protestant Association of Loyal Orangemen of England.

BENJAMIN BAILEY, P. G. S.,
No. 12½, Park Row, Leeds.

[Squire Auty, Printer, Bradford.]

A New Loyal Song

In Memory of the Heroes who Fought at

Derry, Aughrim, and the Boyne.

You true loyal sons of King William I will sing you a new
Orange lay,
Of heroes who fought for our freedom their memory will never
decay;
At the Boyne, Londonderry, and Aughrim, the Orange flag
proudly did wave,
They freed us from traitors like Gladstone, for Britons shall
never be slaves.

Chorus—

Hurrah for the union of England, long live Victoria our Queen;
Parnell and his crew they will never make laws for us in
College Green.

Parnell now and Gladstone may babble, one thing they never
can do.
Break the tie that binds us together and unite the Orange and
Blue;
If they dare to usurp or to trample our rights we together
will join,
And march like the conquering heroes, our fathers who fought
at the Boyne.

Our fathers they fought and they conquered for privilege and
right did combine;
The Army of James they encountered and victories were at the
Boyne,
The Prince of Orange commanded; King James that day took
to flight,
While King William cried No Surrender, and led on his men
to the fight.

The day of that historic battle, history recalls us to mind,
James and his army encampted on the south bank of the
Boyne,
At sunrise our bugle sounded, each hero for action prepared
Our Artillery well in the centre, the Cavalry close in the rere.

Our cannons like thunder did rattle, musketry showered like
hail,
Our Cavalry forded the river and the south bank did regain,
A cheer and a charge of our heroes completely forced them to
yield,
We captured their guns in position, in disorder they fled from
the field.

Gladstone is still agitating Morley, Parnell, and Co.,
The Union they want for to sever, that we all very well know,
Ere submit to injustice, united again we will join,
Like the heroes that fought with King William, and conquered
that day at the Boyne.

Nicholson, Printer, 26, Church Lane, Belfast.

The SHANKHILL ROAD HEROES.

Loyal Orange Lodge, No. 1923.

———:o:———

Unfurl the banner now, my boys,
Unfurl the banner blue,
Come rally round the dear old flag
Like loyal men and true;
Like loyal men and true, my boys,
Like loyal men and true—
Ye heroes of the Shankhill Road
Be ever firm and true.

The number Nineteen Twenty Three
May it have a spotless fame—
Orange heroes of the Shankhill Road
Knox, the worthy master's name.
In history's page may they ever shine
Like Derry's sons of old,
Inspired by such valiant deeds,
May their hearts be ever bold.

May they ever on the dear old Twelfth
The banner blue display,
To the merry tune of fife and drum
May they ever march away.
Like William's sons who at the Boyne
Did James's men defy,
May they ever hoist their banner blue
On the 12th day of July.

In the year eighteen and eighty-two,
The 11th time they unfurled their flag,
When fifty chosen men and true
With fife and drum they marched away,
Their wives and sweethearts with them
went,
The day being very fine—
The tune they played when going away
Was the Battle of the Boyne.

———————

Orange Cards for Ball Anniversaries, Soirees.
Circulars for meetings, &c., can be had on the
shortest notice and most reasonable terms at
J. NICHOLSON'S, Printer, Cheapside, Church
Lane, Belfast.

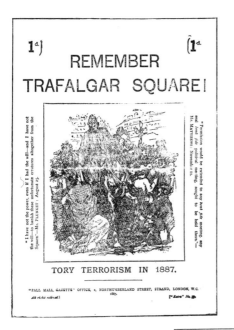

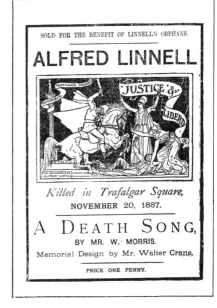

DECIMAS

JOHN F. KENNEDY presidente de los Estados Unidos de Norte America,

FUE ASESINADO EN DALLAS, ESTADO DE TEJAS

La muerte del Presidente
de los Estados Unidos
todo el mundo la ha sentido
en Oriente y Occidente.

1

Llora una madre querida
entre amargura y dolor
por el hijo de su amor
que triste perdió la vida
y la esposa entristecida
sufriendo valientemente
consuela sus inocentes
y pequeñas criaturas
que lloran con amargura
la muerte del Presidente.

2

John F. Kennedy murió
en Dallas Tejas señores
que entre vitores y flores
alegre le recibió
mas lo que allí sucedió
dejó a todos sorprendidos
cuando este fué abatido
de dos certeros balazos
siendo el mas complejo caso
de los Estados Unidos

3

En medio del estupor
Kennedy se reclinaba
y su esposa le aguantaba
sufriendo el mas cruel dolor
cuentan que el Gobernador
Conolly fué grave herido
todo acto fué suspendido
grande fué la confusión
ya que la vil agresión
todo el mundo la ha sentido

4

Una mano criminal
cuentan que un rifle esgrimía
el viernes a medio día
con fanatismo infernal
y el hombre que fué mundial
ante el peligro valiente
saludando sonriente
los disparos recibía
y la tristeza cundía
en Oriente y Occidente

5

Al hospital fué llevado
se le hicieron transfusiones
según las informaciones
Kennedy ya había expirado
su espiritu había marchado
hacia Dios Omnipotente
se fué repentinamente
cuando menos se esperaba
y todo el mundo lloraba
la muerte del Presidente

6

La Alianza para el Progreso
y los Derechos Civiles
fueron sus temas sutiles
por la paz del universo
que destino tan adverso
le acogió desprevenido
cuando un pueblo reunido
lo aclamaba alegremente
cayó herido el Presidente
de los Estados Unidos

7

Mami donde está papito
preguntan dos criaturas
y en medio de su amargura
clama una madre ay bendito
no se apuren mis hijitos
que su papito ha salido
así es amigos queridos
que entre la pena taladre
la tristeza de una madre
todo el mundo la ha sentido

8

Oh Dios Padre Soberano
acoge en Tu Santo Seno
aquel hombre que fué bueno
tiéndele Tu Santa Mano
quien por el orbe mundano
luchó tesoneramente
Kennedy el gran Presidente
que tan vil fué asesinado
por el que el llanto ha brotado
en Oriente y Occidente.

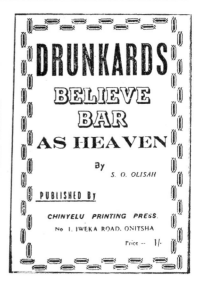

CHAPBOOKS (pages 151–152)

The Lover's Magazine ($5'' \times 7\frac{1}{2}''$) is an Aldemary Church Yard publication some time after 1760 (one sold is 'God bless great George the Third') of the type called a 'garland'—a collection of songs. *The Appearance of An Angel to a Minister* ($4\frac{1}{2}'' \times 7''$) would appear to be the short title of a late eighteenth century tract which tells the story outline in one breathless cover sentence. *Seven of the Most Popular Songs* ($3\frac{3}{4}'' \times 6''$) is one of a long series of late nineteenth century song and ballad chapbooks. *Mary, the Maid of the Inn* ($3\frac{3}{4}'' \times 6\frac{3}{4}''$) is a single sheet folded into 24 pages. The miniature novel is followed by a poem of Southey on the same theme. Davison of Alnwick published in partnership with James Catnach's father.

The Famous History of Friar Bacon ($3\frac{3}{4}'' \times 6\frac{3}{4}''$), a favourite chapbook subject, relates folk legends of the medieval Roger Bacon, probably deriving from Greene's play *The Honourable Historie of frier Bacon, and frier Bongay* circa 1594. *The History of Jack & the Giants* ($3\frac{3}{4}'' \times 6\frac{3}{4}''$) is from the press of John Turner, Coventry, who printed many ballads and chapbooks. *The Pilgrim's Progress* ($3\frac{3}{4}'' \times 6''$) is a late chapbook version of Bunyan's masterpiece, the one book next to the Bible which had the greatest influence on the common people and was most often found in cottage libraries. *The Colrain Lass* ($4'' \times 6\frac{3}{4}''$), printed in Ireland, is typical of nineteenth century chapbooks which used old woodcuts.

CHILDREN'S LITERATURE (pages 153–154)

The Child's Easy Primer ($3\frac{1}{2}'' \times 5\frac{9}{16}''$) is an attractively printed and illustrated item, deriving from similar chapbooks produced by Davison of Alnwick. *New & Improved Battledore* ($8\frac{1}{4}'' \times 5''$) is a nineteenth century variation of the old horn-book, by which children learned their alphabet. Cardboard battledores are said to have been invented circa 1746 by Benjamin Collins, who sold more than 100,000 in ten years.

Nursery Poems and *An Elegy on the Death and Burial of Cock Robin* (both $2\frac{9}{16}'' \times 3\frac{7}{8}''$) are well printed and illustrated. Both Kendrew and Rusher were noted for such small children's chapbooks. The device on the cover of *Nursery Poems* is also found on a trade token of W. Rusher, 'Hatter, Bookseller & Stationer', who was the father of J. G. Rusher. *The Babes in the Wood* ($3'' \times 5\frac{7}{8}''$) is another Davison of Alnwick chapbook, with charming title lettering and decorative border. *History of Cinderella* ($3\frac{7}{8}'' \times 6''$) lists over a hundred penny 'Histories, Religious Tracts, Song Books, &c.' on the back cover. Basic motifs of the Cinderella story have been traced back to ancient Hindu myths.

HANDBILLS (page 155)

The two enticing Lottery advertisements were printed by Evans & Ruffey, London. *The Battle of Neuve Chappelle* ($4\frac{1}{4}'' \times 5\frac{5}{8}''$) is a late example of the old tradition of using 'A Copy of Verses' for begging purposes. *Juliet* ($2\frac{7}{8}'' \times 5\frac{3}{4}''$) is an advertisement for Warren's Blacking, in the style of the Lottery advertisements. This was the business where young Charles Dickens slaved before he became an author, and he mentions that Warren employed a poet for publicity.

ALMANAC (page 156)

Vox Stellarum ($4'' \times 6\frac{1}{4}''$), a forerunner of 'Old Moore's Almanack', first appeared in 1700. It became a best-seller of the Company of Stationers before they lost their monopoly of almanacs. Moore died circa 1715, but a succession of ghost-writers has continued his Almanac into present times.

STREET NOTICES (pages 157–159)

The Speech of the Prince of Orange ($7\frac{1}{2}'' \times 11\frac{3}{4}''$) marks a critical stage in English history, with the landing of William of Orange. This speech was cited by Macaulay as 'short, dignified and well considered'. *The Old Grey Tory* ($11'' \times 8\frac{3}{4}''$), an election poster of 1836, was printed by Rusher of Banbury, who also published children's chapbooks. *Diarrhoea* ($11\frac{3}{16}'' \times 17\frac{5}{16}''$), a street notice of 1866, recalls the epidemic problems of nineteenth century London life. The main heading is in the 'Playbill' typeface associated with theatre bills.

BROADSIDE BALLADS and PROSE BROADSIDES
(pages 160–186)

Oppertunity Lost ($13'' \times 8\frac{1}{2}''$) is a Black-Letter ballad that illustrates typical 'general purpose' woodcuts suitable for many different occasions. For the tune, see Claude M. Simpson *The British Broadside Ballad and its Music* (1966).

Lord Thomas and Fair Eleanor ($14\frac{1}{2}'' \times 10\frac{1}{4}''$) is a nineteenth century reprinting of this old ballad, using a copy of the woodcut on *Oppertunity Lost*, possibly descending to John Pitts from a Dicey and Marshall original. This ballad was often sung to the tune of *Chevy Chase* (see Simpson, *The British Broadside Ballad and its Music*).

Chevy Chace ($10\frac{1}{4}'' \times 14\frac{1}{2}''$) is an early nineteenth century reprinting of a broadside first registered 14 December 1624. Prior to the broadside version, there was an earlier traditional ballad of *The Hunting of the Cheviot* (Child, No 162) relating to the great battle of Otterburn in 1388. Addison's famous appreciation of the ballad in *The Spectator* (Nos 70 and 74) probably derives from the broadside version. *Chevy Chase* also has pride of place as the first item in Percy's *Reliques*; Percy had dedicated the work to the Countess of Northumberland.

The Just Judgment of God shew'd upon Dr. John Faustus ($12\frac{3}{4} \times 8\frac{1}{2}''$) circa 1690–1700, was a popular subject, often used in prose chapbooks. The woodcut also appeared on an earlier broadside *The Tragedy of Doctor Lambe* (1628) on a similar theme.

The Wandering Jew ($13\frac{1}{4}'' \times 8\frac{1}{4}''$) is an eighteenth to nineteenth century reprinting of a ballad first registered 1 March 1675. The legend circulated in the thirteenth century and became a popular chapbook subject.

Jockey's Escape from bonny Dundee ($12\frac{1}{2}'' \times 8''$) is sometimes ascribed to D'Urfey, but may be earlier. It is printed in D'Urfey's *Pills* (V, 17) with music. The ballad inspired Scott's 'The Doom of Devorgoil', to be sung to the same tune.

The Faithless Captain, Or Betrayed Virgin ($14'' \times 9\frac{3}{4}''$), printed by John Pitts, was a popular eighteenth century piece.

Death and the Lady ($12\frac{3}{4}'' \times 8\frac{1}{4}''$) was first printed in the seventeenth century with a solemn homily after the title: 'From whence it appears that Death is no Respecter of Persons, either for Birth or Beauty; so that, as sure as we are born, we shall certainly die: Therefore let us prepare ourselves against that Hour and Time, so that he may appear as a welcome Messenger [who] brings glad tidings.'

The Bloody Gardener's Cruelty ($9'' \times 13\frac{1}{4}''$). This pathetic eighteenth century ballad has been recorded by A. L. Lloyd in the LP album *English Street Songs*, Riverside [USA] RLP.12–614.

Reason: or, the Unwilling Maid and Amorous Squire ($4\frac{3}{4}'' \times 13\frac{3}{4}''$), *The Beaver's Prize* ($4\frac{1}{2}'' \times 14''$), and *William Far Away* ($3\frac{3}{4}'' \times 11\frac{3}{4}''$) are typical eighteenth century single slip ballads.

The Beggar ($3\frac{3}{4}'' \times 9\frac{3}{4}''$), *The Belfast Mountains* ($3\frac{3}{4}'' \times 10\frac{1}{4}''$), and and *Cold Winter is Past* ($3\frac{1}{2}'' \times 9\frac{3}{4}''$) are typical of the nineteenth century single slips published by John Pitts.

The Maiden's Bantam Cock ($3\frac{1}{4}'' \times 9\frac{1}{2}''$) and *Vilikins and His*

Dinah (3″ × 10″) are single slip ballads from another printer, probably J. Harkness of Preston. The former title is a popular piece of folk bawdry, the latter is a comical version of the tragic song 'William and Diana'.

Chanting Benny, or the Batch of Ballads ($7\frac{1}{2}$″ × 10″) is a 'medley'— a song made up from cross readings of titles of other songs. This type of broadside was known as early as 1620. Such medleys are valuable in indicating titles of songs that were popular in their time.

Uncle Tom's Cabin/The Pope He Leads a Happy Life/I Cannot Mind My Wheel ($7\frac{1}{2}$″ × 10″) was printed by J. O. Bebbington, Manchester. This is a type of broadside common in the latter half of the nineteenth century, printing three songs on one quarto sheet. Although such sheets would not cut down the middle into two self-contained halfpenny ballads, they appeared special value as three songs for one penny. Sometimes the two smaller songs were cut off and pasted on to larger slips. *Uncle Tom's Cabin* brings the story of Mrs Stowe's substantial best-seller into the compass of a short song.

I Shall Be Married On Monday Morning/The Pope He Leads a Happy Life ($7\frac{1}{2}$″ × 10″) is typical of the way country and town songs were coupled on one sheet, rather like the 'A' and 'B' sides of a 78 rpm gramophone record. This sheet is one of a series using very decorative titles and borders.

The Banks of Inverary/The Constant Lovers ($7\frac{1}{2}$″ × $10\frac{1}{4}$″) bears the Catnach imprint on both columns of the sheet, designed to be cut down the middle into two halfpenny ballads if need be. Both items are good country style songs. *The Constant Lovers* was mentioned by Samuel Lover in 1837, who heard it sung in Dublin with the second line rendered 'That lived *convaynient* to the Isle of Man'. This prompted an amusing parody by song writer Percy French, whose 'Come-All-Ye' opens:

> Oh! a sailor courted a farmer's daughter;
> Who lived contagious to the Isle of Man

Sale of a Wife ($7\frac{1}{2}$″ × $10\frac{1}{4}$″) was printed by Walker of Ottley. It refers to a folk belief that it was legal to sell your wife provided that you put a rope round her neck and auctioned her in the market-place, thus putting her in the category of cattle. Unbelievably, this practice persisted into the late nineteenth century. In 1882, one woman was sold by her husband for a glass of ale, and another husband disposed of his spouse for the bargain price of one penny and a dinner.

Uncle Ned's Description of the Bloomers ($7\frac{3}{8}'' \times 10\frac{1}{8}''$). The reform dress of nineteenth century Women's Lib advocate Mrs Amelia Bloomer included a short skirt, with loose trousers gathered round the ankles. This costume was introduced in 1849 and was inevitably named 'bloomers'. It became a favourite topic for humorists of the day.

Baby Farming ($7\frac{3}{8}'' \times 9\frac{3}{4}''$) deals with a very real problem of nineteenth century Britain. George Moore's novel *Esther Waters* tells the heartrending story of a young unmarried mother obliged to hire herself out as wet-nurse and deny her own child.

The Ivy Green/Woodman Spare that Tree ($7\frac{1}{4}'' \times 9\frac{3}{4}''$). Charles Dickens's song *The Ivy Green* was set to music by no less than four composers, and the words pirated by many broadside ballad printers. The most popular version was that of Henry Russell, who made the song known in America as well as London. The words of *Woodman Spare that Tree* were written by American poet George Morris, and the music composed by Henry Russell, who popularised the song on both sides of the Atlantic. On one occasion when Russell was singing this item, a man in the audience stood up excitedly and demanded, 'Was the tree spared, sir?' 'It was,' replied Russell. 'Thank God for that!' said the man, resuming his seat with a sigh of heartfelt relief.

God: a poem, by Derzhavin ($9'' \times 10\frac{1}{8}''$). I have been unable to discover the printer, or any other information concerning this broadside, but it must be the only such poem to be translated into Japanese (embroidered with gold), and Chinese and Tartar languages.

The Wonderful Adventures of Mr. O'Flynn in Search of Old Mother Clifton! ($7\frac{1}{2}'' \times 10''$). Such nonsense pieces are related to the speech of the character the Doctor in folk mumming plays, and to the mountebank speeches of early medical charlatans.

The Pig-Faced Lady ($11'' \times 16''$). A nineteenth century survival of a legend that was old even in 1639, when Henry Glapthorne, in his play *Wit in a Constable*, has this crushing rejoinder to a vendor of new ballads':

> There you lie, boy.
> I doubt it is some lamentable stuff,
> O' the swine-faced gentlewoman, and that you'll grunt out
> Worse than a parish boar when he makes love

Unto the vicar's sow; her story's stale, boy;
 't has been already in two plays.

Nearly three hundred years later, the Fairburn broadside attempts to give verisimilitude by a coloured portrait and an address in Manchester Square, London.

The Royal Fortune Teller! ($9\frac{1}{2}'' \times 15''$). An attractively printed catchpenny from Catnach. In spite of the occult atmosphere of the sheet, the verses simply give witty commonsense advice.

The Evergreen ($9\frac{3}{4}'' \times 14\frac{3}{4}''$). A carol sheet with quaint old woodcuts, hand-coloured. Some of the verses are old folk carols, such as 'As I sat on a sunny bank' and 'The Joys of Mary'. There were also carol sheets twice this size.

The Ladies Concert ($7\frac{1}{2}'' \times 19''$). A 'long-song sheet' published by Pitts, containing fourteen separate songs.

D'Goliath-Risewal-Stinkballade ($4\frac{1}{2}'' \times 19''$). A modern long-song sheet of irreverent verses from the Basle Fastnacht festival 1960, printed on pink paper.

NEWSPAPERS (pages 187–188)

The London Gazette, No 1659, 10 to 13 October 1681 ($7\frac{1}{2}'' \times 11\frac{1}{4}''$). The first newspaper, as distinct from news pamphlets. It began on 16 November 1665 as *The Oxford Gazette* and was renamed with issue No 24.

The Tatler, No 34, 25 to 28 June 1709 ($7\frac{3}{4}'' \times 12\frac{5}{8}''$). Richard Steele was editor of *The London Gazette* in 1707. *The Tatler* first appeared 12 April 1709, and most of the early numbers were all written by Steele. After No 18, Addison began to write for it.

Both official and literary newspapers were unattractive to the man in the street, as well as expensive.

THE NEWS IN VERSE (pages 189–195)

A group of nineteenth century penny news ballads:

Copy of Verses on the Late Dreadful Fire ($7\frac{1}{2}'' \times 10''$), *Long Life to Captain Webb!* ($7\frac{1}{2}'' \times 9\frac{7}{8}''$), *Lord Palmerston He is a Clever Man* ($7\frac{1}{2}'' \times 10\frac{1}{8}''$), *We'll Not Forget Poor Roger Now* [the Tichbourne case] ($7\frac{1}{2}'' \times 9\frac{3}{4}''$), *The Outrage & Murder on a Little Child at Purfleet* ($7\frac{1}{2}'' \times 9\frac{3}{4}''$), *Murder at Cambridge* ($7\frac{1}{2}'' \times 10''$), *Murder of M. Marten, by W. Corder/Wilt thou say Farewell Love* ($7\frac{3}{4}'' \times 9\frac{11}{16}''$).

EXECUTION SHEETS (pages 196–199)

The Condemnation of Oliver Plunket ($8'' \times 12\frac{1}{8}''$). Accused of complicity in a 'Popish Plot', Plunkett was convicted on the flimsiest of evidence, and duly hanged, drawn and quartered at Tyburn in 1681.

An Account of the Execution of Brigadier Rookwood, Major Lowick, and Mr. Cranburn ($7\frac{1}{2}'' \times 12''$). These Jacobite conspirators planned an assassination of William III. The sheet gives a clear factual report of their last hours before being hanged and quartered at Tyburn, 1696.

The Last Dying Words and Confession of Benjamin Wike, alias John Smith ($8\frac{7}{16}'' \times 14\frac{11}{16}''$). According to what is presented as his own account, Wike was a pedlar who took to highway robbery, and the story is told with much skill. This detailed narrative abruptly goes into third person as 'the unhappy culprit' in the last paragraph, which describes how Wike was hanged. The woodcut at the head of the sheet is a stock one, used for any execution.

Execution of Five Pirates ($7\frac{1}{2}'' \times 9\frac{3}{4}''$). Five foreign sailors on the vessel *Flowery Land* committed mutiny and murder on the high seas, were tried at the Old Bailey, London, and executed 22 February 1864.

THE IRISH QUESTION (pages 200–201)
Grand Protestant Association of Loyal Orangemen ($5\frac{1}{8}'' \times 7\frac{1}{2}''$) and *The English Murderer at Work* ($5'' \times 7\frac{1}{2}''$) are two rival political handbills that make interesting comparison. The pro-Orange bill proclaims civil and religious liberty and tolerance to all—except to its 'disgusting, obscene, and filthy' enemies! The Republican bill follows the equally well-established propaganda convention that all revolutionaries and terrorists are heroes, and those who imprison them are murderers.

A pro-Orange ballad-sheet of the 1880s with a song about 'The Shankhill Road Heroes' exhibits a hard-line sentiment still propagated in 1972.

DEMONSTRATION IN TRAFALGAR SQUARE 1887
(page 202)
In 1886, following widespread unemployment and hardship, William Morris championed the cause of free speech in Trafalgar Square. A year later came the great demonstration of Irish and Radical protest against the arrest of Mr W. O'Brien, MP. *Reynold's News* and the *Pall Mall Gazette* upheld the right of free speech, and denounced the undoubted brutality of the police on 'Bloody Sunday', 13 November 1887. Three people were killed, and over two hundred admitted to

hospital with injuries. Mr Cunninghame Graham, MP, later to be famous as an unconventional author, was arrested and imprisoned for two months. Alfred Linnell, an innocent bystander at the demonstration, was trampled by a police horse and his thigh broken. He died in Charing Cross Hospital a few days later from 'blood-poisoning'. William Morris and Walter Crane collaborated on a memorial pamphlet to raise money for Linnell's family. It is ironic that some present-day demonstrators now claim the freedom to make unprovoked assaults on police and property, describing all restraint as 'brutality'.

MODERN BROADSIDE BALLAD FROM PUERTO RICO
(page 203)

Decimas on the assassination of President John F. Kennedy ($8\frac{1}{2}'' \times 11''$). Verses printed on a sheet of pink paper, and sold in the street for 5 centavos.

MODERN CHAPBOOKS (page 204)

Beware of Harlots and Many Friends and *Drunkards Believe Bar as Heaven*. Two cheap pamphlets of a modern literacy explosion, sold in the market at Onitsha, Nigeria.

A Morte dos 12 Pares de Franca ($4\frac{3}{16}'' \times 6\frac{1}{4}''$) and *O Fim do Mondo* ($4\frac{1}{4}'' \times 6\frac{1}{4}''$), two cheaply printed chapbooks in traditional style consisting of a single sheet folded into 32 or 16 pages, sold uncut and unstitched. *A Morte dos 12 Pares de Franca* tells an ancient story of Charlemagne and the twelve Peers of France. *O Fim do Mondo* is typical of modern apocalyptic religious cult literature of Brazil, and describes the end of the world.

Appendix

Appendix

JAMES CATNACH was established at No 2 Monmouth Court, Seven Dials, London, in 1813, after the death of his father John Catnach who had come to London from Alnwick. The Catnach Press soon outpaced that of John Pitts, previously the leading Seven Dials publisher of street literature.

The original Catnach press could turn out 200 copies an hour, with a top rate of 300. In 1823, with a sensational murder case, Catnach used four presses, and by working day and night for a week, produced 250,000 copies of one broadside.

Catnach retired from business in 1838, when the press was managed by his sister Mrs Anne Ryle with James Paul. Catnach died in 1841. Paul retired from partnership in 1845, when the business continued as A. Ryle & Co. It was eventually acquired by W. S. Fortey, who revived the Catnach imprint as 'The Catnach Press (Established 1813)'. About 1882 Fortey gave up the old Catnach and Ryle premises at Monmouth Court and moved to No 4 Great St Andrew Street, only a couple of doors from the original 'Toy and Marble Warehouse' of John Pitts. Fortey died 14 April 1901.

The Catalogue of James Catnach in 1832 gives an excellent impression of the range of traditional and topical street ephemera of the period, reminiscent of the Dicey and Marshall catalogues of Aldermary Church Yard in the previous century. Old traditional ballads and children's chapbooks are listed side by side with the new songs of the day.

CATALOGUE

OF

SONGS AND SONG BOOKS,

SHEETS, HALF-SHEETS,

CHRISTMAS CAROLS, CHILDREN'S BOOKS,

&c. &c. &c.

PRINTED AND PUBLISHED BY

2, MONMOUTH COURT, SEVEN DIALS.

1832.

Established in 1813.

2   *CATALOGUE.—SONGS.*

ARCHER Boy
   Arab Steed
Auld Lang Syne
All's Well
Arthur O'Bradley's Wedding
Alice Gray
All the Lads in the village come wooing, &c.
American Stranger
Answer to garden gate
—— to light guitar
—— to heart and lute
—— to Home, sweet home
—— to Isabel
—— to the lamenting maid
—— to Old England for ever shall weather
    the storm
—— to the blue eye'd stranger
—— to Oh no, we never mention her
—— to Barney Brallaghan
—— to Burns's lovely Jane
—— to Colin and Phœbe
—— to Kate Kearney
—— to the Bloom is on the Rye
Affectionate soldier
A red, red, rose
Alne's Vale
Allan Water
Around the huge oak
Auld Robin Grey.
Allen A-Dale
And has she then fail'd in her truth
Amynta
Adieu my native land'
An old man was wooing
Away with Melancholy
Arethusa
Adieu to Old England, or the Transport's
    farewell
Battle Field
Blue bonnets over the Border
Buy a broom
Billy Barlow
Banks of the Dee
Buffalo
Betsy Baker
Ballenden Braes
Barclay & Perkins's drayman
Black-eye'd Susan
Blue bells of Scotland
Bold Robin Hood
Barney Brallaghan's courtship
Banks of the Band
Britons, strike home
Banks of Claudy
Blue tail'd fly
Blackbird
Banks of the Suir
Butcher turned devil
Ben Block
Bread, Cheese, and Kisses.
Battle of the Shannon and Chesapeake
Be careful in choosing a wife
Behold how brightly breaks the morn
Banner of war
Bright Phœbus
Belfast Mountains

Billy O' Rooke's the boy, sir
Beverley maid and the tinker
Betsy of Dundee
Breeches
Brighton Camp, or the girl I left behind me
Ben Backstay
Bold Pedlar and Robin Hood
Banks of Allan Water
Banks of the Clyde
Braes of Birneybouzle
Banks of Forth
Border widow's lament
Billy Taylor
Bonny Dundee.
Bonny Tweedside
Blythe, blythe, blythe was she
Bower, The
Bannocks of barley meal
Bush aboon Traquair
Braes of Yarrow
Birks of Aberfeldy
By the gaily circling glass
Blow thou winter wind
Bonny breast knot
Barney Brallaghan's wedding
Bonny Roy
Bonny lass o'Branksom
Banks of Banna
Bold dragoon
Buy a mop
Bottle o' Rum
Blanch
Birds of a feather
Beautiful boy
Banks of Doun
British true blue
Bow Bells
Bonny blue handkerchief
Bonny blue jacket
Baran doun braes
Battle of the Nile
Bold farriers
Bold Irishman
Bold privateers
Bailiffs have been
Bedlam City
Britannia's revenge
Braham's Beautiful Maid
Begone Dull Care.
Brown jug
Banner so blue
Beautiful maid
Bay of Biscay O
Bid me discourse
Billy Barlow's wedding
Blue eye'd Mary
Bunch of rushes
Butterfly was a gentleman
Bold General Wolfe
Bill Bounce, the swell cove
Billy Barlow's wedding miseries
Bound prentice to a waterman
Bewilder'd Maid.
Captain Bell, a parody on Isabel
Cupid the pretty plough boy.
Come landlord fill a flowing bowl

CATALOGUE.—SONGS.   3

Cottagers Widow
Cabin Boy
Curly Hair
Crazy Jane
Cherry Ripe
Canadian boat song
Colin and Phœbe
Cottage near a wood
Caledonian maid
Curly headed plough boy
Croppy boy
Cries of London
Come where the Aspens
Cottage on the moor
Castilian maid
Content, a pastoral
Cookey's courtship
Chapter of noses
Cuckoo
Constant lovers
Cold winter is past
Cruel ship carpenter
Cottage in the grove
Country Girl
Carpet weaver
Cowden knows
Calder fair
Colin stole my heart away
Cold flinty rock.
Cottager's daughter
Coversation between the Monument and St. Paul's
Countryman's rambles in Cheapside.
Christening and diversions of Ballyporeen
Deserter
Dashing white sergeant
Death of Parker
Distressed Maid
Devil and Mike
Donald of Dundee
Dame Durden
Draw the sword Scotland
Dunois the brave
Drink to me only
Deep, deep, Sea
Death of General Wolfe
Duke of Marlborough
Dark eye'd sailor
Drowsy Sleeper
Down in our village
Disobedient daughter
Death of Nelson
Down Hill of life
Disconsolate sailor
Dusky night
Doating old man
Duke William
Don't let me die a maid
Dustman
Deploring damse.
Down the Burn, Davie
Dear Creatures
Dolly Duggans
Dulce Domum

Each has a lover but me
Ettrick banks
Evelyn's bower
Endearing young charms
England is the land we love
Exciseman
Evening Star
Exile of Erin
Effect of Love
Englishman's wife, God bless her
Fly from the world, oh, Bessy to me
Flowers of Dumblane
Frozen river
Fly not yet
Fly away pretty moth
Fairest Flower
Fall not in Love
Firm as Oak
False lover
Female drummer
Farmer's boy
Fair Zephyr
Fanny Blair
Follow over mountains
Female auctioneer
Fighting for the breeches
Flounce to your gown
Fanny in the valley
Feyther's old sow
Fireman waterman
Forsaken Shepherdess
Friend and pitcher
Flowing bowl
Fair Susan
Follow the drum
Fit comes on me now
Faint and wearily
Farmer's Son
Four Seasons of the Year
Farmer's courtship
Fox chase
Fair Flora
Farewell he
Fisherman's boy
Great Flopping Bonnets
Gay Guitar
Girl of my heart
Golden glove
Garden gate
Galley slave
Green bushes
Girl I left behind me
Good husband
Grand conversation under the rose
Glasses sparkle on the board
Gentle Moon
Goddess Diana
Good old days of Adam & Eve
Garland of love
Guy Fawkes and the Parliament
Grandfather's pet
Gown of Green

Gilderoy
Generous farmer
God save the King
Gallant sailor
Gosport beach
Gallant Mars
Grumbling Farmers
Green grow the rushes O
Gallant Troubadour
Green Hills of Tyrol
Ground for the floor
Glorious Apollo
Going to Chelsea to buy buns
Gipsey Laddie
Gleaners
Golden vanity, or the low lands low
Glorious victory of Navarino
Highland home
Here's a health to all good Lasses
Hurrah for the bonnets of blue
Huge Oak
Harry Bluff
Heart of Oak is King William
Hunter's horn
Heart that can feel for ano ther
He was fam'd for deeds of Arms
Heart and Lute
How to change a sovereign
Highland Mary
Harry Hawser
Health to the Ladies
Henry's gone to the wars
Henry Martin
Hope told a flattering tale
Hurrah for the Jackets so blue
Home, sweet home
Home, love is home, be it ever so homely
Heat'y good fellow
Happy shepherd
Hearts of Oak
Honour calls me to the field
Her mouth with a smile
Health to Fair Scotland
Huntsman's chorus
Highland minstrel boy
Hot codlings
Highland Kitty
Henry and Nancy
Here we meet too soon to part
Hounds are all out ·
Is there a heart
I'd be a butterfly
In my cottage near a wood
Incontrovertible facts
I never says nothing to nobody
I love thee night and day love
I'm in haste
I've been roaming
I hae seen the roses blaw
Isabel
Is not it a pity
Irish stranger

4   *CATALOGUE—SONGS.*

If I had a donkey wot wouldn't go
Innocent mirth
I'm often drunk
I love somebody
Isle of St. Helena
I sowed the seeds of love
Irish School
I stood amid the glittering (throng
Jolly Jack Tar
Judy's black eyes
Jack Robinson
Jack of Ambrose Mill
Johnny Lowre
Jack on the Green
Jemmy is slain in the wars
Johnny to the fair
Jack of all trades
Jeremy Diddler, the fiddler
Julia to the Wood-robin
Jerry Duff
Jack Williams, the boatswain
Jack's the lad
Joe of the Bell
Jack returned from sea
Jolly sailor
Jockey to the fair
Joe, the marine
King, God bless him
King of the Canibal Islands
Keel Row
Kate of Aberdeen
Knight of the Golden Crest
Kitty of Coleraine
King and the countryman
Kennedy I O
Kiss dear maid
Knight of the Cross
Kate Kearney
King William IV. for ever
King, Heaven bless him
King and Sailor
Lash'd to the helm
Lady fell in love with a 'prentice
Labourer's welcome home
Love Sick Policeman
Lovely Ann
Lament foo Georgy
Loss of one hero
Lilies and roses
Larry O'Gaff
Loch Erock side
Lass wi' the bonny blue 'een
Light Guitar
Lass of Richmond Hill
Let us haste to Kelvin grove
Last Rose of Summer
Love has eyes
Light bark
Little dun mare
Lubin is away
Lord Bateman
Lass of Teviot side
Lovely sailor
Legacy
Live not were I love

Last farewell
Land, boys, we live in
Love's a Tyrant
Lilies in the valley grew
Lads of the village
Lamenting maid
Love sick maid.
London heiress
Love's roundelay
Lovely Joan
Lord Thomas & Fair Eleanor
Lass of London City
Life let us cherish
London merchant
Landing of Royal Charlie
Love's Ritornella
Love in Long Acre
Long time I've courted you,
Lass o'Gowrie (miss
Lasses, lasses, listen
Little Lowland Queen
Leicestershire Chambermaid
Little Mary, the sailor's bride
Love in a hayband
Lullaby
Lass of Hazledean
Love was once a little boy
Lover's meeting
Lucky farmer's boy
Lass that loves a sailor
Lumpkin and Fan
Lass of Dundee
Lamentations of poor old Father Thames
Moon is up
Mary's Love
Minute gun at sea
Mad-brained King of the Frenchmen
My own blue bell
Merry row bonny bark
Merry Swiss boy
Major Longbow
Mary of the Moor
Merry little soldier
My village fair
Mountain Maid
Mower
Meet me by moonlight
May pole
Mr. December
My lodging is on the cold
Mary, list, awake (ground
Merry Swiss Girl
My friend and pitcher
Maiden of Staffa
Mistress Judy Minningen
Mr. Lowe and Miss Cundy
Milkmaid of Blackbury Fold
Monkey turned barber
Mountains high
Milkmaid
Milkmaid coming from the wake
Marian's my Lily
Money is your friend
Maid of Langollen

March for the red, &c.
Moon is on the hill
Minstrel boy
Maid of the Mill
Mary's Lament
My Highland Home
Mary of the Dale
My dear little girl that lives in yon cot
Mermaid
Molly Popps
Mrs. Munday
Mary's dream
Merchant and Shepherdess
Men, what silly things you are
Merry Hay-makers
Mariner's Compass
My father kept a horse
Maid's Lament for her sailor boy
Maria Louisa's lament, or the green linnet
New landlord of the Crown
New version of Adam & Eve
Nancy of Yarmouth
Not a drum was heard
Never marry a Charlie
New fashioned farmer
Nan of the Valley.
New God save the King
Newgate walls
New Mary Neil
Nut girl
Nosegay girl
No we never mention her
Nothing, a new song
New sailor's farewell
New Jack of all trades
Nightingale
New mown hay
Our Queen is the wife of a sailor
Oh say not woman's heart is
Old Towler (bought
Old Adam
Old England for ever shall weather the storm
Oh lady fair
Our King is a true British
Oyster girl (sailor
One day while working at my plough
Orphan wet with rain
O 'tis Love
Old miser
Old commodore
Our cottage lay distant a mile
Oh, how I love the ladies
Old Man's Petition
Oh no, my love, no
Oh come to me when daylight sets
Oh! Nanny, wilt thou gang with me
Oh, if I had such a lassy as
Outlandish Knight (this
Oxford City

CATALOGUE—SONGS. 5

6   *CATALOGUE—SONGS.*

Wealth of the cottage
Wild and wicked youth
What will old England come to
Witty shepherd
When the trees are all bare
When pensive I thought on my love
When the rosy morn
Welsh harper
When William at eve
Way worn traveller
What a shocking bad hat

Wild guitar
We met
Willow Tree
Wolf
Wallace bled
What a shocking bad bonnet
When a man's a little bit, &c.
Welchman's leek, or St. David's day
Wandering girl
Wilt thou say farewell, love
Worth of a woman
Worth of a husband

Woodmam
Willow (Old)
We tars have a maxim
World turn'd upside down
Ye banks and braes of Bonny Doon
You shan't come again
Young Love
Young Riley
Young Morgan
Young Colin stole my heart
Young squire   (away
You don't exactly suit me

ADDENDA.

Albion the pride of the Sea
Away to the mountain's brow
Boys of Switzerland
Bonny Maggy Lauder
Britons united
Bonny light horseman
Battle of Algiers
Bold boatswain of Dover
Barnet races
Behold the man that is unlucky
Batchelors Hall
Burns's Farewell
Bold Turpin
Chapter of Cheats
Curious love letter
Conversation between Old & New London Bridge
Comforts of man
Cottage that stands by the sea
Dido and I
Elwina of Waterloo
Fairlop Fair
Fame sound the Trumpet
Free and Easy
Farewell, my trim built wher- (ry
Flowers of the forest
Greenland whale fishery
Giles' Scroggins' Ghost
Goddess of the silver stream
Grand battle of the tally man.
He'll come if he can
Husbandman & Farmingman
Isle of Beauty
Irish girl

Innocent mirth
It was a winter's evening
Johnny Cope
Jane of Tralee
Kentish Cricketers
Kent tragedy
Kitty Jones
Lover's downfal
Loss of the Betsy
Lovers Lament for her Sailor
Listen, dear Fanny
Love and Glory
Marriage of the rose
Maid of Lodi
Maria Martin
May we ne'er want a friend nor a bottle to give him
Mouth of the Nile
Mary the maid of the green.
Milton Oysters
Maid's lamentation
New York streets
New Chapter of Cheats
Now by the waving greenwood tree
O my Love is dead
O take me to your arms, my
Old Conwell, the pilot (love
Overseer outwitted
On board the victory
Pensioner's complaint
Punchinello
Ploughboy's dream
Quite politely

Row with me down the river
Rolling down Wapping
Rest thee, babe
Roving Batchelor
Ribbon stuck in the cap border
Red Cross Knight
Samuel Wright
Sylvia's request
Sailor's home
Sailor's Farewell
Sun that lights the roses
Shipwreck of the Rambler
Sale of a wife
Swiss toy girl
Tobacco's but an Indian weed
The Model
Tom Starboard
The Indian lass
There you go with your eye out
The Fox
Thorney Moor wood
They marched through the town
The Thrasher
Two wenches at once
Valiant soldier
Victim of seduction
Wealthy farmer's son
Word of Advice
We're a' noddin
What won't money do
Weaver's daughter
Will the Weaver

Barbara Allan
Poor Mary Anne
Banks of Blue Moselle
Heavenly Home
Chapter of Accidents
Bonnet so Blue.
Jane of Tyrone
Kelly the Pirate
Brigand's Ritornella
Pretty Page
Soldier's Dream
Soldier's Boy
Girl I adore
Dandy Husband
Dandy Wife

Scotch Blackbird
Advice to Farmers
Devil and Hackney coachman
Child of a Tar
Pretty Chambermaid
Blind Beggar's Daughter
Buy Broom Besom's
Huntsman is winding his horn
Robin Roughhead
Poor Jack
Blue-ey'd Stranger
State of the Times
Dawning of the Day
Finikin Lass
Battle of Trafalgar

Think on the Poor
Pigeon
Lamentation of an Old Horse
Ramilies
High Germany
Humphry Duggins
Castle Hyde
Ri-fum ti-fum
Pennyworth of Wit
Erin go Brah
Young Tyler
Henry the Poacher
Lad that I love
Jolly Toper
Jolly fellows follow plough

N. B.---The Trade and the Public are respectfully informed that an addition to the above Catalogue of Songs takes place every month

CATALOGUE. 7

SONG BOOKS.

Northern Garland
The Guitar
The Nightingale
The Skylark
Golden Harp

Charmer
Minstrel
Neptune's Wreath
The Evergreen
Musical Syren

May Flower
The Lyre
British Songster
Comic Songs and Recitations
Winter's Amusement.

SHEETS or ROYALS.

The Last Day
Elijah fed by ravens
Star of Bethlehem
Noble army of Martyrs
Sun of Righteousness
Travels of the Children of Israel
The Morning Star
The Life of Joseph
The Glory of Solomon
Vanity of Human Life
The Seraphim, or Hymns for youth
Golden Grove
Daniel in the Lion's Den
The Rake's Progress
Fall of Man
Stages of Life
History of London
Prince of Israel
To-day and To-morrow
Elizabeth Watson
Prodigal Son
Affectionate Daughter
Ambrose Guynett
The Dutiful Child

Tree of Life
Creation
Victim of Seduction
Pilgrim's Progress
Crucifixion
Destruction of Babylon
Adam and Eve in Paradise
History of England
Tom and Jerry, or Life in London
Captain Parry's Voyages
The Child's Dream
Pennyworth of wit
Effects of Gambling
Scarborough Tragedy
Prophecies of Isaiah
The Star of Israel
Life and age of man
Life of Abraham
Dance of Death
Golden Chain of Salvation
Young man's dream
King and Christian.
Faith, Hope, and Charity
Lost child restored
Shipwreck of the Flora

Rose of Sharon
Lives of the Apostles
Industry rewarded
Cruel stepmother
Leading events in the life of Joseph
Sabbath breaker
Watts's Hymns
Christ in the storm
Solomon's Proverbs
Harlot's progress
Evening Hymn
Our Saviours' Letter
Atheist converted
Nixon's Prophecies
Children at their mother's grave
Belshazzar's feast
Death of Abel
Blasphemers punished
Holy Bible
Great and terrible wonder
Children in the Wood
Fatal book opened
Destruction of Babel
Unhappy Transport

HALF SHEETS.

Our Saviour's letter
Pious Hymns
The fifty-six wants of the children of Zion
Dying pilgrim
Ploughboy's dream
Village bell
Songs in the night
Christ in the storm
A present for a good child
The Two Orphans
Henry's Lamentation
The wandering Jew
A voice from the grave
The great concern
A warning from Heaven to England
Worthy is the Lamb
Prodigal daughter
The Great Assize
Soldier's Almanack
The Holy Bible
Life and sufferings of Jane Wade

The two wonderful prophets
The Tailor's funeral
The dead alive
Dialogue between a Miller, a Baker, Butcher, &c.
Dialogue about a tea and toast party
John Joblin
Matthew Grey and Susan Smith
Twelve young women smothered
Sufferings of Mary Howard
Dreadful shipwreck
Gambler's fate
Old Mother Clifton
Boxing ladies
The lady eloping with her handsome footman
Beggar's Wedding
Royal Fortune Teller
Execution of Dorothy Jennison
The Four Monsters

Execution of Fanny Amlett
Execution of Mary Higgins
Horrid murder discovered by a waggoner
Murder by Martha Alden
—— near St. Albans
—— by a father on his own daughter
—— by David Gaskell on his sweetheart
—— by Roger Davison on his child
—— by John Day on his father and mother
Funny Wedding
Pat Carol's goat's adventures in a Church
A copy of verses on Mary James
Lady of the cave
Crim. Con.
Miraculous Preservation of a babe
Angel appearing to a Minister

8   *CATALOGUE.*

CHRISTMAS CAROLS.

Divine Mirth	Crucifixion	Twelfth Night Amusements
The Evergreen	Resurrection	Rose of Sharon
Plants of Paradise	Lyre of Zion	Christmas amusements
Star of Bethlehem	Harp of Israel	Moses striking the rock
Golden Chaplet	Christmas drawing near	The Nativity
The Black Decree	Christmas Amusements	*The three last are sheets.*

Halfpenny & Farthing Books.

A. Apple Pie	Goody Two Shoes	Old Mother Hubbard
Babes in the Wood	Jack and Gill	Old Dame Trot
Blue Beard	Jerry Diddle	Old Woman of Stepney
Butterfly's Ball	Jumping Joan	House that Jack Built
Cock Robin	King Pippin	Mother Muggins
Cries of London	Tom Tucker	Picture Alphabet
Jenny Wren	Mother Goose	Whittington and his Cat
First Step to Learning	Nurse Lovechild's Legacy	Tom the Piper's Son
Golden Pippin	World turned up side down	Easter Present

Simple Simon, and others preparing for publication, the cuts of which are already engraved.

₊ Sheet Songs and Valentines, between Twenty and Thirty different sorts.

J. CATNACH, most respectfully begs leave to inform Country Dealers, Proprietors of Toy Shops, and the Public in general, that in addition to the above, he has a great variety of Penny and Two-penny Primers, Battledores, &c. Also a number of Sheets and Half-Sheets, which being only of temporary interest, are not enumerated in the above Catalogue.

Printed by J. CATNACH, 2, Monmouth Court, Seven Dials.

Glossary of Terms Relating to Street Literature

advice
: Seventeenth century term for newspaper advertisement.

ballad
: Originally a traditional narrative song associated with dancing, later applied indiscriminately to any song composition, especially those printed on broadsides.

Stall ballad—a term used to indicate broadside ballads or ballads in chapbooks, purchased from markets or fairs.

Slip ballad (or *Single slip*)—a single column ballad-sheet, usually cut from a double column sheet; halfpenny ballad-sheets were cut from a double-column sheet costing a penny.

Pasteup—short ballads which have been cut from a sheet with three or four items, and pasted on a sheet of waste paper.

battledore
: A folding cardboard sheet (usually approx. $8\frac{1}{2}'' \times 5''$) with printed alphabet, syllables, simple sentences, and woodcut illustrations, used up to the late nineteenth century in teaching children to read.

Black-Letter
: 𝕲𝖔𝖙𝖍𝖎𝖈 style typeface used on early broadside balladsheets, pamphlets, and books.

broadsheet
: Often regarded as synonymous with *broadside*, but strictly applied to a sheet with printing on both sides.

broadside
: An unfolded sheet with printed matter on one side only—a proclamation, poster, handbill, or ballad-sheet.

Broadside ballads are sometimes referred to by size: 'sheets'—approx. $20'' \times 30''$, or $20'' \times 15''$; 'half-sheets', and 'quarter-sheets'.

catchpenny
: General term for deceptive or hasty literary work got up for mere profit; specifically applied to deceptive narratives on broadsides.

chapbook
: 'cheap book'. A pamphlet formed from a sheet folded

into four, eight, twelve, or sixteen, i.e., a 4to, 8vo, 12mo, or 16mo booklet, usually sold uncut and unstitched. Chapbooks contained romances, fairy-tales, riddles, jokes, superstitions, stories, or ballads. Chapbook collections of ballads were often called *garlands*.

chaunt　　　To sing or chant prose or verse broadsides in the street.

cock　　　Used as synonymous with 'catchpenny', but specifically a timeless broadside of fictitious news which could be revived whenever real news was scarce.

coranto　　　('Current of News'); an early news-sheet or pamphlet.

long-song sheet　A penny sheet approx. $7\frac{1}{4}'' \times 20''$ containing many short songs, sometimes cried as 'three yards a penny', but actually referring to three columns rather than the overall length.

mercury　　　Popular term for a news pamphlet in the seventeenth century, deriving from such publications as *Mercurius Aulicus*, *Mercurius Civicus*, *Mercurius Britanicus*, etc. Also used to describe a seller of news pamphlets.

pamphlet　　　An unbound book. Pamphlets usually dealt with topical subjects for middle- and upper-class readers; chapbooks circulated amongst poor people.

patter　　　Street speech or oration by traders. (Possibly derived from 'Paternoster'.) Nineteenth century patterers sold verse or prose broadsides, either from a fixed pitch (*standing patterer*), or whilst moving down the street (*running patterer or flying stationer*).

pinner-up　　　A seller of street literature who pinned up his stock on twine suspended between railings or against walls.

siquis　　　Early term for advertisements using the opening formula 'If any one. . . .'

tract　　　Often used loosely of pamphlets; specifically a religious pamphlet or chapbook.

Bibliography

TRADITIONAL BALLADS AND SONGS

BARING-GOULD, S. *et al. Songs of the West* (nd)

BELL, Robert. *Early Ballads, illustrative of History, Traditions and Customs; Also, Ballads and Songs of the Peasantry of England* (1877)

BROADWOOD, Lucy E. and FULLER MAITLAND, J. A. *English County Songs* (1893)

BRONSON, B. H. *The Traditional Tunes of the Child Ballads* (Princeton, New Jersey, 1959–72, 4 vols)

CHILD, Francis J. *The English and Scottish Popular Ballads* (Boston, 1882–98, 5 vols; The Folklore Press/Pageant Book Co, New York, 1957, 5 vols in 3; Dover Books, New York, 1965, 5 vols)

DEAN-SMITH, Margaret. *A Guide to English Folk Song Collections 1822–1952* (Liverpool, 1954)

Journal of the Folk Song Society, 1899–1931, continued as *Journal of the English Folk Dance & Song Society*, in progress

KIDSON, Frank. *Traditional Tunes* (Oxford, 1891)

[Percy, Thomas]. *Bishop Percy's Folio Manuscript*, edited Hales and Furnival (1867; Singing Tree Press, Detroit, 1968, 4 vols in 3)

PERCY, Thomas. *Reliques of Ancient English Poetry*, edited Wheatley (1886, 3 vols; Dover Books, New York, 1966)

REEVES, James. *The Idiom of the People* (1958)

REEVES, James. *The Everlasting Circle* (1960)

SHARP, Cecil J. *English Folk Songs* (1921, 2 vols)

WHITE, Rev. E. A. and DEAN-SMITH, Margaret J. *An Index of English Songs contributed to The Journal of the Folk Song Society 1899–1931 and its continuation The Journal of the English Folk Dance & Song Society to 1950* (1951)

WILLIAMS, Alfred. *Folk-Songs of the Upper Thames* (1923; Singing Tree Press, Detroit, 1968)

BROADSIDE BALLADS AND CHAPBOOKS

ASHTON, John. *A Ballade of the Scottysshe Kynge. The earliest known English printed ballad* (1882; Singing Tree Press, Detroit, 1969)

ASHTON, John. *A Century of Ballads* (1887; Singing Tree Press, Detroit, 1968)

ASHTON, John. *Chap-Books of the Eighteenth Century* (1882; Blom, New York, 1967)

ASHTON, John. *Humour, Wit, & Satire of the Seventeenth Century* (1883; Singing Tree Press, Detroit, 1968)

ASHTON, John. *Modern Street Ballads* (1888; Singing Tree Press, Detroit, 1968)

BAGFORD BALLADS, edited Ebsworth (The Ballad Society, Hertford, 1876–80, 2 vols; AMS, New York, 1968)

BLAND, Desmond S. *Chapbooks and Garlands in the Robert White Collection in the Library of King's College, Newcastle Upon Tyne* (Newcastle upon Tyne, 1956)

BRYANT, Beth. *Broadside Ballads for Christmastyde* (Folk World Inc, New York, 1963)

(A) COLLECTION OF SEVENTY-NINE BLACK-LETTER BALLADS AND BROADSIDES, PRINTED IN THE REIGN OF QUEEN ELIZABETH, BETWEEN THE YEARS 1559 and 1597 (1867; Singing Tree Press, Detroit, 1968)

CRAWHALL, Joseph. *Chap-book Chaplets* (1883)

CROPPER, Percy J. *The Nottinghamshire Printed Chap-Books with Notices of their Printers and Vendors* (Nottingham, 1892)

CUNNINGHAM, Robert H. *Amusing Prose Chapbooks Chiefly of Last Century* (1889)

D'URFEY, Thomas. *Wit and Mirth: or Pills to Purge Melancholy* (1719–20, 6 vols; Folklore Library Publishers Inc, New York, 1959, 6 vols in 3)

(THE) EUING COLLECTION OF ENGLISH BROADSIDE BALLADS (University of Glasgow Publications, 1971)

FAWCETT, F. Burlington. *Broadside Ballads of the Restoration Period from the Jersey Collection, known as the Osterley Park Ballads* (1930)

FEDERER, Charles A. *Yorkshire Chap-books* (1889)

FIRTH, C. H. *The Ballad History of the Reigns of Henry VII and Henry VIII*, reprinted from *Transactions of the Royal Historical Society*, 3rd series, vol 2 (1908)

FRASER, John. *Scottish Chapbooks* (New York and Glasgow, 1873)

FURNIVALL, F. J. *Captain Cox, his Ballads and Books: or, Robert Laneham's Letter* (The Ballad Society, Hertford, 1871)

GERRING, Charles. *Notes on Printers and Booksellers with a Chapter on Chapbooks* (London and Nottingham, 1900)

GOMME, G. L. and H. B. Wheatley. *Chapbooks and Folk-lore Tracts* (1885, 5 vols)

HALLIWELL-PHILLIPS, James O. *A Catalogue of Chap-Books, Garlands, and Popular Histories* (1849)

HARVEY, William. *Scottish Chapbook Literature* (Paisley, 1903)

HEALY, James N. *The Mercier Book of Old Irish Street Ballads* (Cork, 1967–, 7 vols)

HENDERSON, W. *Victorian Street Ballads. A Selection of Popular Ballads sold in the Street in the Nineteenth Century* (1937)

HINDLEY, Charles. *Curiosities of Street Literature: comprising 'Cocks', or 'Catchpennies', a large and curious assortment of Street-Drolleries, Squibs, Histories, Comic Tales in Prose and Verse* (1871; The Broadsheet King [John Foreman], 1966, 2 vols)

HINDLEY, Charles. *The History of the Catnach Press, at Berwick-upon-Tweed, Alnwick and Newcastle-upon-Tyne, in Northumberland, and Seven Dials, London* (1887; Singing Tree Press, Detroit, 1969)

HINDLEY, Charles. *The Life and Times of James Catnach (Late of Seven Dials), Ballad Monger* (1878; Singing Tree Press, Detroit, 1968)

JOHN CHEAP THE CHAPMAN'S LIBRARY: The Scottish Chap Literature of Last Century, Classified. With Life of Dougal Graham (Glasgow, 1877–8, 3 vols; Singing Tree Press, Detroit, 1968)

LAWS, G. Malcolm, Jr. *American Balladry from British Broadsides* (American Folklore Society, Philadelphia, 1957)

LEMON, Robert. *Catalogue of a Collection of Printed Broadsides in the Possession of the Society of Antiquaries of London* (1866)

LINDSAY, J. L., Earl of Crawford. *Bibliotheca Lindesiana. Catalogue of English Broadsides, 1505–1897* (Aberdeen, 1898; Franklin, New York, 1965)

LOGAN, W. H. *A Pedlar's Pack of Ballads and Songs* (Edinburgh, 1869; Singing Tree Press, Detroit, 1968)

MAC GREGOR, George. *The Collected Writings of Dougal Graham, 'Skellat' Bellman of Glasgow* (Glasgow, 1883, 2 vols)

NATIONAL LIBRARY OF SCOTLAND. *Catalogue of the Lauriston Castle Chapbooks* (Boston, Mass, 1964)

NEUBURG, Victor E. *Chapbooks: A Bibliography of References to*

English and American Chapbook Literature of the Eighteenth and Nineteenth Centuries (1964; new edition 1972)

NEUBURG, Victor E. *The Penny Histories. A Study of Chapbooks for Young Readers Over Two Centuries* (1968)

O LOCHLAINN, Colm. *Irish Street Ballads* (Dublin, 1939)

O LOCHLAINN, Colm. *More Irish Street Ballads* (Dublin, 1965)

PEARSON, Edwin. *Banbury Chap Books and Nursery Toy Book Literature (Of the XVIII. And Early XIX. Centuries)* (1890; Franklin, New York, nd; Seven Dials Press, Welwyn Garden City, 1970)

PHILLIPS, Ambrose(?). *A Collection of Old Ballads* (1723–5, 3 vols)

PINTO, V. de Sola and A. E. Rodway. *The Common Muse* (1957)

ROBINSON, Clement, *et al. A Handefull of Pleasant Delites*, edited Rollins (Cambridge, USA, 1924)

ROLLINS, Hyder E. *An Analytical Index to the Ballad Entries, 1557–1709 in the Registers of the Company of Stationers of London* (North Carolina, 1924; Tradition Press, Hatboro, 1967)

ROLLINS, Hyder E. *The Black-Letter Broadside Ballad* (Publications of the Modern Language Association XXXIV, USA, 1919)

ROLLINS, Hyder E. *Cavalier and Puritan. Ballads and Broadsides Illustrating the Period of the Great Rebellion 1640–1660* (New York, 1923)

ROLLINS, Hyder E. *Old English Ballads, 1553–1625, Chiefly from MSS.* (Cambridge, USA, 1920)

ROLLINS, Hyder E. *The Pack of Autolycus or Strange and Terrible News . . . as told in Broadside Ballads of the Years 1624–93* (Cambridge, USA, 1927)

ROLLINS, Hyder E. *A Pepysian Garland. Black-Letter Broadside Ballads of the Years 1595–1639. Chiefly from the Collection of Samuel Pepys* (Cambridge, USA, 1922)

ROLLINS, Hyder E. *The Pepys Ballads (1553–1702)* (Cambridge, USA, 1929–32, 8 vols)

ROTH, H. Ling and J. T. Jolley. *War Ballads and Broadsides of Previous Wars, 1779–95* (County Borough of Halifax, Bankfield Museum Notes, 2nd series, no 5, Halifax, 1915)

ROXBURGHE BALLADS, edited Chappell and Ebsworth (The Ballad Society, Hertford, 1871–99, 9 vols; AMS, New York, 8 vols)

SHEPARD, Leslie. *The Broadside Ballad. A Study in Origins and Meaning* (1962)

SHEPARD, Leslie. *John Pitts, Ballad Printer of Seven Dials, London, 1765–1844, with a short account of his predecessors in the Ballad & Chapbook Trade* (London and Detroit, 1969)

SIMPSON, Claude M. *The British Broadside Ballad and its Music* (Rutgers University Press, New Brunswick, NJ, 1966)

THOMSON, Frances M. *Newcastle Chapbooks in Newcastle upon Tyne University Library* (Newcastle upon Tyne, 1969)

THE UNIVERSAL SONGSTER OR MUSIC OF MIRTH, forming the most complete, extensive, and valuable collection of Ancient and Modern Songs in the English Language (nd, 3 vols)

WEISS, Harry B. *A Book About Chap-books, The People's Literature of Bygone Times* (Trenton, New Jersey, 1942; Folklore Associates, Hatboro, 1969)

WEISS, Harry B. *A Catalogue of the Chap-books in the New York Public Library*, reprinted with revisions and corrections from the *Bulletin of the New York Public Library*, January, March, October, 1935 (New York, 1936)

WELSH, C. and W. H. Tillinghast. *A Catalogue of English and American Chapbooks and Broadsides in Harvard College Library* (Cambridge, USA, 1905; Singing Tree Press, Detroit, 1968)

WRIGHT, Thomas. *Political Ballads published in England during the Commonwealth* (1841)

PROCLAMATIONS, EARLY NEWSPAPERS, PAMPHLETS AND OTHER EPHEMERA

ARBER, Edward. *An English Garner, Ingatherings from our History and Literature* (1895, 8 vols)

CATALOGUE OF THE COLLECTION OF BROADSIDES IN THE UNIVERSITY LIBRARY (*Goldsmith's Library of Economic Literature*) (University of London Press, 1930)

CATCHPENNY PRINTS, 163 Popular Engravings from the Eighteenth Century (Dover Books, New York, 1970)

COLLET, C. D. *History of Taxes on Knowledge* (1899, 2 vols)

DAHL, Folke. *A Bibliography of English Corantos and Periodical News-books 1620–42* (1952)

DRAPER, John W. *A Century of Broadside Elegies, being ninety English and ten Scotch broadsides illustrating the biography and manners of the seventeenth century* (1928)

FRANK, Joseph. *The Beginnings of the English Newspaper 1620–1660* (Cambridge, USA, 1961)

HALKETT, S. and J. Laing. *Dictionary of Anonymous and Pseudonymous English Literature* (Edinburgh, 1926–, 9 vols)

HODGKIN, John Eliot. *Rariora* (nd, 3 vols)

JACKSON, Mason. *The Pictorial Press, Its Origin and Progress* (1885; Gale Research Co, Detroit, 1968)

LEWIS, John. *Printed Ephemera* (Ipswich, 1962)

MORISON, Stanley. *The English Newspaper. Some account of the physical development of journals printed and published in London from 1622 to the present day* (1932)

SAMPSON, Henry. *A History of Advertising from the Earliest Times* (1875)

[THOMASON, George]. *Catalogue of Pamphlets, Books, Newspapers and Manuscripts relating to the Civil War, the Commonwealth and Restoration, collected by G. Thomason, 1640–61* (1908)

TUER, Andrew W. *1,000 Quaint Cuts* (1886; Singing Tree Press, Detroit, 1968)

TURNER, E. S. *Boys Will Be Boys* (1948)

WATT, William H. *Shilling Shockers of the Gothic School* (Harvard Honors Theses in English, Cambridge, USA, 1932)

WILLIAMS, J. B. (pseudonym of J. G. Muddiman). *A History of English Journalism to the Foundation of the Gazette* (1908)

WOOD, Robert. *Victorian Delights* (1967)

LITERACY AND CHEAP PRINTING

ALTICK, Richard D. *The English Common Reader: A Social History of the Mass Reading Public, 1800–1900* (Chicago, 1957)

CHAMBERS, William. *Memoir of Robert Chambers, with Autobiographic Reminiscences of William Chambers* (Edinburgh and London, 1872)

CLARKE, W. K. L. *A Short History of The SPCK* (1919)

CRUSE, Amy. *The Englishman and his Books in the Early Nineteenth Century* (1930)

HOPKINS, Mary Alden. *Hannah More and Her Circle* (New York, 1947)

JONES, M. G. *The Charity School Movement: A Study of Eighteenth Century Puritanism in Action* (Cambridge, 1938)

KNIGHT, Charles. *The Old Printer and the Modern Press* (1854)

KNIGHT, Charles. *Shadows of the Old Booksellers* (1865; 1927)

LACKINGTON, James. *Memoirs of the Forty-five First Years* (1794)

MATHEWS, H. F. *Methodism and the Education of the People, 1791–1851* (1949)

MUMBY, Frank A. *Publishing and Bookselling* (1934)

WEBB, Robert K. *The British Working Class Reader, 1790–1848* (1955)

PEDLARS

GULIELMUS DUBLINIENSIS HUMORIENSIS. *Memoir of the Great Original Zozimus (Michael Moran)* (Dublin, 1871)

HINDLEY, Charles. *The Life and Adventures of a Cheap Jack* (1881)

LOVE, David. *The Life, Adventures and Experience of David Love* (Nottingham, 1825)

MAYHEW, Henry. *London Labour and the London Poor* (1851–64, 4 vols; 1968; Dover Books, New York, 1969)

SPURGEON, C. H. *et al. Booksellers & Bookbuyers in Byeways and Highways* (1882)

STRATHESK, John. *Hawkie: The Autobiography of a Gangrel* (Glasgow, 1888)

STREET LITERATURE FROM OTHER COUNTRIES

BUMGARDNER, Georgia B. *American Broadsides* (Imprint Society, Barre, USA, 1971)

DUCHARTRE, Pierre-Louis. *L'Imagerie Populaire Russe* (Paris, 1961)

FERRAND, Louis et Edmond Magnac. *Guide Bibliographique de L'Imagerie Populaire* (Auxerre, 1956)

FORD, Worthington C. *Broadside Ballads . . . Printed in Massachusetts, 1639–1800* (Massachusetts Historical Society Collections LXXV, Boston, 1922)

FORD, Worthington C. *The Isaiah Thomas Collection of Ballads* (Worcester, USA, 1924)

HORAY, Pierre. *Canards du siècle passé* (Paris, 1969)

JANDA, Elsbeth and Fritz Nötzoldt. *Die Moritat vom Bänkelsang oder Das Lied der Strasse* (München, 1959)

(*THE*) *LUBOK*, *17th-18th Century Russian Broadsides* (Moscow, nd)

MISTLER, Jean, François Blaudez et André Jacquemin. *Epinal et l'imagerie populaire* (Librairie Hachette, 1961)

NISARD, Charles. *Histoire des livres populaires: ou, de la littérature du colportage, depuis le xve siècle jusqu'à l'établissement de la Commission d'examen des livres du colportage* (Paris, 1854, 2 vols; New York, 1964)

TINKER, Edward Larocque. *Corridos & Calaveras* (University of Texas, 1961)

TOSCHI, Paolo. *L'Imagerie populaire Italienne* (Paris, 1964)

VAN VEEN, C. F. *Three Centuries of Pictorial Broadsides for Children* (Amsterdam, 1971)

WÄSCHER, Hermann. *Das Deutsche Illustrierte Flugblatt* (Dresden, 1955–6, 2 vols)

Index of Names